YOU'RE DOING *WHAT* TO THE MAPES?

Karl Breckenridge
November 2005

YOU'RE DOING *WHAT* TO THE MAPES?

By

KARL BRECKENRIDGE

Jack Bacon & Company
Reno Nevada
2005

ISBN 0930083180

Special thanks to
The Reno Gazette-Journal
for permission to print these columns.

Designed by Jim Richards

Jack Bacon & Company
516 South Virginia Street
Reno, Nevada 89501

www.JackBacon.com

Cover photo by the author.
Cover background photo, Mapes window coin,
courtesy of Kim Bacon.
Back cover author photo by Jack Bacon.

Table of Contents

Foreword

If the term anthology is indeed defined as a "collection of works," the business card of Karl Breckenridge should identify him as an anthologist.

For years, from the Reno office of Breckenridge Realty, he self published and freely distributed his *Blue Plate Special.* Each edition allowed him to share a bit of local history humorously recalled from personal experience and indelible observation.

During this same period Karl successfully authored and had published three books offering tongue-in-cheek guidance to prospective Realtors; few know one of them made the *Chicago Tribune* best-seller list in 1990.

As Karl's academic credentials were in journalism rather than economics, it took him a while to realize that meeting the demand by locals to get on the *Blue Plate Special* mailing list, along with the increased postage and publication costs were knocking hell out of the residuals he was receiving from his three books.

Reno's daily newspaper, The *Reno Gazette-Journal*, served as a transition vehicle. Karl stopped the *Blue Plate Special* presses and started furnishing a weekly column for the paper's Saturday real estate supplement, the *Homefinder,* later to become just *Homes.*

Notwithstanding an occasional shot at contemporary targets, Karl's writings remind locals of people and places as they used to be, at the same time introducing newcomers to the thread of historical continuity that will eventually fasten them to their new community.

The collection offered in *You're Doing* What *To The Mapes?* allows the reader reflection and insight relating to the creation of the attitude of today's Reno area residents... Surely you have noticed that Reno has an attitude!

– Lewis E. "Red" Kittell, Commissioner
Reno Historical Resources Commission

Tom McGuire with Bertha the elephant, 1975.
Courtesy John Ascuaga's Nugget.

Dedication

I've dedicated four books in the past, and their dedications always posed a dilemma.

Happily, choosing the honoree in this book was a no-brainer from the git-go. Tom McGuire rolled the dice one day over a dozen years ago, when I submitted a column that was a complete departure from what I was supposed to be writing about – this caprice is detailed in the Readers' Guide. That aside-look led to a new direction for these columns, and it's safe to say that without Tom's help this book would never have been published.

Tom worked for Reno's Gannett papers for over 31 years – the *Nevada State Journal,* the *Reno Evening Gazette,* both later combined into our present *Reno Gazette-Journal.* He wrote for every desk in the newsroom at one time or another, and in later years served as editor for almost every department. His moment in the sun, actually in the chilly darkness of a January night in 1985, came when Galaxy Airline's propjet Electra crashed into the motor home sales lot on South Virginia Street. Tom was the officer-of-the-deck that night, and marshaled every one of the paper's news, photo and support staffers into action for the morning paper already heading for the presses, and an extra edition later on the morning of the crash. His final effort, a happier assignment, came in 2004, overseeing the Fifty-year Anniversary of John Ascauga's Nugget compendium of news clips, Nugget archives, and a heartwarming collection of nostalgic photographs.

He's a pro, the model of what the Fourth Estate is all about, yet all the while an inveterate punster. I'd fire in an e-mail that the chicken crossed the road to see his brother Gregory peck, and he'd retaliate in a heartbeat that that was sheer poultry in motion. The score stood stalled at McGuire 1, Breckenridge 0, for a dozen years. I could write a column of some of our goofy exchanges that never saw print. And I might.

Tom relocated in January of 2005 to a similar position at the RGJ's sister newspaper, Gannett's *Statesman Journal.* On this dedication page I thank him for his friendship, and the incredible knowledge of the craft that he brought me. And I extend to him the Homefinders' gratitude for making our Saturday mornings a little brighter.

The Reader's Guide

> **"I am remembering now in ever increasing detail, events which I'm not sure ever happened…"** ***Author unknown, passage unearthed by Gordon Chism***

A dozen years ago, I had already been writing of real estate matters in the *Reno Gazette-Journal* for some time. But soon after beginning that undertaking, I discovered that there are only four root facts to be known about the craft, and that's probably a stretch, but write, I did, on Saturday mornings, each column a rehash of another I'd already written.

Coming up on a deadline one evening, I lost it. My digits, acting on their own, struck several lines about old Reno streets on my old Mac keyboard: "We have an Elm, a Persimmon, an Apple, a Pine, a Cottonwood, a Vine Street – why do we misspell the name of one of our busier streets, Plumb Lane?" (Knowing full well the answer; the lane was named for the Plumb family and ranch.) "And we have street patterns named after universities – Harvard, Vassar, Auburn, by the airport; Citadel, The Strand, College, by the university (never UNR in my columns.) We have goofy alleys: Alley Oop, and Bowling Alley, (for my friend, the late Monsignor Bob Bowling). And we have a street named LaRue, French for Street-Street."

And a dozen more oddities, in that fateful column. My phone rang, and I received mail. (All this was far before e-mail.) Reader responses. I called my editor, Tom McGuire: "Readers are writing me and calling me about last week's column. What the hell do I do now?"

"Dunno," Tom replied. "No one's ever read your column before."

But the responses encouraged me, and the non-real estate writing in the real estate supplement continued. For the next dozen years, the weekly column explored the origins, history, heritage, and caprice of Reno and Sparks and their denizens. While most great literary works have a theme that holds them together, this column didn't. Text was often inspired by the day's news on the day I was writing it, usually Tuesday evenings to meet a Monday noon deadline. Or by events – Hot August Nights cruising downtown? Let's do a 1959 cruise in the paper, and see what we'd see when I was in high school. The Olympics in progress somewhere? Well, let's look at our own Squaw Valley 1960 Winter Olympics, in retrospect. A forest fire? You'll read of several major fires in the pages that follow.

Some of the more popular topics were the walks – we'd start, all together from some corner, call it North Virginia and West Fourth, and walk west, visiting some old shops and landmarks, and return the following Saturday morning eastward to that intersection. Or, we'd go to an old restaurant – Eugene's or the Bundox, to name two, and examine the bill of fare. One of the proudest moments of my writing career came at a meeting of the Good Old Days club at the Liberty Belle, and with Neal Cobb's help I put on a slide show of the old Eugene's restaurant. The kicker was bringing about 20 of the original Eugene's staff together, some of whom hadn't seen each other for a decade. Their were few dry eyes in the group – old staffers or G.O.D. club members – who had been waited on by these fine folks so many years before.

The original columns were grouped by subject in the manuscript's initial layout – by fire, restaurant, walk, by event. I realized early on that following a sequential read of the Lake Street fire, the Sierra Street fire and the Golden Hotel fire, the text ran together into a jumble in my mind and would certainly do so in yours. If I wrote it and still couldn't keep them straight, heaven help you the reader. You'll find them spread out in the pages.

We all came to be known as the "Homefinders" on page 8 on Saturday mornings, that appellation rooted in the name of the Saturday real estate supplement where the column appeared (at press time it's now called simply "Homes.") I have been asked, "How do I join the Homefinders?" We meet every Saturday morning, the dues are cheap – four bits for a copy of the RGJ – and the qualification is easy: A love for our valley, and tolerance of my long, run-on sentences in the columns.

Your comments and correspondence kept it alive – it takes a village to chronicle the heritage of a village, and I could not have written it alone. Quite often I'd throw a topic out, sit back and read the mail, and over a fortnight hammer an accurate account of how something came to be into our trove of local history. This little book is the work product of us all; the readers contact me with some tidbit that I'd have never in a million columns struck on myself if unassisted, and we are all the richer for it. And, while some questionable facts occasionally snuck into an original column, by the time they reached this book, they have been verified several times over. *(Well, mostly...I've written before that drive-by writers who chronicle the minefields of churches, railroads, architects and irrigation ditches need to have their heads examined.)*

As humans first and Homefinders secondarily, our methodology for recalling the past is revealing, and often amusing. In one column I wrote that the Lancer (restaurant, earlier the Mesa, on the rise across from present Galena High School) burned to the ground, on ~ ~th, 19xx. The contacts were many, and not untypical of how we all remember events: "It couldn't have been 19xx; we took our daughter to the Lancer when she graduated from Wooster in 1972." "I remember it well; we drove up there when my 1970 Pontiac was brand-new and I had to chain it up!" "My wife and I went to the Lancer when she was pregnant with our son, who was born in 1973."

The Lancer burned on July 30, 1971. And if anyone believes that after over 220 columns that I haven't made the same associative mistakes many times over, the Easter Bunny will autograph this book for you. But hopefully – by the time you read this, it's fixed.

The book is laid out in "segments," rather than chapters – each segment substantially contains the text as it appeared in one or more columns – in some cases, three or four, as in the El Reno Apartment segment, combined from five different columns. The Roman text, like you're reading now, approximates the verbiage as it appeared in the *Reno Gazette-Journal.* *[Bracketed text in italics, as this appears, contains supplemental information which might have come along later and strengthened the work, or was withheld from the print version for space considerations.]*

All of the columns are protected by the *Reno Gazette-Journal*'s copyright, and it is here that I extend my most sincere appreciation to the RGJ, and particularly to Christine Thompson, the editor of the RGJ's Custom Publishing Group that publishes the *Homes* real estate supplement, for allowing a one-time release of the copyright so that this book could become a reality.

I hope you will enjoy this book even a fraction as much as I have enjoyed writing the columns that comprise it. Each of you snuck into the pages of this book in some manner, and you all share my gratitude for making it possible. A final note, as seasoned Homefinders have come to know: On the dark Saturday following 9/11/2001, the final words in that column, and all that followed, became, God bless America.

Enjoy!

A local dinner house that will never be replaced...

(June 23rd, 2001)

Homefinders, your table is ready...

Eugene Jarvis turned a classic old ranch house a fur piece south of Reno into a elegantly appointed restaurant after the end of World War II. He might have called it "Jarvis's," but owing to either caprice or the awkward apostrophe, he elected to go with "Eugene's," thus bestowing one of the most instantly identified and enduring names in Reno's heritage.

Jarvis picked the name, but it took two young men who met in New York at the 1939 World's Fair and journeyed – separately – to Reno, to get the restaurant underway. Joe Patrucco was the affable bartender at the Riverside Hotel's well-known Corner Bar, while Gilbert Vasserot had opened the Moulin Rouge restaurant on Sierra Street. Their youthful careers were interrupted by a world war, but they rejoined and in 1947 bought the restaurant from Jarvis, retaining the Eugene's name and assembling a world-class staff that would give Reno a restaurant that would rival the finest in cosmopolitan San Francisco. (Eugene Jarvis, possibly to create confusion for 50 years to follow, would open a second Eugene's on a promontory above Lake Tahoe's Crystal Bay.)

Gilbert, a Swiss culinary *artiste* trained in Europe, donned the chef's toque, a hat he would wear six nights a week for years to follow, while Joe handled the "front" duties – also six nights a week. And Joe greeted all equally – Eugene's had the local reputation that a guest was a guest and none were treated better or more quickly than others; that all would receive old world hospitality be they Dennis Day sneaking in for dinner before his show in the Mapes Sky Room, or the local couple taking their daughter out to dinner on her 16th birthday.

• • •

The town embraced Eugene's with civic pride, and eleven years after it opened in Eugene Jarvis' ranch house, local architect Frank Green was commissioned to design a new restaurant building.

Premier local builder Allan Gallaway finished the new restaurant on a spot now near the domes left over from the Century Theater south of the Peppermill, and Gilbert and Joe reopened Eugene's on May 14th, 1958 (a great photo of Joe and his wife Lucia, and Gilbert with his Lucienne, taken on the steps on opening night, will magically appear on my website soon...) *[Lucienne passed away shortly after this column appeared.]* The original ranch house restaurant had been moved a few hundred feet to the west to free up the site for construction. That structure burned a few years after the new restaurant opened. And it wasn't the old James McKay house, as I and many others originally believed; the McKay home was a long block to the south.

What a place the new restaurant was! A classic bar with a beamed ceiling, leaded glass windows and thickly padded leather banquettes, and a bartender named Cliff Challender who prided himself on committing regular diners' cocktail preferences to memory (Gilbert points with great pride at his sommelier – wine steward, to some of us – well-remembered by many as Antoine Balducci, who handled the patrons' wine orders with uncanny knowledge, freeing up the waiters to provide better service.)

The main room was quiet and open, with rich paneling and more leather – chairs and banquettes – and chandeliers with bulbs hand-painted by Gilbert himself for just the right effect. Pianist Del (few knew his last name was Dellaquadre) could be heard around the room, subtly, but less subtly when somebody would roll in with a party of eight and no reservations. Del would break into *La Vie En Rose*, to some a charming love song, but to Joe Patrucco, somewhere out in the room greeting guests, a code to come to the front pronto and deal with a problem.

One didn't hear *La Vie En Rose* too often at Joe and Gilbert's…

• • •

The bill of fare rivaled any fine dinner house in America, garnering Holiday Magazine Five-Star awards year after year when fewer than 75 were conferred in the whole country. In 1960, Eugene's hosted the City of Reno's welcoming luncheon for the International Olympic Committee during the Squaw Valley Winter Olympics. Business soon came from one interesting market, the airlines. United Air Lines, three words in the 1960s, began with meals for two flights a day to solve a logistical problem and found that the food was so popular on those runs that they eventually selected Eugene's to prepare meals for twelve flights a day. Years ago the rumor was that United changed their schedules just to use food from Eugene's. Bonanza Airlines also served Eugene's fare enroute to Las Vegas. Gil and Joe did take-out judiciously; for a good customer a little under the weather, a Broiled Langoustine Eugene's or a Filet of Sole *Meuniere*, with Foigras du Perigord or Zabalione might appear on their sickbed tray. Or, for Charles Clegg and historian/raconteur Lucius Beebe's St. Bernard – all three fairly frequent diners — a nice dish of Skippy a la Comstock for the beast.

There's too much on the menu here to cover in one week. Soon, we'll name names: the long-time employees who bought it from Joe and Gilbert in 1961; about photographers Gitta and Jimmie Smith, old-world names like Madalaine Chamot, Annie Creux, Walter Zhand, Rene Jacquemin, Raymond Capitaine, Sergé Nussbaum, Don Richter and Dave Blakely (*Richter* and *Blakely*? Well, not all of them were old-world...) I'll include some anecdotes from a recent visit with Gilbert Vasserot, some more from the late Joe Patrucco's daughter Linda, about Eugene's guests, staff, and great times in a Reno landmark, and finally about Joe and Gilbert's Continental Lodge.

And now, dessert...

In a recent column, we spoke of what I boldly labeled the finest restaurant that ever graced local nightlife – Eugene's – and I braced myself for a spate of e-mail pointing out a few other classy places, of which there are many in town. That argument never arrived (a lot of agreement did, however.) On the other hand, I heard from all 1,704 people, to listen to them, who had dined in the old house out by the present Peppermill that housed the original Eugene's on the night owners Joe Patrucco and Gilbert Vasserot closed it in 1958. And all of the 3,214 first-nighters when the restaurant reopened in the new building across the parking lot on May 14th the same year. *[Sarcasm herein missed by some readers – the new place sat about 130 diners.]* Gitta was there that night and took many photos of the diners, as she did almost every night, trundling off to her studio downtown to process and print them and return before her subjects left for a nightcap at the Riverside.

I promised in that column that in this sequel I'd name names and here we go, with little regard to sequence or grammar:

It's hard to think of Eugene's without thinking of Gil and Joe, then almost automatically of the tall, ethereal waiter-turned-host-turned-owner, who approached Joe Patrucco in 1946, he looking for a job as a waiter, Joe then in the process of buying Eugene's from Eugene Jarvis. His name was Walter Zhand (still is) and this "skinny kid," as Joe described him once in a letter to his daughter, became synonymous with wonderful service and food, first at Eugene's, then at the Continental Lodge that Joe and Gil opened in 1963 (that's a column for another Saturday), and later when he built the Galena Forest restaurant on the Mt. Rose Highway. (Walter, with Raymond Haas and chef Raymond Capitaine, bought Eugene's in 1971 and operated it into the early 1980s.) Walter still walks from his home by Virginia Lake, ramrod-straight, still a great guy.

Many readers wrote of their favorites: Angelo Buccalari tended the bar in the earlier years; Cliff Challender, of the masterful memory for patrons' favorite drinks, took over later. Armand was the wine steward of long standing; Raymond Haas was originally a waiter, becoming the lead wine steward when Antoine Balducci, who took over from Armand, retired. Sergé Nussbaum, Walter Dixon, René Jacquemin, and Carmen. Waiter Heinz Sauer's name came up, as did a chef named Mel, and another named Steve LePochat. Here's a surprise: Retired Carson City dentist Tom Horgan, who bussed tables while in school.

• • •

The patrons were myriad and far-flung to Reno from around the world: During the Squaw Valley Olympics, Joe and Gilbert hosted Lillian Crosa, the figure skater from Gilbert's native Switzerland, her coach Annie Creux, and ladies downhill contender Madelaine Chamot. During the filming of *The Misfits*, Clark Gable, Marilyn Monroe and most of the cast made

Eugene's their home-away-from-home for dinner (a photo in Gilbert's scrapbook which he so kindly loaned me depicts our own Betty Stoddard in a page near the Misfit cast, and most people I've shown the scrapbook to at first see Betty as Marilyn. Their 1960 resemblance was amazing…)

It should be noted that the inspiration for this column came from two fronts occurring within a week of each other: the first, the aforementioned Betty Stoddard sitting with Bob Carroll in a Bonanza Inn TV commercial chatting about great old restaurants – the Lancer, Vario's, Eugene's, etc. Almost simultaneously a lady e-mailed me about a restaurant that her father co-owned, out South Virginia by the Peppermill, a long time ago. Might make a good column. "Yeah, I've heard of it once or twice," I answered Linda Patrucco Doerr, and I was off and running.

Gilbert's book contains dozens of other neat photos, most from Gitta, Reno's pre-eminent nightlife photographer, a few from Jimmie Smith and a few more from Don Dondero. One is of Reno mayor Len Harris and his wife, another of Mike Mirabelli, the music man and state treasurer, one of my old friend Dave Ginsburg and his parents, yet another of Eddie Questa, Jordan Crouch, and a few other First National Bank honchos who I can't recognize. And one real treasure: How many people remember Reno's first TV news anchorman? I picked him out of a shot, when others couldn't: His name was, and remains, Durward Yasmer, the voice of KZTV. *[later KOLO-TV.]*

• • •

Finally, the guys who parked the cars. There were a few, I'll name two old fraternity buddies: Don Richter, who prided himself on lurking around the restaurant watching for a party to get ready to leave, then bringing their car to the door as they walked out (he used his free time to dump the ashtrays and wash the windshields, and reportedly later took three years in the insurance business to get his income back up to what he made in tips at Eugene's.) A later valet was Dave Blakely, whose late parents Bill and Maryalice were steady diners at the restaurant.

I'm indebted to many for the background for this yarn; to Gilbert Vasserot, who with Joe Patrucco – who passed away in 1994 – set the standard against which local dining class and elegance will be measured for years to come. To Joe's children, Linda Patrucco Doerr and her brother Bob (and Wendy) Patrucco. And to Josette Jacquemin, Christiane Balducci Markwell, Denise Haas Hastings, and Carmen Buccalari Borges, for their reminiscences.

Reno's answer to Wrigley, Fenway and Forbes Field...

The Boys of Summer

The outlook wasn't brilliant for the Mudville nine that day;
the score stood stalled at four-to-two with but an inning to play...

As I write, the Series score stands stalled at one-to-one, Angels-to-Giants, with five more games to play. *[Anaheim won; and this was my last World Series prediction ever in a column.]* Anything other than a trip to a ballpark by the Homefinders this fine October morning would be unthinkable. On Saturdays past it could be Threlkel's or the one at West First and Chestnut (Arlington), or Reneva Park at East Sixth and Valley Road. But this morning, Moana Ballpark it will be. It might be worth mentioning for the newer readers that the name "Moana" was the choice of pioneer Reno landowner William Short, who visited Moana Beach in Honolulu in 1904, and it's probably a damn good thing for some local merchants that Short didn't vacation at Ho'noali'iani Beach on Maui or they'd have been forever hung with that moniker for their businesses. The *Ho'noali'iani Lane Nursery?*

The history of our ballpark is rich, nearly a hundred years old since 1906 when Louis Berrum laid a streetcar line from downtown Reno to Moana Springs, which then included mineral baths, a dance hall, a movie theater, ice skating, and of course, a ballpark, albeit not in its present location. And occasionally, a circus or a prizefight, a trap shoot or a rodeo. I relied on Jack and Ed Pine for some reminiscences about the ballpark; turns out that their grandfather, Harry Plath, by coincidence was a conductor on that Moana car line. Spanning a century makes for a tough column so this morning we'll stick within the years following World War II through the early 1950s when the park stood in its present location west of the original Moana Springs.

The old ballpark was aligned with home plate at the southeast corner of the park, the batter facing northwest to the pitcher and Peavine Peak. (If you haven't been out to the park lately, home's now southwest looking northeast, more about that later.) In right center field backing up to Moana Lane – then a two-lane dirt road – was a flagpole and the scoreboard. It was a classic ballpark scoreboard, like old Mackay Stadium's or Wrigley's, with guys working feverishly on platforms behind the board changing numbers by hand for balls, strikes, outs, the inning and the score. A hectic job, but fans today wait in line for the honor of doing the same job for free at Pac Bell Park's *[OK – now SBC Park]* "other games today" board in San Francisco.

Along old Moana's right field foul line fence was "Sunset League, Class D," painted in large block letters.

There was a snack bar under the wooden grandstands, and for a time our classmate Rob Johnson's mother Dell ran that show. On the corner of the right field fence and the foul line was Monty Montgomery's popular post-war restaurant – the "Steakhouse" – with a patio on its south side where patrons could dine and watch the action.

• • •

And now the leather-covered sphere came hurtling through the air, and Casey stood a-watching it in haughty grandeur there. Close by the sturdy batsman the ball unheeded sped – "That ain't my style," said Casey. "Strike one," the umpire said...

Well, any good ballpark needs some noise. Let's fill the wooden planks in the grandstand with fans and fannies, their cars parked alongside Moana Lane with a few unwary souls' windshields off the left field fence about to get smacked with a foul ball. We need a P.A. announcer, so we'll put Reno's sportswriter and columnist *extraordinaire* Ty Cobb Sr. behind the stadium's raspy microphone. We were hashing this yarn out at an early-morning coffee klatch – the aforementioned Pine brothers plus stockbroker Johnny Heward plus Craig Morrison, who batted the University of Arizona into the College World Series in his heyday – and we agreed that Ty missed very few, if any games, for a long span of time in the 1950s. Alongside Ty in the pressbox was the venerable Bob Stoddard, the Voice of the Silver Sox, calling the game for KOH or KATO radio. (That's right, KOLO-TV weatherman Dick Stoddard's father.) Let's put a kid on the roof to shag high pop-foul balls for a dime a ball, and to direct the less-lucky guy working the alfalfa field to the south to the fouls that landed out there. The ballplayers? Park their buses at the Moana plunge, the old one next door; they can use those lockers and showers.

Even the Little Leaguers got to play in Moana Ballpark; 'twas in 1952, we think, during Little League's second year in Reno. They shortened the baselines from 90 to 52 feet, ran a temporary fence behind the full-size field's infield and played just like the big guys.

• • •

With a smile of Christian charity great Casey's visage shone; he stilled the rising tumult, and bade the game go on. He signaled to the pitcher, and once more the spheroid flew; but Casey still ignored it, and the umpire said, "Strike two."

The City of Reno bought the Moana Baths from the Berrum family in 1956 (and I also thank Washoe County Treasurer Bill Berrum for his input into this column.) The City bought the ballpark in the following year. The plunge, by then probably 50 years old, was razed and replaced. The old ballpark burned in a spectacular fire on Hallowe'en of 1958 and the replacement diamond was realigned southwest-to-northeast when the park was rebuilt.

Epilogue: On June 3, 1888 *Casey at the Bat: A Ballad of the Republic,* penned by 20-year-old sportswriter Ernest L. Thayer on his lunch hour, appeared in the San Francisco *Daily Examiner.* Enjoy it on the Web at www.baseballscorecard.com/casey1.htm, or call Bud Beasley; who still occasionally recites it from memory at age 91 (we suspect that Bud knew Thayer personally…) Enjoy the World Series, *Giants in 6 games*, and God bless America. *[refer to comment above, how 'bout Anaheim all the way.]*

Oh, somewhere in this favored land the sun is shining bright; the band is playing somewhere, and somewhere hearts are light; Oh, somewhere men are laughing, and somewhere children shout; but there is no joy in Mudville – mighty Casey has struck out.

• • •

A followup e-mail from my friend Bill Cobb:

"Remember how the crowd would immediately yell "SCOREBOARD" whenever the score keeper (usually me whenever I got to do it) made a mistake? Speaking of the pressbox, I can still remember it perched on the top of the roof of that rickety stadium. But it really had the flavor of a baseball stadium, didn't it?

"Thanks for your including my father [Ty Cobb Sr., longtime RGJ sportswriter and columnist] as the announcer. Boy, did he do that for many years. Remember the old metal gong that they would ring at the end of the inning – one gong for each run. I remember my dad would hold the microphone by the triangular iron piece that was hanging there as someone would wallop it with a metal rod. How about my dad's favorite song that he would play to get the crowd going – Rebel Rouser *by Duane Eddy. [made famous again later in the redneck scene in the Forrest Gump movie.]*

Good memories, William – thank you. When we get Triple A ball downtown or by the Sparks Marina we'll already have a bunch of tradition to build on. And Phil and Gregg Zive can do the play-by-play.

When Fourth and Virginia was the center of town...

Walkin' North Virginia Street, ca. 1955

It's a grand autumn morning to take a stroll downtown along North Virginia Street to the Truckee River. The year is 1950 or a bit later, when trees still line the street by the apartments along North Virginia – fifty years later others will be struggling to recreate the downtown we're so taking for granted on this fine morning. The shops and used car dealerships between West Fifth and Fourth were moved out a few years ago to make room for the new Sewell's market we're passing, probably the first grocer in Reno to take up a full half-block. The Federated Church on the northeast corner of Sewell's lot is being razed as we walk; a few architectural features salvaged and moved to the new church 'way out on West Seventh Street. On the corner at Fourth – the confluence of two major highways, US 40 and US 395 – is a Standard Oil service station, the busiest in northern Nevada until well into the 1960s.

Across Fourth Street on the corner lies the Grotto Bar, where the cowboys from the cow counties frequently confronted the judo instructors from newly-renamed Stead Air Force Base, and that wasn't sawdust on the floor, it was last night's furniture.

Walking south, the food purveyors to our city: the Purity Bakery, a fruit market, Pettis' Pharmacy, Bill Pettis a popular druggist in Reno for decades to follow (Reno Drug). The California Market, not to be confused with the California Avenue Market on California and Lander – this downtown one a wholesale meat market.The legendary Little Waldorf Saloon, the unofficial watering hole for the University of Nevada student body. Welsh's Bakery. Flagg's Furniture, Rauhut's Bakery, which would later move down South Virginia to the FNB office to built on Arroyo, then north almost to Mary Street (where there's still a shell of a building next to the motel.) Then on the corner of Plaza a professional building, where ace architect Russell Mills practiced, and Reno Sporting Goods. Some of my placement may be off; I've a conflict in the City directories, phone books, and a collection of ads from stuff like old papers, Reno High and U of N yearbooks and Reno Little Theater programs. I tend to go with the ads as being the most accurate…

Let's cross Plaza Street and the tracks – a few years ago we could have used the pedestrian tunnel that once existed under that route, until some bad guys started rousting tourists in the darkness of the tunnel – hard to believe, isn't it? On Commercial Row, a classy joint, the Stag Inn, not to be confused with the later Stagger Inn on West Second, or Raymond Stagg's Roaring Camp. No connection. In that block next was Heaney's Loan and Jewelry, George Heaney a fine guy who a few years later would loan his red '32 Ford roadster to the "Rebel Without a Cause" filmmakers – James Dean himself got to drive it. In that building, with mostly stockbrokers upstairs, was Southworth's Cigar Store, with an honest-to-God cigar store Indian at its Douglas Alley entrance, no more politically correct than the savages attacking the cowboys on the roof of Harolds Club across the street. But this was 1950, and scant commotion was made of all this. *[That cigar store Indian is now displayed in the Wells Avenue window of a paint store on the corner of Wells and East Second Street.]*

Across Douglas Alley, the Primadonna; owner Ernie Primm named it; statuesque showgirls adorning the roof. Then R. Herz & Brother Jewelers, who would soon move south by the river. Next, the late columnist Ty Cobb's favorite restaurant, Tiny's Waffle Shop, a classic. Paterson's Mens Store, who with Sunderland's, a few doors to the south, would soon move to West First and Sierra, later to burn down in the 1957 explosion. The popular Monarch Café and Toby's Ladies Wear were in this block. Roger's Jewelry, next the DeLuxe Taxi office, where the dispatcher had a window to the street and a half-dozen phones. Both cabs sat ready at the curb. On the north corner, a Walgreen Drug (these latter few businesses were in the present building, known then as the Byington Building.) *[OK – still is.]*

Crossing West Second Street, Edise's Jewelers, Leeds and Lerner's ladies wear, with varying apostrophes, a Colbrandt's Tavern which I think at one time was the Cameo but I can't prove it. And the Games family (some of my most loyal readers who dine every Saturday morning at the south Truckee River Bar and Grill) owned the Washoe Market next door – in a few years they'd relocate 12 blocks south on South Virginia Street. These buildings were the financial heart of Reno: the Clay Peters building, four stories, the Wonder Building (a dress shop on the street floor), the Cheney building, then the Hilp's Building (Hilp's Drug on street level), where my mother opened an origami shop but it folded. On the street, the magnificent old clock in front of Ginsburg's Jewelers that took a lickin' with floods and fires downtown and keeps on tickin' in Park Lane. And yes, there was a similar clock across the street also, at Gensler-Lee Jewelers, its fate unknown. Ending this block, the Mapes building that housed the now-closed Woolworth's on street level (this an earlier building than the present one.)

Crossing West First and down to the river, Wilson Drugs, Morrill and Machabee office supply, and the Nevada Bank of Commerce in the Masonic

Building. Across the river, in the Riverside: United Air Lines, three words, operated a ticket counter for its daily DC-3 flight out of Hubbard Field to San Francisco, and the Riverside Florist, in a tie with Glenn Turner's as the greatest florists in town. And – old-timers get ready for this: Hans Lugin-Buehl's gift store, a pricey place with the cachet of Gump's in San Francisco. Any wedding gift from Lugin-Buehl's given in 1950 is probably a treasured possession of some couple now celebrating a Golden anniversary.

• • •

Space draws short; let's rest at the powerhouse Corner Bar in the Riverside and start back north soon. 299 Safe Days at Ralston Food Company, congratulations hometown boy/Arizona Diamondback Matt Williams, and God Bless America!

Walking the east side of Virginia Street

Ok, Homefinders, we've been lollygagging for a week in the lobby of the Riverside Hotel, even enjoyed Dennis Day's singing one night in the showroom, but the hour has come to journey north by Shank's-Mare back along the east side of Virginia Street to our cars in Sewell's parking lot. It's 1950+, and after Thanksgiving next week the carolers will be on the lawn of the State Building across the street, but the activity south of the river will be another column all its own some Saturday.

Walking north, the grand lady of the Truckee, the four-year old Mapes Hotel, hard to elaborate on too much anymore. The hotel was home to Dean Witter's stockbrokerage office, an Arthur Murray dance studio, Virginia Stevenson's Ladies Store, George Benioff Furs, operated by Les Conklin the Senior before he opened his own store, and KATO radio on the mezzanine – Bob and Betty Stoddard at the mike. Walter Ramage ran the hotel, Harry Spencer garnered the publicity masterfully, and I should mention that the corner entrance at East First Street was a Rexall Drug store.

Across East First Street, the First National Bank building dating to 1913. A new building would be built in 1953, four stories, to be later replaced by the present onyx-and-stainless building built in 1963, now occupied by the Reno Chamber of Commerce. *[And now, Reno City Hall. Copious parking next door…]*

Everyone remembers the Arcade Building, with its first couple of stories open to all its shops like a Spanish plaza, some the sporting goods store and Joseph Magnin's. The upper floors were professional offices. The Medico-Dental Building – a curious name (when I was young Medico was a popular maker of smoking pipes, and the connection to dentists always eluded me.) It seemed that half of Reno's doctors and dentists practiced in that four-story building (the other half across the street in the Hilp's Building!) Walking past the Arcade, the four-story Clay Peters Building, its tenant directory on the street containing many of the Who's Who in Reno business and legal circles. The best-informed people in Reno were the little ladies, both under five feet tall, who ran the elevators in those buildings, and knew pretty well who was visiting their attorney, their shrink, or both.

The Waldorf – an elegant nightclub in the mainstream of downtown Reno. A great piano bar, and scene of Jack Joseph's late-night celebrity drop-in radio show. Good food, and not to be confused with the Little Waldorf across the street and tracks. Next, Armanko's – tied with Morrill & Machabee across the street as Reno's leading office supply houses. At the East Second Street corner, Skeel's Drug. And we can't stand at this corner too long without looking up at the red light hung over the street that summoned the duty cop downtown to call the dispatcher.

Across East Second Street in the Harrah block, another First National Bank, the tiny main office for the whole state. Strange, until one looked at the tenant list and noted that the bankers, miners, captains of industry and law firm – Woodburn, et al – were the backbone of Nevada's growth during the 1920s and '30s, and they *liked* this little building. (It would later become the head office of Harrah's, including Mr. Harrah's own office.) North of FNB I invade Reno historian Dwayne Kling's turf, his great book *Rise of the Biggest Little City* the defining story of Reno gaming. Go to Sundance Books and buy a copy for your spouse for Christmas, then you can read it yourself. [Or follow it up with Dwayne's later *All The Lights Were On*.] I will note that as we walk, we pass Harrah's only casino in the whole world in 1950, then only four years old. The Frontier Club. The Nevada Club, with the best coffee shop in town (whatever happened to decent coffee shops?) Then Harrah's Bingo Parlor, a popular game for people not comfy with table gaming. And mighty Harolds Club, no apostrophe. As we walk past it, look up at the mural – created in 1949 by San Francisco artist Theodore McFall, who also did some artwork in the interior of the club. Last I heard, McFall was still alive, living in Pacific Grove, California. In 1950 you could still see some detail that was lost forever when some later signage obscured it (that coiled, hissing rattlesnake – ouch!!) *[Mr. McFall later passed away. See the Harolds Club Mural chapter…]*

Across Douglas Alley, the Colony Club, one day to become part of Harolds, and upstairs in that building, a "T and that rhymes with P and that stands for Pool" (parlor.) Trouble. On the roof, the Indians, attacking the pioneers in the Harolds Club mural. Beyond Commercial Row and the railroad tracks, a used car lot and Reno Vulcanizing, where they'd bond new rubber onto your old tires and off you'd go up the Lincoln Highway. Then, the Sportsman sporting goods – Swede Christiansen behind the counter, best-known salesclerk in Reno, a popular guy. *[A gratifying number of readers remembered Swede – the consummate salesperson – after this piece ran.]* On the corner, Silver State Appliance on the ground floor of the Ross apartment house – Silver State would move in later years to the building kitty-korner behind the Standard Station. *[I wrote cater-corner just once and no one knew what the hell I meant.]*

Crossing West Fourth Street, Jack Reifschnieder's auto body shop, earlier, Rissone's auto service. Then Reno Furniture – "Your home should come first" was Kelly and Margie Eccles' motto in their ads. Nice people. Patricia Stevens' Girls Charm School, not a bad concept to bring back today. Then McKesson Liquor and Safeway in a picturesque old brick building still standing on the corner at Fifth Street but probably doomed. *[Still there.]* Safeway, who built the building, was about to depart that corner as we walk in 1950, driven out by the huge new Sewell's built in 1948 across Virginia Street. And north from there, just small apartment after apartment, on tree-lined North Virginia Street, all the way to the University campus and the Wolf's Den bar on East Ninth Street.

• • •

It's been a good walk, thanks for tagging along. We'll organize another 1950s walk soon, up and down Center Street or maybe along Second Street. Until then, Happy Thanksgiving, and God bless America…

[appeared November 9th and 16th, 2001)

Great piles of bricks and stones all over the town...

SOME NIFTY BUILDINGS...

The days grow shorter, the crisp of early autumn hangs over our early mornings; HAN, RTO, ArTown and the rodeo are in the past, and the kids are back in school – (do modern schools have the permeating, almost pleasant odor of fresh wax and polish on the hardwood floors we returned to after summer vacations?) I've learned that no one reads this column anyway on Labor Day or the Fourth of July weekends, so right now I'm having a little fun with my solitude, kidding on the keys, just the RGJ's linotype operator and I.

Many notes collected over the summer went into an "unsung treasures" file, most subtitled "bricks and stones" – buildings we'd pay an arm and leg to replicate today for our new office or home. Reading this column any further creates the implied promise that you'll go out and visit them on your own. Study the workmanship on... The Belmont Apartments at California and Arlington (once "Belmont Street"). The old industrial buildings and hotels on East Fourth Street. Incredibly complex masonry on so many homes in the Academy Heights area by the University – hobbit doors, columns, variegated colors of brick – Imperial Way, Codel, The Strand, Citadel, Seminary, College – park on any of those old streets and just take a fall walk. And if you're that far north, go a block or two west to "little Italy," generally Washington and Bell Streets north of Whitaker Park and check out the rococo interlocking of multicolored bricks and wood, the arches and fenestration (OK, OK: windows, sills, and lintels.)

Downtown now, and remember you made a promise to go: The Triune Building at Pine and Center, named by attorney Clel Georgetta for the Triune Ranch he grew up on in eastern Nevada – great brickwork – across from the Pioneer Theater (can you implode a round building...?) Check out the former Skaggs-Safeway market at Fifth and North Virginia, SE corner, and the old National Dollar Store/Parker's downtown. Under a half-century of bad paint jobs lies a wonderfully designed classic auto dealership at 500 South Virginia Street, reminiscent of many on San Francisco's Van Ness Avenue auto row. It was for many years the Dick Dimond Dodge and the Cyrillic or Hebrew letters on some of the blocks continue to elude me, and others I've asked. Were it to be sandblasted back to its postwar red brick it could be one of the prettiest buildings in downtown Reno, and here you never even noticed it.

In the Saturday morning treasures, rock division, are the old guardrails along the University Terrace curve by the Lambda Chi house, and the big stone mansion at the southwest corner of Keystone Avenue and Kings Row, built almost a hundred years ago by Chinese laborers – note the vents to free evil spirits on the roof crown – great rockwork, no spirits. Right house, wrong lot: The Steinheimer, Hill, later Redfield house on Mt. Rose Street. Picture that baby removed to the long-vacant bluff in the 800 block of Marsh Avenue overlooking Reno High and the Village Center, with extensive landscaping and a big matching rock-and-wrought iron fence along the street. Now *that* would be a showplace. But – the granddaddy of rock, the sovereign of stone, is on Hillcrest, a block south of West Plumb Lane and a half-block west of South Virginia. A drum roll please: the Alamo Lodge. And remember, you're on your honor to go there, and tell me if you've ever seen finer stonemasonry in the world, including the lighthouse with its stained-glass lens and the little wishing well in the front yard. And it's unbelievable how few Homefinders ever see it, and, sadly, that it can't be relocated. In the same architectural vein, check out the El Borracho lounge a few blocks to the north on South Virginia Street. *[And since much of that block has been cleaned up, one can actually see the Alamo looking past the Mark Twain Motel from South Virginia Street.]*

While they're not ornate masonry, we must be happy as connoisseurs of old structures that the ornate original entrances of sprawling Washoe Med and ditto St. Mary's hospitals have both been mercifully preserved in spite of a dozen expansions of each facility. Well done, trustees. And we just have to include the former Mary Ann Nichols School on Pyramid Way, and the Robert Mitchell School on Prater, for their cool brickwork.

Now – while you're committed to a mandatory, self-guided tour of neat stuff to see, we'll depart brick and stone for Lincoln logs – piles of them, we call it the Silver State Motel on West Fourth Street, built when the Lincoln Highway (40) ran in front of it. Fifty years from now some real estate broker-turned-drive-by-columnist will play the game I played five years ago with the El Reno Apartments – how many were there? – When were they built? – Where are they now? So, my counsel to some seven-year old who likes to write would be, go out and count them so you'll be prepared when I retire. Soon they'll likely be dismantled and rebuilt, maybe all over town like the El Reno apartments have been. There was lots of history in that little "auto court," as it was called. And I can't omit that my classmate, Pat Reynolds Ferraro Klos, the grand diva of the Historical Reno Preservation Association, grew up with her family in the Silver State Motel;

her late parents, Rod and Peg owned them for many years. *[Sorry, young writers – they were demolished – no salvage – in 2004.]*

A few more treasures, seldom visited: Oxbow Park and the Dickerson mansion, on Dickerson Road, where else; another is the University Farm, one of the last places around to take the little ones to see herds of sheep and cattle. They've a great butcher shop there, known only to a few, and your child could take a little lamb to school (between two slices of bread) *[Several readers complained about "herds" of sheep. When writing a column, one economizes on words. How 'bout a "flock," or a "band"?]*

Final unsung treasure for the weekend: train whistles. (never *horns.*) In a year or two we'll miss them. Does anyone else wish that they'd just left Lawton's Resort alone? A great swimmin' hole, far better than what's there west of town on the river now. And while speaking of the river, one squawk: Kayakers must have better lobbyists that the Virginia Lake joggers and walkers – the Truckee is being turned to a rehearsal stage for World War III to accommodate kayaks, yet we can't get more than one working drinking fountain at Virginia Lake. *[It gets worse: At production time there's rumor of removing two of the four Wingfield tennis courts, to create parking for kayakers.]*

Go forth in safety and good cheer for the next three days; watch out for self-expressionists rejoining society from Burning Man, have your hat blocked at Peerless Cleaners, sign up for the Historic Preservation fall tours, floss, know where your children are, buy a home through a Realtor, and God bless America.

Labor Day, 2002

Before the supermarkets and two-car families...

Ten items or less, and other myths...

Maybe you've already had your turkey, pilgrim, but I write this Tuesday with visions of drumsticks dancing through my head, and hearken back to an era when 90 per cent of the grocery stores in Reno weren't much bigger than a Seven-11 convenience store. I mentioned a fortnight ago that families 50 years ago had refrigerators only slightly larger than the little countertop units we have in our offices, and even after the World War II many weren't even mechanical refrigeration – the Iceman cometh. Thus, we visited the market several times a week, and many shoppers were limited to buying only what they could carry or wheel home.

Markets sprang up around town, their locations dictated by demographics. Travel back with me now to a smallish postwar Reno and we'll visit a few markets – many little more than a room added on to the storekeeper's home, often on a corner. Some had enough room for temperature-controlled boxes for meat and produce brought in daily from the wholesale grocers, and a few stores were large enough to sublet space to an actual butcher shop on the premises. Let's mosey around town and revisit a few stores. I'll probably miss a few; so don't be bashful about filling in the gaps. You probably think this is easy – just go through the 1950 City Directory, right? It don't work that way, boys and girls. Many listings are just "B. Akert" or "J. Barnes," and it takes a little scratching around to find it was "Akert's Market" and "Barnes' Cash Grocery." And some have had a slew of names over the years – I'm gravitating toward the names they were known by in 1950, when the mom-and-pops last proliferated.

The southeast quadrant of our Reno was populating close to South Virginia and Wells, only starting to sprawl south of Vassar. Washburn's Market was on Wilson Street, later a radio shop. Kearns' was far southeast at Kirman and Vassar by the new Veterans' Memorial School. A couple on South Wells Avenue – a redundant address in 1950, as there was no North Wells Avenue – Reid's, and Polli's a little further south. Glubrecht's was far south on Wrondel near Hubbard Way, and as I recall there was a chinchilla farm across the street. With a name like Glubrecht's it has to be good.

Organizing these markets, I tended to put the South Virginia Street markets together, and they were for the most part walking distance from southeast and southwest Reno homemakers. At the end of Wells Avenue at South Virginia was Black's, a fairly comprehensive market with a butcher shop. A little to the south at Linden was the Twentieth Century Market, next door to Harris Meat, owned by Len Harris who would later be mayor of Reno. The Old Orchard Market across from the present Park Lane Center lasted well into the 1960s; to the north was the Mt. Rose at 711 South Virginia. The Farmer's Market was exactly that, a little north of the Old Orchard by the present Peppermill, serving retail customers and wholesale to other Reno markets.

Southwest Reno, as we've learned in past columns, wasn't exactly overdeveloped in 1950 – picture the town with no Plumb Lane east of Arlington Avenue and little development west of Hunter Lake Drive. (The Corner Market at Hunter Lake and Mayberry was rural, as in "dirt roads.") The California Avenue Market (known for a time as the "South Side Market") was the venerable grocery in that part of town, a full market with a popular butcher shop that went well into the 1970s – George Minor, later Charlie Bradley, finally Fred Antoniazzi – the legends of lambchops. A kid named Karl Breckenridge the Elder delivered groceries for them on a bike with a huge basket in the early 1930s. (It should be mentioned that most of these markets survived by running an efficient and speedy delivery trade, filling a good percentage of their orders by phone. Ergo, some stores were called "cash grocery" – no delivery, cash on the barrelhead, no charge accounts.) Still in the southwest was Clark's Market, east on California Avenue in what would become Powell's Drugs at Humboldt. To the south, Collier's, on Mt. Rose Street by the present Seven-11, and the Lander Street Market, which closed only last spring *[2002],* near Mount Rose School. *[Mt. Rose Street, Mount Rose School. Fourth Street in Reno, 4th Street in Sparks. Wanna be an editor…?]*

As we travel to northeast Reno I realize we've a long way to go and space grows short, but we'll get to northwest Reno and Sparks next week or my name isn't Don Jack. I mentioned Akert's Market on East 4th and Alameda (North Wells) Avenue, where the Akerts' son Ben learned the grocery trade decades before opening Ben's Discount Liquors. On East Sixth, Meffleys, further out was Mathisen's, later a catering hall *[the late Swede Mathisen, mentioned in a license plate chapter].* On East Fourth, the Lincoln, Pinky's, and further out the M&M and L&H Meats. Davey's, on Quincy by the future freeway. Muenow's, on East Seventh.

Downtown, where a lot of people worked then shopped on the way home, was Ring-Lee with one store on Mill Street and the other in the block now occupied by the Bank of America Plaza on Liberty. In the Liberty block also was a Safeway, and Frank's on the corner of Sierra. Safeway had another store in the classic brick building that remains on the southeast corner of North Virginia and 5th Street that opened before WWII as a Skaggs-Safeway. That store would survive until the Sewell family opened the "super-store" in 1948 across Virginia Street, demolished in 1995 for the Silver Legacy. Lemaire's was a little north of that on Virginia; Louie Piazzo's across the tracks to the south in a space later occupied by The Sportsman. The Reno Public Market was on East Second at Lake. A little larger than a mom-and-pops were the Eagle Thriftys (later Raley's), the aforementioned-Sewell's, and the Games family's Washoe Market, still all downtown. We had a little confusion in town, and more in this column, over the California Market across from Piazzo's – often confused with the California *Avenue* Market named above (that one often called the California Avenue Grocery.

Next Saturday morning, we'll watch Santa arrive at the Sparks Hometowne Parade, then visit the mom-and-pop groceries in the Rail City, and go west on Highway 40 to the many stores in northwest Reno.

• • •

Paper or plastic?

Last week we plied the streets of 1950s Reno touring little markets. Some wrote, "you missed Washoe Market, Eagle Thrifty and Sewell's Markets" *[their names above didn't appear in the column but were added to the book]* – but we were spotlighting the smaller stores. We ran out of steam as we left populous northeast Reno nearing the Sparks neighbor-hoods, so we'll pick up the beat there and stop in the express lane of the Stop 'n Go on the corner of East Fourth and Coney Island, then I'll say this one last time and you'll never have to read it again in a *Homefinder* column: When we're recalling the old days, the present Victorian Avenue shall for-ever be known as B Street. (I've grown weary of making that distinction week-after-week.)

Down the road to Sparks, in no particular order, we have Kellison's on B Street, a block from Baker's Grocery and butcher shop, and I have a deal with the guy who assembles the *Homefinder* each week that on the Saturday following his retirement from the RGJ, which will coincide with my final column, I will print for you all to read the motto on the side of Baker's 1950 Chevy panel delivery truck. *[I'll keep the deal, but their motto started "You can beat our prices, but you can't….," and here remind you that they were also a butcher shop.]* Pay 'n Save was a little to the east on B Street; as we learned last week most grocery stores carried charge accounts and delivered – the name Pay 'n Save indicated that it was a no-frills store.

"Conductor Heights" – the residential area south of the S.P. tracks – was well served by Gomes' Grocery on South 17th Street (now Rock Boulevard). On Prater and 15th Street was Kendall's, nearby the Wright Way Market, a classic that Washoe County Clerk Amy Harvey would shoot me for not mentioning. Smitty's Market (Lody Smith's family) was on B near Pyramid Way (OK, "8th Street" in 1950). How could we forget the Midget Mart on B near 2nd Street – one of the earliest "mini stores" and still in business today as "Litke's," tied with the Wright Way as the oldest markets in Sparks.

• • •

Just as some theaters have poor acoustics, I think some of these columns suffer from a failure to communicate clearly. Last week's "we'll go to northwest Reno next week" text failed to prevent about ten people from calling or emailing "How about the Santa Claus" or the "Ralston" or some such. All together we go now, west along Highway 40 but we can't stop for coffee at the Gold-n-Silver because it won't be built for seven more years. (Some reader will probably suggest Hale's Drug's fountain at West Fourth and Vine, for the best hamburgers in town in 1950.)

It's nearing Christmas, so I'll mention the Santa Claus Market first – a tiny little rock building on the corner of Vine and West Sixth, the native stone spray painted bright silver and not likely to be confused with any other structure in Reno. Across West Fifth Street from Mary S. Doten School was the Cottage Grocery, Johnny Beetchen, proprietor, who was also the butcher (as I mentioned last week, a butcher shop was a rarity in these little mom & pops.) A block north on Washington Street at Seventh was the Quality Market and gas station – known to most as "Quilici's" – and many of us aging northwest Reno denizens long for the chance to have grabbed up their gray '40 Ford pickup with "Quality Market" on the doors, always parked alongside the antique hand-operated, glass-reservoir gas pump that really belongs on someone's, say my, patio. It probably got carted off as junk when the I-80 freeway ate the old Quality Market site. I can say with authority that the Quality, Cottage and Santa Claus sold one hell of a lot of Bazooka bubble gum, licorice ropes and banana Popsicles after school

Ralston Street? You bet – three markets I know of: the Ralston Market at the foot of the hill by West Sixth Street *[gone]*, Maynard's at Tenth Street, (now the Pub-and-Sub, Sigma Nu fraternity's beer garden branch office) and the University Market two blocks to the north of Maynard's. On West Fourth Street, Reno's apartment row, the Elmwood Market at 435 West Fourth and Churchill's across Highway 40 from old Reno High (in 1950, a year later Central Jr. High, now the Sundowner site.) Barnes' Cash Grocery, a block to the west on the ol' Lincoln Highway.

On West Second Street, (Brickie) Hansen's Market, across from Bello's tamale factory, best in the west. Vanoni's Market was further west at Arletta (Gardner?) Street. While noodling around West Third at the site of the present Sands Resort we find the Porta family's market, stocking every manner of pasta for the "little Italy" district north on Washington Street. I'd mention that it was later the first location of Porta Subs, but Lee Green, *neé* Lina Porta, wife of our favorite Central Jr. High vice-principal Chet Green, wouldn't want me to do that. So I won't. And on Sierra Street serving Academy Heights, as in "University of Nevada's faculty enclave": Rommelfanger's, 'way north by College Drive, and DuPratt's, nearer downtown at Sierra and West Sixth. That was the town's only Rommelfanger's, by the way.

There are others, like the Ferrari family's Food Store on West Second Street, so stay tuned – we're not done shopping yet.

Bringing the Sparks Nugget to the pages of the San Francisco Chronicle...

Happy Bill Howard, The Flagpole Sitter

'Twas in the year of 1955 that battleship gray and black-and-green high-reach trucks – Sierra Pacific Power and Nevada Bell's respectively – set a spindly 60-foot pole on the north side of B Street in Sparks just across the street from the Sparks Nugget's brand-new building, set guy wires to keep it vertical, and then lifted a replica of a shiny gold nugget as big as a Chevy Suburban to the top of the pole. On that nugget they set a platform, and finally a canvas tent on the platform, then aimed floodlights up to illuminate it.

The Nugget casino south of B Street was tiny compared to the Nugget of today; no I-80 freeway over the building, just B Street out in front doubling as transcontinental Highway 40. No elephants; this was pre-Bertha. Last Chance Joe had just arrived to keep an eye on the happenings out in front. And pilgrim, did he get an eyeful as Happy Joe Howard, the last of the great pre-war flagpole sitters arrived on August 4 to begin his ascent to the platform atop the tower where he would stay longer than any flagpole sitter would ever sit. Flagpole-sitting was a rage that died out somewhere in the 1930s, probably for good reason, but the Nugget's then-owner Dick Graves, already well-along in the process of selling the Nugget to John Ascuaga, was a showman, attuned to every PR stunt in the book.

Howard soon became accustomed to life on top of the highest building in Sparks. He became the darling of the local media and the West Coast scribes when his time on top of the gold nugget started to look like a serious attempt. A month, two months, dragged by, the number on the base of the "flagpole" being changed daily to indicate the number of days he had stayed there. The summer of 1955 arrived and the world was in turmoil, but local notice was paid first to Happy Bill Howard, so high above B Street, drawing crowds of people who would stop on the highway to look in wonder at how he could possibly keep doing it.

Casual visitors could speak to Happy Bill on a phone provided by Nevada Bell, from the base of the tower to his lofty perch. Several times daily a truck from the Nugget arrived to lift a basket of grub – the best fare of the Roundhouse Room or an Awful-Awful burger from the Coffee Shop, maybe an iced pitcher of piçons from the Nugget's long-gone Basque Bar, the day's edition of the *Reno Evening Gazette*, and letters from his fans. He had a radio, no TV. For reasons unknown to anyone, a band of local idiots tried to incinerate Happy Bill by burning down his tower, forgetting that the Sparks Fire Department and Police Department were housed nearby on C Street then. The fire laddies doused the fire and Sparks' Finest threw the perpetrators into the hoosegow for a few nights.

Time marched on into the late autumn. The West Coast press still loved it, and afforded the Nugget the ongoing publicity in the Bay Area that Dick Graves had hoped for. Happy Bill's birthday arrived, with accompanying hoopla and a cake from the Nugget's bakery, songs from the local media and fans. Rumors abounded – was Happy Bill happy because a truck would arrive by dark of night to hoist a comely visitor to his lonely perch, to share the aura of the Southern Pacific railyard and other local attractions with him, to then be lowered and escape just as the dawn of a new day broke over "S" Hill east of town? Seven months is a long time.

And the unexpected occurred – Happy Bill woke up with a hell of a toothache one morning, and the Nugget summoned respected Reno dentist Arnold Johannes to his aid. In a display of humanitarian emergency not one bit concealed from the adoring press, Dr. Johannes was lifted in a Jacob's Chair-harness with his black bag of drills, pliers, wrenches, laughing gas and an HMO form to Happy Bill's side, to administer on-the-pole medical aid. I suspect that the rest of the late Dr. Johannes' career, excitement-wise, was downhill after that procedure…

As the leaves turned to gold on the trees lining the Reserve in Sparks, the evening winds turned wintry. Happy Bill's reign over the little town was coming to a close, although not for lack of interest – the town and the media continued to embrace his effort, but the simple fact was that his flagpole had no heat, and the night was rapidly approaching during which he'd freeze his celebrated buns off. Leaving on a high note started to become realistic.

In a round of PR embraced by Reno and Sparks and the San Francisco press, by then including Herb Caen and Terrence O'Flaherty, Happy Bill Howard was returned to Mother Earth by the same Nevada Bell snorkel truck that had set him atop the flagpole, 204 days – almost seven months – before.

Bill's work on earth, or in this case above it, was done – his effort was vastly successful in putting the little burg of Sparks, known before by very few in the Bay Area as being a little east of Reno, wherever that was, permanently onto the map. For his efforts he was awarded a sterling silver belt buckle as big as a penny postcard engraved with *Thanks from the Sparks Nugget* in a very public ceremony. To our knowledge, he never sat flagpoles again. And Sparks, whatever it been before that, was defined as a destination town; Dick Graves departing, a legend named John Ascuaga soon to arrive.

I thank several readers for inquiring about Happy Bill Howard and inspiring this story, Fred Davis – the Nugget's longtime (1958-1972) publicity director, Sparks native Don Stockwell, he of the ironclad memory, the Nevada Historical Society, and John Ascuaga, Nugget executive secretary Nancy Trabert and publicist Beth Cooney for their help with this yarn.

What the cruisers would see at the 1941 Hot August Nights...

Cruisin' in our '41 Chevy

An old friend offered me a yellowed copy of a Nevada State Journal – "Nevada's Only Morning and Sunday Newspaper," according to the masthead. Since there's some readers in town engaged in the current Hot August Nights nuttiness that drives sane people to live in the past, and since there's readers who would actually pay good money today for a car with a flathead-6 engine, no heater, vacuum window wipers that died going up the California Avenue hill, a carb that needed choking before it would start and steered like a John Deere baler, then it follows that they might also enjoy reading some of what was happening in town when that same car was built, and retracing their car's old path. The paper was interesting to me because it went to press the day I was born in Santa Barbara, six Sundays before Pearl Harbor. I left Cottage Hospital in a '41 Chevy coupe. I remember it well.

• • •

Perspective established, here we are seated now in our brand-new '41 Chevy, a slick little car like a hundred others that will be in town sixty years later on a Saturday morning at a Show 'n Shine or a Poker Run to Tahoe. There's no drive-in theaters in Reno or Sparks yet, but a good choice of flicks, with the Sparks Theater; in Reno the shaky Majestic that defied attempts at demolition 40 years later. Or the Wigwam near where many of us remember the Crest, and the Granada, the Reno, and the Tower –"Reno's newest and smartest show house," according to the ad. I didn't know that; I did know that kids my age went to the Tower in droves on Saturdays for a morning of movies for 14¢ and an Old Home Milk bottle top. But I've written about that before, so we'll keep driving.

Our date might want to stop by Hilp's Drug Stores for a jar of Marie Earle's Essential Cream for two bucks, this week only, on North Virginia Street in Reno (phone 6104) or 938 B Street in Sparks (333, free delivery.) Whatever essential cream is, it sounds important, a chick thing. Hilp's was a great old store… R. Herz Jewelers was a block south of Hilp's in Reno, Credit Available, wedding rings $7.50 to $300, "You can pay by the week or month." They must know what they're doing, they were "Established 1885"and still going at press time. A little low on gas in the Chevy? Among other service stations in this paper, try Krieger's, 14¢ a gallon, which is interesting, but the real item is the address, 111 West First Street – a service station near where the downtown parking garage is today at Sierra. Want a ride out into the country? Head out past the County Hospital on the Mill Street Road to the Reno Riding Stables, "also renting horses for the upcoming deer hunting season." (The hospital would later be Washoe Med.)

Here's an intriguing establishment: the Carlisle Bar & Service Station, corner of Wells and Second Street, and another, Dougherty's, South Virginia and Mt. Rose Streets, featuring a bar, dancing, and Richfield Oil Products. Buying gas was once fun, apparently, beating the hell out of sitting in line at Costco. Lyons & Maffi Signal gas advertises its address at 1111 California Avenue and Granite Street; hearken back to past columns speaking of Sierra Street once being known as Granite. *[The address is really 111, not as typoed at 1111. These old typos are what make nostalgia columnists crazy... And, the astute reader will note that that this is on the site of the Levy Mansion, detailed in another chapter.]*

Ramos Drug was a favorite, first on the corner of Second and Virginia Streets, after 1952 at midblock between Hill and Flint Streets on California Avenue. Genial Bill Ramos was a great friend to many, and the interior of his drug stores looked like a soda fountain background for a Hot August Nights poster. *[More of Ramos Drug on the California Avenue walk chapter.]* In this particular newspaper the Ramos ad is for "the Bracer, the First Step Toward That Well-Dressed 'Executive' Look, to trim the waistline, pull in the stomach muscles, and eliminate the 'bay-window' for the vital, up-and-coming look." (In my experience, the *muscles* aren't the problem.) Two bucks for a Bracer, for the very few *Homefinder* readers whom that might benefit, this week only at Ramos'. Cheaper than going to the gym.

Heading for the barn in this ride in our Chevy, we find a foreboding ad from John Whitmire Motors on South Virginia Street: a full half-page layout, depicting an Oldsmobile (with *HydraMatic*!), with a license plate lettered *New 4-42* in the artwork. Why foreboding? Two reasons: Many years later, Olds would introduce a muscle car called a "4-4-2" – four-on-the-floor, four-barrel carburetor, and dual exhaust. That 4-4-2 thing was surely a coincidence that had nothing to do with the 1941 ad. But ponder this: The ad's text reveals that the *4-42* plate was to indicate *New for 1942*.

Remember, this paper came out six Sundays before Pearl Harbor. *Oldsmobile never made a '42 model....*

[And it gets weirder: As I assemble this book, the last Olds ever are coming off the assembly line.]

• • •

Thanks to my childhood buddy Mike Lindeman for the old newspaper, welcome to Reno and Sparks if you're in for the weekend, and happy cruisin' to all!

The first downtown fire that most readers can remember – 1948

The Lake Street Fire

Few who lived in our little valley on that August midmorning didn't hear – or feel – the thump coming from downtown Reno, that by the end of that sunny Sunday would leave five people dead and well over a hundred injured.

On the heels of mentioning the YMCA explosion a week or so ago, several readers pitched the Lake Street, or Greyhound building fire as a topic candidate for a future *Homefinder* column, so grab your turnouts and the Dalmatian – here we go, Code Three…

•••

It was August 15th, 1948, a bright morning in a small town where most of the churches were close to the downtown area, bringing a lot of people there on a Sunday. Up at our family home on Ralston Street we could hear sirens congregating at the origin of a smoke column that was evident from all over town.

The people downtown – arriving or departing from their churches – walked the three or four blocks to East Second and Lake, or down Plaza Street to Lake Street. Almost immediately, there were hundreds of onlookers; some said a thousand. Many beat the second wave of fire trucks coming from the old Commercial Row main station.

It was apparent that this was a gnarly conflagration, involving several buildings just south of the Santa Fe Hotel (that's right, northern Nevada's Piçon headquarters; or at least tied with Louis' Basque Corner.) There was a print shop, a leather tannery with a few retail products, and a Farm Labor office within the burning buildings. Just south of those buildings were the storied Mandarin Café and the Alturas Room – I found this building named in two sources as the "Van Buren Building."

Pacific Greyhound Lines and J. M. Hiskey, a local entrepreneur who owned or managed several small bus and freight lines, owned the burning buildings. In 1948, Greyhound coaches and the smaller V&T Lines, Hiskey Stages, NCO Line and a few other carriers' buses used a station in the 200 block of North Center as a terminal, that location now in back (due west) of the fire, across the alley. Hiskey had bought the Lake Street buildings to allow expansion directly through and across the alley to a new terminal to be built on Lake Street.

Point being that the fire was forever after known by many as the Greyhound *terminal* fire, but in truth that's not where the problem started… (The "Lake Street" fire found the most acceptance with the locals.)

• • •

The crowd gathered, together with every fireman and engine in town, with the Civil Air Patrol and local contractors soon bringing heavy equipment on lowboy trailers, the Salvation Army bringing food, the Red Cross medical supplies. Washoe General Hospital and St. Mary's Hospital sent on-duty employees and called in off-duty medical people. Sparks Fire sent two engine companies. Sierra Pacific Power was there. The *Reno Evening Gazette* prepared for an extra, Sunday evening edition and massed their writers, photographers and linotype operators.

All were prepared for a long fight – the fire was between two old buildings on Lake Street with yet another to the north. Across the alley to the west were many more old buildings on Center Street. And the crowd was growing, breaking police lines at both ends of that block of Lake.

Someone cried out, "One of the buildings has dynamite in it!" – a statement heard by a few but not enough spectators to scare anybody back and away. The dynamite angle was never backed up by any evidence in the days to come, but still flares up with the old timers.

But – one of the buildings sure as hell had something explosive in it, because after burning for about 25 minutes, all the while laying a thick black smoke cloud over all Reno and Sparks and attracting an ever-growing crowd, a massive explosion ripped through the Lake Street block. The concussion blew windows out of the Mizpah Hotel, the Liberty Garage and other buildings across Lake Street and north and south from the intersection. And, remnants of the burning buildings and shards of glass flew over a three-block radius.

Inevitably, the injuries numbered well into the hundreds. Smoke inhalation, cuts, abrasions and a few fractures stretched St. Mary's and Washoe General's troops thin. Major injuries resulting in the necessity of victims to be hospital-admitted numbered into several dozen (reading the injury list in an old *Gazette* brought an eerie reminder of 9/11 in New York City: The bulk of the major injuries were to firemen.) Many had Chinese surnames, indicating involvement of the Mandarin Café to the south, and a few Nevada Basque names surely were in the Santa Fe Hotel to the north. (That building survived the fire.)

Several readers reminded me that the Reno fire chief also was killed, and I confess that this was my recollection also. In fact, it was the Sparks Fire Department's chief, Frank Hobson, who died in the explosion. Frank was a longtime resident of Sparks, at the time of the fire living in Reno, who at one time in his youth worked for Southern Pacific Railroad. Two other firefighters also died: Reno Captain Glen Davis, and Fireman Earl Platt. To round out the thought, Reno's fire chief at that time was Karl Evans, a fine guy who would always let us kids climb around the old LaFrance and Seagraves engines at the main station. *[Hobson figures in* The Guy On The Bench *chapter.]*

We all learned a lesson – don't get close to fires. We kids still had a bunch of big fires out in front of us, and it's amazing how fast a Schwinn can get around town to a column of smoke: the YMCA explosion, the Elks' Home, the Masonic Temple, the Golden Hotel, and the Sierra Street mid-block fires. If I wrote about all those, I'll be out of business, modern downtown disaster-wise.

•••

Endnote: Greyhound Lines later built on that site. That building is still there, now painted to match the Harrah's tower to the south. The bus station's relocation to West First and Stevenson Streets bespeaks Reno's municipal land use at its finest. We'll write about that stroke of genius too, someday.* Have a good week, and God Bless America.

•••

**[OK – no time like the present; let's write about it right now: Harrah's needed the bus line's building so they could close the alley and join their two hotel towers. They acquired the Stevenson/Riverside corner and built a suitable building for Western Greyhound, amid a brace of public squabble over putting a bus station so close to the river. A concession by Greyhound was to agree to plant and maintain decorative vegetation sufficient to enable the station to blend into the pastoral river setting. They didn't.*

A tremendous amount of public money being spent to improve Wingfield Park and river path for kayaking. (And I'm leaving out that zilch has been spent on my childhood stomping ground, Virginia Lake.) But – as this book is prepared, the bus station, bereft of the obligatory landscaping, looks from across the river like a World War II warehouse in Herlong.

Remember that, next time a developer promises the moon – once it's built, regulatory oversight ends and we're stuck with it.

This rant is now complete. Thank you for your attention.]

It didn't always look like a castle...

The house on the hill by Virginia Lake

Luke Hancock struck oil in Oklahoma many years before J.R. and Daddy built the South Fork, and after parlaying the gusher into the Hancock Oil Company, he elected to move to sunny Southern Cal and commissioned his San Francisco architect to design a fine home for himself and the wife.

But Luke visited Reno before construction began in Beverly Hills, some say drawn here by our favorable tax climate. He stood on a barren bluff overlooking a big hole in the ground a mile around, watching WPA crews planting trees by the dirt road ringing what would soon be Virginia Lake. Luke bought two lots and told his architect to redesign the Mediterranean Villa-style home for the acre-and-a-half Reno site.

Luke never made it to the country club nearby – the place burned down, leaving only Country Club Drive as a reminder of its brief existence. But Virginia Lake finally filled to the rim and the home at 2301 Lakeside Drive was finished – the last major structure to be completed in Reno before World War II.

And what a dandy it was! A mansion with a grand staircase winding up to three huge bedrooms. (The little oval Arabesque window in the master bath fascinated all those who strolled around the lake until the home was totally remodeled in the early 1980s.) A living room with an incomparable view of the growing city – beautiful inlaid parquet hardwood flooring and an egg-and-dart coving around the ceiling. A dining room with frescoed walls depicting sunlight radiating through a shadowy bayou, the magnolia trees laden with Spanish moss. The bright little breakfast room on the curved wall on the southeast corner of the home, with similar frescos, a little livelier. We talked to a craftsman who worked on the home, who recalled the fresco artist came from Europe just to do the Hancock home – not just a red-eye flight in 1940.

• • •

But the remaining piece de resistance in the home was and is the library. Imagine a stuffy Fortune 500 boardroom like the late John Houseman strode into, "making money the old fashioned way" ad you'll have a fair picture of the library: a huge fireplace, comparable in Reno only to the fireplace in the adjacent living room. Beveled glass beam trusses resting on ornamental iron corbels to the cathedral ceiling. I turned a crank (in 1974, this), gently against the resistance of 20 years of inactivity. High above, shutters slowly creaked, then narrowed around the stained-glass skylights– as an iris closes over the pupil– and the room fell to darkness.

In 1962 a two-bedroom home for the domestic help was added, just south of the original structure. A prewar-tech Kohler generator was shunted to run the furnaces, refrigerators and the three-level elevator during power outages. (The elevator hoistway had been dismantled when I listed the home for sale in 1974.)

The southernmost of three garage bays was converted in 1952 to a Civil Defense-approved bomb shelter, with jail-style barred door, designed to allow the nuclear blast to blow through the shelter without imploding it, then keep neighbors away from the goodies when the Russians were coming – the goodies consisting of stored provisions, most tagged with Sewell's Market, the supermarket of the era. The shelter had, still intact in 1974, a self-contained toilet, a water supply, filtered ventilation, cooking facilities, books, bedding and power from the generator outside. It appeared to be an ideal place to go completely bananas within the first 24 hours of occupancy. The treasure that got away was the classic Zenith Transoceanic long/short wave/AM, battery-or-AC radio – state of the radio art in 1951 and for many years to follow. The 1974 buyer, (who's not the present owner), trashed everything in the shelter.

It was a fine old house, built before the war rearranged upscale housing concepts, difficult to sell during the realities of the 1970s. We listed it for $215,000, the price held down by the extensive landscaping needs, the interior designed to be maintained by domestic help, and what we call in the real estate biz "functional obsolescence' – small closets in the bedrooms, for example. One shining moment in the selling experience was the local doctor who tired to get his 40-foot, three-axle Greyhound-turned-motor home up the curved driveway from Lakeside Drive, to see if it would fit if he bought the home. He got the bus up there, but his wife hated the place, Milne Towing got the bus back down the driveway, and we sold the home to somebody else *[not the present owner]* who wallpapered over the irreplaceable frescos – the rough equivalent of winning the gold medal in the Olympics and having it bronzed.

• • •

[It sold, by the way, for $205,000, (1974) and we were mighty glad to get that after five months on the market.]

Well, it could have happened this way, and some early Nevada history...

OL' VIRGINNY

We all know that our main drag, Virginia Street, our once-signature park, Virginia Lake, and our Virginia & Truckee Railroad, suspended in 1950, were named for Virginia City. And, we all know that Virginia City took its name one night in the early 1850s when James "Ol' Virginny" Finney, one of the first miners in the not-yet-named Comstock Lode who had roots in the State of Virginia, maybe, partied hearty until the wee hours of a morning, probably, then smashed an empty hooch bottle to the earth and proclaimed, "I name this 'Virginny Town!'," an epic pronouncement witnessed by a half-dozen other miners as toasted as he was from emptying that bottle and several before it. If you believe all that, you'll also believe that the Easter Bunny filed an account of the proceedings with the *Territorial Enterprise* the next morning, and straightened the minutes out to read "Virginia City."

(Why do readers of this column take me to task on an event that happened in 1998, yet the whole of the State of Nevada's residents buy into a tale witnessed only by six inebriates and a rabbit, a 150 years before...?)

It doesn't matter – that's the commonly accepted version of the naming of Virginia City, and the references to Virginia to follow for the next half-century. Our ties to that state run deep – the Civil War Union general from whom we take our "Reno" name was born a Virginian. The picturesque Quadrangle – the "Quad" – on our University of Nevada campus emulates the design, landscaping, building placement and ambiance of the University of Virginia's quad and is said to be a duplicate of it; that campus designed by no less than Thomas Jefferson. And now, following a plea in this column last week for writers and historians to perpetuate the name of the island that Wingfield Park rests on – Belle Isle – comes forth Red Kittell, whose hobby of Civil War research has placed him as a formidable authority on that war's history.

Red tells me that a "Belle Isle" is located west of Richmond, Virginia on the James River. During the Civil War the small island was used to house Union prisoners-of-war. There were few structures on the island, and the prisoners, all enlisted men, were afforded no protection from the elements, which at times were savage. The number of captured Union soldiers grew to almost 10,000 by 1863 and a hospital was finally built, but the death toll continued to rise. The island, belying its idyllic-sounding name, became the dread of the Union troops. Walt Whitman gave some insight into the suffering going on within, saying "Can those be men? Those little livid-brown, ash streaked monkey-looking dwarves? Are they not really mummified, dwindled corpses…?"

We have very few names of French origin in our Spanish land-grant-heritage town. The existence of Belle Isle in Virginia coincides – chronologically – with the naming of some of Reno's early features in a period dominated by the war's aftermath, and our Belle Isle beneath Wingfield Park stands almost alone in its French-name extraction. I'll pose the question to readers, seeking an answer to what I've never been able to determine: Was the name Belle Isle for our Truckee island a local tribute of some fashion to Union soldiers who died in the heinous, insidious conditions of Virginia's Belle Isle? And, I'll stick my neck out even a little further: I've spoken to groups in the past, and probably written in these pages that Belmont Street, the former name of Arlington Avenue from the Truckee up the bluff southward to California Avenue, was a derivative of "Belle," as in Belle Island at its northern terminus, and "mont," French for "high place." Bel-mont. Readers? (That's what Ann Landers writes, translating to "I don't know either…")

In a similar vein, Red answered a question that has bugged a number of Reno residents my age for years – those of us that had heard all through school that our town was named for a Union Army officer named Jesse Reno (which we actually learned as "Reynaud," or occasionally "Renault," Anglicized to "Reno.") Reno, we learned in school, was an Army surveyor, sent west to complete the Congressionally-mandated national survey – the section, township and range system, with one section set aside for a schoolhouse.

"How did so many teachers and texts go so wrong?" asked I of Red. "He was a general who died in battle, one of the major battles of the war."

"In the 21st century, we call it political correctness," Red answered. "When you heard the 'surveyor' bit, was the 1940s, maybe '50s. A few of the soldiers who actually fought in the war, and many of their children who had learned of it first-hand from their fathers, were still alive – some wore blue, others wore gray. To call Jesse Reno – the namesake of our town – a conquering hero, would have polarized Reno residents and the nation. Only in years to follow could his true accomplishment could be popularized…"

I thank Red for this Jesse Reno and Belle Isle insight.

[A follow-up e-mail to the Belle Isle inspiration came in, from a man I respect greatly, and who has provided our state with an incalculable amount of Nevada – and railroad – history. His name is Richard Datin, and his name appears elsewhere in this book.

Richard disputed the Belle Isle-explanation for the park's name, inasmuch as our strong Union state, Battle Born, would not deify such an ugly memory of the Civil War, and a Confederate facility. My words, with Red's, were that it was in tribute to the Union troops who suffered or died there, not an effort to memorialize the prison camp.

I respect his opinion. No other explanations came in, and this book draws no conclusion as to Belle Isle's name origin.]

• • •

Before this gets too cerebral, I better paw through the ol' e-mailbag: Two readers wrote that the duplex on the northwest corner of Mt. Rose and Arlington Avenue was moved onto the site, and was an El Reno apartment. It was indeed moved onto the site after it was built in the NAPCO building on Timber Way, as were a lot of other Reno structures built in that old building in the 1950s. But it's not an El Reno.

Last week's column mentioned Russ Sheldon's early KZTV/KOLO-TV show "Snootrac," and a few readers cried "misprint." "Snootrac" is the Yiddish word for "Cartoons," Yiddish being a language read right-to-left.

As a 26-year finish judge at the Air Races what do I think of the Air Races' ad "It could hit the fan anytime"? We had 50,000 fans sitting across from our home pylon, and didn't want even one to be hit. Bad ad.

In Sparks across from my office on Pyramid and McCarran, the "Yankey Country Store," selling "lamps and candels," per their commercially lettered sign. Get them to a spellchecker. Or their own real estate column. *[They fixed it. Nice people; fun little store the former Peggy O'Neal's Gifts.]*

Have a good week; go buy a house, Race for the Cure – (this may be the year) – and God bless America.

"Now, what was it you wanted on that personalized plate?"

A star is born

"Why," several e-mailers have asked, "don't you ever write about personalized plates…?"

First, I've revered the late RGJ columnist Ty Cobb from a time dating back to my early 1950s Reno Rec youth baseball days (before Little League), and it's still a bit early to invade that popular milieu in his Cobbwebs columns. Secondly, I walk a tight line even on my most disciplined days by stretching your vision of real estate matters in this-here real estate supplement 'til they squeak, and I'm afraid if I launch off into license plates now I'd be 'way over that line. Or gone.

That said, this Saturday morning we'll read of a personalized plate that has prompted some calls and comments over the years. It was attached fore and aft to a late model Cadillac parked at Longs Drug in the Village Center last Monday, so I laid in wait for the owner.

I first saw this plate in the early 1970s on a red Caddy, and often through the years on a number of intervening Cads, always red. I thought back then "How in the world did he get that plate?" Over the years occasional column mentions of blue license plates have sparked inquiries about this unique one from some of the Homefinders.

Soon a couple exited Longs; a nice-looking couple who could pair in any TV commercial as the all-American, picture-of-health grandparents, and they fortunately also had a great sense of humor when this total stranger/drive-by columnist told them that the time was here and now, to speak of their license plate for a hundred thousand-or-so waiting *Homefinder* readers. We talked for a half an hour.

A little background is required here: Before World War II Nevada plates used just numbers, and shortly before the war they received a county prefix, in our local case a "W." Fast forward to the late 1960s when the connoisseur of all things automotive, William Fisk Harrah, wanted something a little more unique than "W23743" or whatever on the tail end of his hopped-up Chrysler 300. He dispatched his minions out into the hinterland with orders to bring the casino every plate in Washoe County from W1 to W100, car and truck alike (trucks wore "WT" back then), and use any asset in Harrah's arsenal to convince the plate' owners to cough them up. There were a whole lot of Nevadans winding up with everything from trips to the club's Idaho Middle

Fork Lodge retreat to showroom tickets for life to a date with Olivia Newton John in a chauffeured Harrah Rolls Phantom V, and acquire almost all the double digit "W" plates for his execs and truck fleet, Harrah did.

One such plate was W7, whose owner resisted early efforts by club delegates. "Do you like to hunt?" they asked. "Why sure," the owner said, "but what I really want is one special plate." "We can get it," the suits promised. "We otter just hop in the club's Twin Otter and fly up to Idaho and get acquainted. We'll get you an Idaho elk tag, pack horses and a guide and have a little barbecue for a couple of days while we chat. Bring a friend." And so they did, successfully. Harrah's mounted the trophy head, skinned the beast and tanned it, and processed the beef when they got home. "Now, what plate was it you wanted?"

"A star, a simple, five-pointed star, smack in the middle of the plate," said Swede Olsen, aka W7, and as a matter fact, as W76, for Swede owned the Union 76 service station at the Village Center almost since the center was built in the mid-1950s. "We can do it," said the Harrah people, secretly wondering how in the hell they could sell that symbol to the Nevada DMV, but Harrah's had clout then. The craftsmen at the gated community in Carson City that make license plates lacked a star in their font of dies, so they sent it to their branch office at San Quentin to be struck – a star centered in the field of blue, the '69 stamp on the upper left corner (those plates were issued in 1968; 1969 was the expiration year.)

The new plates were returned to Carson City, and Swede and his wife LaRue (retired from Sierra Pacific Power Company) journeyed there to pick up their star plates in trade for W7. It's been on four or five Caddies since, all red. The Olsens have pizzazz.

I asked if it drew any inordinate attention from the fuzz. Once on their way to Portland, Swede recalled, they were yanked over by one of Oregon's Finest, piqued about Swede's mile or two (or 15) over the speed limit. The officer gave him the usual admonitions and checked his license, but as the moment drew closer to putting pen to paper on a ticket he seemed to have second thoughts, something disarming about a sharp, well-spoken driver and his attractive wife in a new clean Caddy with a weird license plate that didn't fit into any highway patrol computer. Who was this guy? He let the roadside visit end with a pleasant "Now you all be careful and keep it down a bit. My wife and I were married in Reno so I want you to enjoy Oregon." Swede and the trooper were both relieved. (Spend five minutes with Swede and you'd learn he'd have just paid the ticket like the rest of us would.) "What happens if you get rear-ended and the plate gets mashed?" I asked.

I'm sworn to secrecy, but an extra might have fallen out of the press that day in San Quentin, just might have.

That started the era that personalized plates started to proliferate, owing largely to, you guessed it, Bill Harrah, who eventually came up with almost all the low numbers save for one – I still smile when I see another Caddy streaking across Washoe Valley to John Ascuaga's Nugget in Sparks, then parking in the Nugget's executive lot – "John" on the parking space, W6 on the car. Perfeck.

Mr. Harrah was eventually able get the low numbers, yet longed to put "CLANG" on the auto collection's cable car, "SAMMY" on Mr. Davis' son's Duesenberg or a lone "H" on his personal Ferrari Boxer (red, natch). He successfully lobbied the Nevada legislature for personalized plates, grist for a future column unto itself. Ty Cobb deciphered them for us in grand style, but it was Swede and LaRue who got the Star of the Show.

• • •

[A week later, I 'fessed up: read on.]

I'll have the crow, and a copy of the wine list

As Jayson Blair *[and you didn't read that name in the RGJ column]* says around the New York Times dayroom, when you make a mistake, make amends immediately. It's easier to eat crow while it's still warm.

Last week I wrote of a Reno couple named Swede and LaRue Olsen, and the convoluted path they took in the early 1970s to get a blue license plate with a star centered on it. The core problem with the column was that I used a name other than Olsen in the text. Later in the week I was having lunch with Reno historian Neal Cobb and we were debating how I was going to get that fixed without looking like a Kentucky Fried Idiot to all nine *Homefinder* readers. Neal remarked "Sure, Swede ran the catering business out on East Ninth Street for so many years; his son Rod flew for the air guard."

"Wasn't that Swede Mathisen?" I countered. "Oh, that's right," said Neal *[Swede Mathisen passed away in May, 2004]*. "Did the Swede with the star plate work at The Sportsman downtown and later at West Fourth and Vine?" "No," I said, "that was Swede Christiansen," and Neal remembered that that Swede sold baseball mitts and fishing lures to every kid in Reno for 40 years. I told Neal that Swede Olsen owned the Union 76 station in the Village Center, and his wife was with the power company. The surname I used in the column was an old friend from San Francisco. Olsen has the star plate, we miss Christiansen and Mathisen, and my S.F. buddy Hansen got his name in the paper by mistake. Swede Olsen's our guy – wave to him and

LaRue when next you see them in their red Caddy with the star plate. They have my sincere apologies.

This gaffé inspired talk at our Bonanza Casino lunch, which didn't include crow, of a column that the late & great Rollan Melton once wrote, an absolutely compelling and moving eulogy of a Reno resident, who, fortunately for the resident but unfortunately for Rollie, was still alive. Now I know how he must have felt bringing him back to life in his next column, a piece as moving as the original. Take heart; at least I haven't killed anyone yet, with the possible exception of the English language.

• • •

OK – I have to deal with a few license plates. Correspondence has been heavy about another plate with a star, like the plate with the lone star that started the whole thing. Recall that I mentioned that Swede and LaRue Olsen, whose surname I booted last week, had plate 7 and W76. While the thrust of that column ran to the one lower-numbered plate, they actually wrangled, or wangled, two plates in the trade, the second one being 7-star-11, the very plate that the correspondence has been about and struck at the same time. Space limited the text and I focused on the lone star, but the Olsens have them both.

I've enough license plate correspondence to start a Cobbwebs redux – the title of the RGJ's legendary Ty Cobb's column, if you're just joining us – and I'll save the notes for a rainy day. But one has to be mentioned. Cheryl Yee's e-mail this week could be fashioned into a column unto itself – great Reno history you'll see more of herein in time to come – but for this week, we'll simply report that her husband, John Doherty, decided some years ago that he'd like a low number plate, so when it came time to renew his registration he asked DMV for the lowest number that was not assigned. He received at random W411, a great coincidence, as he's the Director of Public Information for the Desert Research Institute.

[...and two e-mails came in: "What's so cool about that???"

(response: years ago, we dialed "411" *for* "Information," *and, oh, never mind)]*

• • •

Promising more acuracy I'll move on to a few notes about last week's column, which if you were out of town I'll remind you dealt with Harrah's Club's quest for low-numbered blue license plates. One of the sadder tales it produced came from affable retired Reno entrepreneur Larry Oakley, who in the late 1960s as a college student, through luck, perseverance, karma, kismet and a little je nè cais quà with Pug Chavez at the DMV, possessed license plate -W- and was approached by Harrah's to part with it. Larry read last week of others' trips to Harrah's Middle Fork Lodge in Idaho and a menu of other grandiose inducements to motorists to give up their low plates. I detected a tear falling from Larry's eye as he confessed that he yielded his single-letter plate to the casino for two cases of beer.

On the bright side, he recalled that at least it was quality Anheuser-Busch suds, not Fisher's or Red-White-and-Blue or some of the other inferior rotgut that was in vogue on campus 35 years ago. Larry went on to get three degrees on the Hill, but never made it to Harrah's Middle Fork Lodge.

Two notes beckon: The Nevada DMV office was then on the northwest corner of Mill and Kietzke, in a building now a convenience store, and, the dash-symbol-dash plates were an early precursor of personalized plates, prior to the time one could actually spend 35 hard-earned bucks to get OICUQT or some other foolishness.

As I wrote last week I'm not anxious to include every cutesy vanity plate in our valley individually, but reader responses invited some pleasant recollections. One was that 50 years before one could order a personalized plate, hundreds of folks laid awake nights to get a plate with their home's address – my childhood friend's family had W2240, for they lived at 2240 Plumas. Or to match a phone number – the Reno Bell – precursor of Nevada Bell – customer with phone number 70X6 would garner the matching plate; (the phone number grew to 2-70X6 then FA2-70X6, later 322-70X6. That friend still has the plate and the phone number.) Many of those early plates are still in use. A *Homefinder* contribution to Guy Clifton and Marilyn Melton as they complete the inevitable sequel to their excellent book *You might be a Nevadan if...* might be: "...if you knew someone with a license plate that matched their phone number or street address." Many plates went with numbered organizations: W597 for the director of Elks Lodge #597 and W14, held by Fred Bonnenfant's odd grandfather, the Supreme Poobah of Chapter 14 of the turn-of-the-century Odd Fellows Lodge. Finally, I'm told Harrah's never went after W13 – unlucky in the gaming game. (W13 was held by Clarence Jones, publisher of this very newspaper. And if you had a party line with 70X6 and wanted to call someone else on the same party line, you dialed "1191" then hung up, making both phones ring, then picked it up and said hello when it quit ringing. You just don't get trivia like that any other morning of the week in the Gazoo.

Did someone say a *party* line...? What's *that*...? Housekeeping item: Like other writers, I tire of clarifying "turn-of-the-century." 'Til further notice, on page 8 of *Homes* that phrase connotes 1899-1901 A.D. There.

Once, the railroad tracks followed Prater Way...

THE SPARKS S.P. RAILYARD

While some towns lower their train tracks, others raise 'em: Almost exactly a hundred years ago E. H. Harriman bought the Central Pacific Railroad from the Big Four and immediately started to re-engineer the CP tracks to get rid of some awkward grades and curves to accommodate a new, heavier generation of locomotives and rolling stock.

The main line at that time ran down Prater Way, and engineers decreed that the better route would be south of Prater with a major yard in a lowland area just south and east of the Sparks Nugget's present location. The area south of the Nugget was low and therefore flood prone, but did afford room to expand the train yard, build a first-class roundhouse and locomotive shop, and relocate Southern Pacific's branch operation from Wadsworth to the west, closer to the east threshold of the Sierra and Donner Pass. No sweat; a large community of Chinese laborers were available, the toughest in the world, whose fathers gained experience in creating the landfill Marina/South of Market areas of San Francisco in the 1840s, later in the Comstock mines, their descendants in the Donner Pass railroad tunnels and the Virginia & Truckee Railroad's mountainous right-of-way, and were by 1902 looking for work. *[The Chinese labor picture I wrote was clarified in text that follows – read Dale's labor market language well, as few in the local area, and I include myself, never had an inkling of the nationalities of early railroaders.]*

• • •

Two weeks later...:

I'll reprint what Nevada history writer and my friend of 30 years Dale Darney emailed me; later I'll tell of why when Dale speaks about railroads, Nevadans listen. The [bracketed] language is mine.

"Karl: I read with some interest your article in the RGJ about filling of the Sparks yard in 1903. I have a copy of the original plat filed by the S.P. showing the original line as you describe and the proposed relocation, as was done.

"The project was followed with great interest by the Reno newspapers of 1903 and I have enclosed samples below. Note, that the fill was from a pit just west of Reno. Because of the political situation, Chinese railroad labor (1900–1905) was little used in Nevada as a number of anti-Chinese laws had been passed restricting the use of Chinese labor. Japanese and Greek labors made up the bulk of the labor force on the Harriman [Southern Pacific's new owner] realignment project in Nevada."

A clip from The Reno Weekly Gazette*: June 8, 1903, headline:* Reconstruction Gang:

"Forty-four gravel cars, an engine, steam shovel and eighty men came in from some point east of Reno and pitched tents on the Mary Wall ranch [the present site of the Sparks railyard], one and one half miles east of Reno, preparatory to commencing grading for the new yard. The gravel will be transported from a pit west of town to make the fill required. It is estimated that it will take 300,000 cubic feet of dirt to make the necessary fill. It is thought it will take sixty days to make the fill and level off the yard site." – *Gazette.*

Dale continues: "This pit is still in use, (not by the railroad) it is between Mountain View Cemetery (Stoker Avenue) and the Union Ice Company on Fourth St. A siding was put into the pit in order to assist filling the cars, and a siding for car storage was put in along side the main line. The sixty days estimate was just a bit optimistic."

A clip from the Nevada State Journal*, September 23, 1903, headline*: Its Work is Nearly Done

"The steam shovel at the gravel pit west of town will be through with its labors in about a month. It has already chewed up a good-sized hill of gravel.

"There are 52 cars used in transporting gravel from the pit to the site of the car shops [Sparks railyard]. Two crews are kept working day and night and there are about 135 carloads, or 2700 tons of gravel moved daily. This amount could be increased, were it not for the blockades of trains which [sic] occur so frequently in the Reno yard.

"When the steam shovel ceases its work, the crews will be transferred to the Mayfield pit where gravel will be taken, for ballasting. One engine crew is all that will be employed then." – *Gazette* [The Mayfield pit was near Palisade, a point on the S.P. line in eastern Eureka county.]

Random notes from the *Gazette*:

"The cars were self-clearing bottom dump cars and the steam shovel was one of the first used in this state."

"The steam shovel was a big attraction and drew crowds to watch it operate. A buggy ride out to the pit made a great Sunday outing."

• • •

So there you have it. Now, Dale's response to my question after I received his original email, about why the Vista Cut had been virtually assumed by all that I spoke with and what I read; by records that I had found and assumptions, now obviously disputed, including an old photograph of Chinese working near a railcar purportedly on the Vista site. Dale wrote:

"Karl: I can appreciate the trouble in finding information on many of the events that at the time they were happening were only of passing interest. It seems that the hunt for information starts only after the people involved are gone. For the past ten years I have spent nearly every Wednesday at the UNR Special Collections, or the Nevada Historical Society going through railroad related files and newspapers, not to mention the California Railroad Museum library and the UC Berkeley Bancroft library. I have read nearly every Nevada newspaper north of Goldfield, as well as Sacramento, Truckee and Bishop papers from 1867 to the 1950s. I have spent a small fortune copying items from these papers, and hours putting them in the computer. All this and I still go through newspapers and the files, it never ends. Most of my efforts are railroad related, but all the things that touched on railroads are included in my files."

[signed] Dale

And that, *Homefinder* readers, is a railroad historian. What happened to scar the terrain on *S* Hill above Vista Boulevard? I don't know – maybe Helms Construction, maybe Isbell Construction before Helms, but whatever it is, it can wait for another column. Or book…

•••

I thank the volunteers at the Sparks Heritage Museum for their help, and God bless America.

This column was ready to email – including my thanks to the Sparks Heritage Museum – when I learned that Carl Shelly, the co-founder (with Tom Swart) and driving force behind the museum and the fortunes of the town of Sparks since his childhood, passed away last Saturday

(This originally appeared June 1st, 2002.)

One week, they made the whole base's payroll in two-dollar bills...

Stead Air Force Base

Here's how quickly seven ill-chosen words can germinate into a whole column: Walking Virginia Street in a recent column set in 1950, I alluded to "...the recently-renamed Stead Air Force Base." This elicited several inquiries, all reducible to either "Renamed from what?" or "We're new here; tell us about Stead."

Let's start at the beginning: The facility was commissioned in 1942 as the Reno Army Airport, renamed as Reno Air Force Base in 1948 (when most former Army airbases were ceded to the U.S. Air Force), and finally to Stead Air Force Base in 1951. The Defense Department, in 1949, adopted a policy to name military facilities more after notable people, less after geographic references.

Accordingly, Reno Air Force Base was renamed, not for Spanish Springs rancher/air race co-founder Bill Stead, as many of you thought; rather, for his brother Croston Stead, who crashed into the desert on December 16th, 1948 in an Air Guard Mustang on takeoff, not too long after the Nevada Air National Guard was commissioned at Reno Air Force Base in April of 1948, flying P-51s. (Croston's older brother Bill Stead, a hot-stick, high-time World War II fighter ace, died in an air race in Florida in 1965, flying a midget racer. Go figure...). The third Stead brother is Sparks developer L. David Kiley.

The base's mission over the years was basic aviation training, later rotary-wing training (OK: helicopters), and airport fire suppression – recall the Kaman-built fire-choppers ("Huskies") with the weird twin "eggbeater" rotors that frequently flew over downtown. There were a few uncontrolled auxiliary airports – patch a better word – around our valley, which were associated with Reno AFB in the early years. I lived in the most northwest corner of Reno in the late 1940s and often hiked to a now-long-gone unnamed satellite Reno AFB strip that was between the present Keystone Avenue and McQueen High School. Two youngish cadets in a Beech D-18 trainer with Army tail markings gave three of us kids a spin around Peavine Peak in a 20-minute ride neither our parents nor the flight-line officer at Reno AFB ever needed to hear about. Some things are better left that way for fifty years or so. Another Reno AFB satellite strip parallels Highway 70 at Beckwourth, in use to this day as the Nervino Airstrip. (The bygone Sparks Airport strip northeast of Pyramid Way and Green Brae – the 1950s spelling – in Sparks was not a Reno AFB satellite.)

Stead AFB conducted desert and mountain survival training, for pilots of all branches of the military, other nations, and even for the early astronauts. Later there was a "SAGE" facility, an acronym for Semi-Automatic-Ground-Environment, or whatever paranoids do all day in a great big ugly four-story building with no windows, something to do with global air defense.

One interesting occurrence that some old-timers may remember was when the Pentagon, in a convincing effort to demonstrate the massive economic impact the airbase had on our community, paid Stead troops one payday in crisp two-dollar bills. Those bills circulated around for years, many emanating from the Grotto Bar at Fourth and Virginia Streets, the Stead airmen's hangout. And apropos of probably nothing, I can report that yours truly drove a big bright-yellow, flat-front 66-passenger Cornbinder school bus to the enlisted men's housing area at Stead, and that Ty Cobb Jr., son of the late RGJ columnist, drove a like bus to the Stead officers' housing unit. Between the two of us we delivered every single high school student who lived from the Reno city limits north past Stead and all the way to Bordertown, to Reno High School – the town's only high school until Wooster was built in 1961. *[And I caught Nancy Howell Spina's ire with that: "What was Manogue High, sliced bread?!" Sorry...].* Believe it or don't, only 132 kids, excluding truants, lived north of town in the early 1960s, and we drove them 36 miles a day for three school years, and never harmed a hair on their heads nor creased a fender. Damn, we were good.

The Defense Department began phasing out Stead AFB in 1963 – actually selling off some of the original 20,000 acres as early as 1958 – and it was finally fully decommissioned by 1966 and acquired by the City of Reno. The renamed Reno-Stead Airport once hosted all airline passenger flights into and out of Reno while our downtown airport, at that time hung with the unpopular name of Reno-*Cannon* Airport, was closed for a major runway resurfacing. For five weeks the PSA pilots in their DC-9s raced the AirCal Boeing 737 guys around the Reno National Air Race's 8-mile unlimited-class course pylons at Stead on their way to final approach for runway two-four.

Just kidding...

The Homefinders take a walking tour in downtown Reno...

Walkin' Sierra Street, ca. 1955

Let's play hooky from Central Jr. High on Fifth and West, cut over a block to Sierra Street and head south for the Truckee along the west side of the street.

Across Sierra Street in that block between West Fourth and Fifth is the new Sewell's market, finished in 1948, with an interesting story we'll touch on next column, when we walk north back to school. Coming up on our west side of Sierra now is Ross Burke Mortuary, where Silas Ross received the shamrock from William Blanchfield's mother in Ireland for so many years starting in 1925.

Crossing Sierra at West Fourth Street, which was also Highway 40 – the main drag across the nation – is Daniel's Motor Lodge, which remains even today a first-class operation. (We can see Lee's Drive-In to the west along West Fourth Street.) South of Daniel's was Victor Cleaners, which moved to California Avenue in 1952. Dr. Warburton had his office next door, the Doc an early fixture in chiropractic procedures who would be around for decades to follow. Before he located there, the building was a candy store – "The Sugarie" – before World War II. Anyone remember that? (I don't.)

Guys my age will all remember the neatest store in downtown Reno in the late 1940s –Shim's Army Surplus store – authentic war stuff, hot off the Pacific war theater, just like John Wayne and Dan Duryea wore in war movies at the Tower Theater every Saturday morning. Next to Shim's was Quimby's Awnings – every store in downtown Reno had an awning to extend over a sidewalk, and for years, Quimby made 'em all.

Railroad tracks! *[grade level.]* Teams of new "streamliner" diesel-electric engines started replacing S.P.'s venerable cab-forward steam locomotives right about the time we're taking this walk. The last cab-forwards in revenue service went through Reno in late 1950.*

At the north end of the block at Commercial Row, the Pigley Wigley Market, one of almost a dozen grocery stores in downtown Reno, and later, Fenwick's Art Supply. South of Piggly Wiggly/Fenwick's, the American Fish Market, selling, fish, what else? Another Army goods surplus store, name unclear in the records, maybe Reno Surplus or later the Supply Sergeant, not as good as Shim's (the owner's name was Shimkovsky, actually, great guy, his son Fred is still around.) Next to that store, the Sierra Bar, probably sold Sierra Beer, then Nevada Photo Supply. A good store – the Land Corporation's "Polaroid" was a brand-new camera process as we were walking this 1950s day.

• • •

Across Douglas Alley, the Reno Beauty School – (hairdressers). Next the Sunshine Card Shop; if you wanted a card in 1950 you went to a card shop, not a drug store. On to the Dainty Cake Shop, two cupcakes for 14 cents, no sales tax, then mighty Sears and Roebuck, their farm store backing onto West Street to the rear, the other giant J.C. Penney's filled the block from Sears to the corner.

Across West Second Street, a Hale's Drug, one of many Hale's branches in Reno. A W.T. Grant sundry store, then Spina's Shoe Repair (they moved down the street toward the river in years to follow, read the 1957 Sierra Street fire chapter.) National Dollar Store, in one of those great old two-story buildings with the hardwood floors.

That store's gone now from the American scene, as is Montgomery Wards, their neighbor to the south. United Five and 10 (not *Dime*!) next to Monkey Wards, and Bools & Butler Leather, saddlers to the Hollywood western movie icons who came to town for the Silver Spurs awards during the rodeo each July Fourth. And on that corner, Home Furniture, which would later build directly across the river, later becoming Ardan's Furniture, then to be razed for the present court house.

Across West First Street, Tony's Delicatessen, which was really on West First but how could we possibly leave Tony out of our Sierra Street walk? On the southwest corner, the Federal Store, a kind of latter-day Mervyn's, later becoming Union Federal Savings & Loan's headquarters, later yet rebuilt as Paterson's Men's Store and Sunderland's shoes in the basement, er, lower level. Also Tait's, in that block, another popular upscale shoe store.

Across the Truckee River, on the day we were walking, was Herman & Wilson, our friendly Chrysler-Plymouth dealer, then mostly private homes from there on south to California Avenue. And lest we forget, Sierra Street became Granite Street when we walked across the bridge to the south side of the stream.

• • •

In a week or two, we'll all walk north back to Sewell's, along the east side of the street. And as we walk past Home Furniture and Herman & Wilson, I'm reminded of the devastation that was reaped upon downtown Reno by fire and flood, several of each in recent memory. The time has come that the Homefinders read about the explosion and fire in 1957 that rearranged the landscape of downtown Reno. *[In another chapter]* I'll work on those disasters in the autumn to come. Meet me at the Sierra/Granite Street Bridge soon and we'll walk back to school before anyone misses us.

• • •

Walking North On Sierra Street

The casual reader may recall that we Homefinders cut school en masse from Central Jr. High on West Fifth and walked down the west side of Sierra Street, stopping across the river, where to our good fortune the first-ever local television broadcast of a World Series baseball game was being piped via telephone cable into a half-dozen black-and-white Capehart TV sets in the Riverside's Corner Bar, and a few along the windows by the hotel's swimming pool on Island Avenue. But our education beckons, the ballgame is over (I think the Yankees won the game we watched on that early-1950s fall day), so we'll beat feet over the bridge and back to Central, walking north up the east side of Sierra Street.

Just north of the Truckee we walk past the old brick Elks' Home, whose four stories would be reduced to rubble in a fast fire following a nearby gas explosion in 1957. Faithful reader Debbie Hinman e-mailed me an inquiry this week, about the picturesque old brick Elks Home on the river – what happened to it, she asked? *[She answered her own question, inadvertently, while looking through some other old photos: The original (downtown) Elks' Home was in the same location as it was when it was destroyed by the 1957 fire, but much earlier it had a grand, landscaped entrance to the north, toward West First Street with a quarter-block front courtyard. That courtyard later became the site of powerhouse department store Grey Reid, Wright Co. and the Elks' Home entrance was downsized and realigned toward Sierra Street. Nice research, Debbie.]*

I have a vivid recollection of my dad – and a score of other peoples' fathers, husbands and sons – who customarily had lunch at the Elks and could not be located for a short period of time following the explosion. That specter brings to mind the terror and frustration, multiplied by three-hundred-fold in the missing and by weeks instead of hours, that east coast residents must still be feeling as I write – and you read – this column. *[This originally appeared in the Reno Gazette-Journal on October 13th, 2001.]*

Next to the Elks' Home in the block south of West First, the finest department store in Reno: Gray Reid, Wright, a locally owned treasure. That store in later years would move into a new building that later formed the main floor of the present Circus Circus casino. And the building Gray Reids (its later name) vacated became part of the Granada Theater on West 1st Street. *[The whole quarter-block now under construction as a condominium tower.]*

Across West First, a retail building with clothier Murdock's on the corner, and the Vanity ladies wear, the popular Town House (Al Vario behind the bar!) and jeweler Morgan Smith. *[Later to become in a new building, then close, as J.C. Penney's.]*

Next to the north, the Parkway Hotel, the wonderful Moulin Rouge restaurant on the first floor, the pride of Gilbert Vasserot who would later open Eugene's restaurant we visited in this book. Next door, Karl's Shoes, no relation. Somewhere in there was the old Eagle Bar that moved south to California Avenue in later years, then the southeast corner building with clothiers Leeds, Reeve's and Mode O'Day, and a Payless Drug working their way east on West Second Street.

Crossing West Second, we'll stop for apple pie with Mrs. Lerude's secret topping in the Wigwam Cafe, adjoining what was once the Wigwam Theatre and later the Crest Theatre on Second Street.

Past the Wigwam Café was the Emporium of Music, a popular store founded by Dick and Joe Woodward and later *[still, on Center Street]* owned by the Maytan family, then a ladies store whose name escapes me and everybody else, and venerable Dunseath Key, in another location now on Arroyo Street but still in business *[even after a fire that damn near put them out of business in 2002...]* Across Douglas Alley, Commercial Hardware's back door opened onto Sierra, (the store's main entrance was on Commercial Row, ergo their name, next to Cannan's Drug and Floral and a Sewell's market.) Next, the Society Cleaners.

Stop and take a long look at the building we encounter next, on the southeast corner of Commercial Row and Sierra Street: The building then housed Reno Mercantile, one of the oldest businesses in Reno. But savor today the building itself, for it is surely the oldest building standing in Reno, dedicated on Christmas day of 1873 as Reno's first Masonic Lodge structure (it was almost a year old at that time.) *[And the smart money says the two-year vibration of trains on the shoofly will necessitate its demise. I'm hopeful that this book will be around long enough that some reader will wonder, "what's a shoofly?"]*

As we cross the railroad tracks we can hear cars being occasionally dropped on their grilles by the mechanical monster in the nine-story Harolds Club pigeonhole garage, that slid a frame under a car, and, oh, nuts – that's a whole column all of its own. *[It's all in here.]*

Across Plaza Street was the Plaza Hotel, a building with great charm and a wealth of history to it, historian Phillip Earl wrote the saga of it when it was demolished many years ago. (You probably wondered how Plaza Street got its name – the early Union Pacific Railroad integrated the southern plaza ambiance into its rights-of-way and stations, and the street in the UP's master plan was to be the Reno plaza.) Next to the Plaza Hotel on Sierra Street was electrical motor rebuilder Brown-Milbury, still in business 50 years later on Airport Road.

OK, OK – Gentry Way.

We cross West Fourth Street to Nevada Car, selling Studebakers like hotcakes, and next Sewell's supermarket, remembered by many as the Mayfair market that came later. The real estate aspect of this building is that the Sewell family bought the square-block of land from various owners, but got stymied when the title insurers discovered that the Federated Church, then on the southwest corner of West Fifth and North Virginia Street, received their land by a gift requiring that it "forever be used as a church." A young Realtor named Karl Breckenridge the Elder found a piece of comparable land up West Seventh Street, at that time a fur piece west of Reno, and the Sewell family bought that land for the church and traded with the church, completing their acquisition of the block.

We're late for school; Chet Green and principal Chauncey King will be in a stir if we don't get back the buses will leave without us, so we'll wrap this up. A few landmarks point toward a follow-up column; I'll probably get yelled at for the "first TV in Reno" and "oldest building in Reno" verbiage, but that's what makes my Saturday nights fun. *[no one yelled!]* Have a good week. God bless America.

• • •

**[A reader later sent a question about the old steam engines that's propitious for this nostalgia offering: "Weren't the cab-forward locomotives known as "mallets?" Yes and no; the last loco of the mallet design locomotive probably went through the town in the late 1920s – the name eponymous with Anatole Mallèt, a Swiss mechanical engineer who developed a process for managing high pressure steam in heavy locomotives, having nothing to do with forward or conventional cab placement. The Mallèt design fell out of favor with emerging technology and went by the wayside, but the name stuck as a term of endearment with the old-timers for the cab-forwards, into the 1950s and through to the 21st century, when we still hear "mallet" or see it in print occasionally, often as "mallett." Probably incorrectly, but little worth an argument.*

Visit the retired S.P. cab-forward on display in the California State Railroad Museum in Old Sacramento. The old beauty hasn't been under steam for fifty years, but it's so massive that it's still half-scary to stand next to.]

The 1910 "Spanish Quartette" schools – two still in service...

A TALE OF FOUR SISTERS

If you were one of the seventeen regular readers of this column in September of 1996, you may move right on now to Robert Bruss' piece or the crossword puzzle; if not, welcome – loathe as I am to rerun a column, we've had some questions of late about McKinley Park School on the river, researcher Carmine Ghia is off on assignment, and the column we wrote in '96 *[and '93]* pretty well wove the same tale, so away we go:

McKinley Park School, on Riverside between Keystone and Vine Streets, was one of the original "Four Sisters" built between 1910 and 1912, which operated over a seven-decade span. It's a strong likelihood that native Homefinders who were in elementary school even as late as 1970 attended one of the "Sisters." Their fifth option was Southside School, built in 1903 – the next elementary school built after the "Four Sisters" was Veterans' Memorial, built in 1946.

In 1909, Reno School District #10's Superintendent B. D. Billinghurst negotiated $100,000 to build two of the finest schools in the West Coast, by his description *"...modern and sanitary, eight classrooms and a large assembly room on one floor. A domestic science room for the girls, and a manual arts training room for the boys, are placed in the basement. The assembly hall is 40 feet wide and 80 feet long, including a stage on one end, lighted by electricity, with two sets of scenery. A mechanical fan system of heating and cooling is provided."*

Thus the McKinley Park and Orvis Ring Schools were built (Orvis Ring on the corner of East Seventh and Evans Avenue), and beauties they were – California mission-style, the rooms grouped around three sides of central courtyards, a fountain with a flagpole in the center. But Dr. Billinghurst wasn't through yet; a year later he bargained for another $250,000 for two more similar grade schools and a high school. With these funds Mary S. Doten and Mount Rose Schools, (Washington and West Fifth Streets and Lander and LaRue Streets, respectively), were completed in 1911. For the record, Libby Booth was the first principal at Orvis Ring and Echo Loder the first at Mary S. Doten, Mary's middle name was *Stoddard,* Libby Booth was the last surviving charter member of the 20th Century Club when she died in 1953, and Arlington Avenue was named for the first superintendent of the Reno School District – now where else do you get trivia like that for four bits on a Saturday morning? A junior high named for

Superintendent Billinghurst would be built a block from Mount Rose School in 1930, on land donated by George Wingfield.

So, we have the "Four Sisters" – known also as the "Spanish Quartette," attribution for either name unknown. You'll note a subtle difference between the two surviving schools: The earlier McKinley Park, like Orvis Ring, had a simpler structure over the main entrance and the intake flues for the cooling system were exposed, while the later Mount Rose, the twin to Mary S. Doten, demolished in 1971, has the massive Moorish domes framing the entrance. Mount Rose to most people is more visibly pleasing – owing partially to the baby-poop wall and God-awful roof "tile" colors on McKinley Park that won an architect an award (all four schools were originally dove gray.) At Mary S. Doten School in the 1940s, principal Rita Cannan would banish us to these turrets, up a flight of stairs that was more like a ladder, to a place of penance to reflect upon our misdeeds, little realizing that it was a grand place for a third-grader to just zone out and watch the world go by. We never let on… And, the domes were prescient of the new (1912) Reno High School's design, by local architect George Ferris – (who also designed the Spanish Quartette) – basically a three-story version of the four elementary schools. That school was on the Sundowner's present site.

The modern advances in the schools documented by Superintendent Billinghurst in the 1909 *Nevada State Journal* really worked – the auditorium stage "lit with real electric lamps" and the "central air system, with thermostats in each room." Mary S. Doten was a hell of a lot more comfortable than our later schools, including the present Reno High School which lacked air conditioning in the 1950s, ever were in late spring or early fall. And Mary S. Doten was aesthetically *nice* to attend – big windows, high coved ceilings with huge round suspended glass light fixtures, rich woodwork and brass hardware, and hardwood floors one could only dream of having installed today. Flowering ornamentals and wisteria in the courtyard, water bubbling in the fountain during warm weather, the school names in mosaic tile over the main entry door and a boiler the size of a railroad tank car in the basement warm enough to dry 300 pairs of soggy galoshes on a wintry day.

Mary S. Doten closed in 1971 and was demolished soon after closing (a gleaming brass fire extinguisher from her lunchroom mysteriously appeared as a lamp in my office a month or so later.) Orvis Ring was demolished three years later. McKinley Park became the headquarters for some City of Reno rec and arts programs. Mount Rose, through the mega-efforts of some parents and neighbors – notably Ted and Sue Schroeder, for two – was modernized and reopened in 1977, and remains an active school in the district.

While traveling back in time for this column in 1996 and refreshing my memories, I visited Mount Rose School and looked at the courtyard in full autumn foliage (the fountain's gone), through the ornate railings to the manicured lawn and mature trees lining Lander Street, and was reminded that Mount Rose School remains today a timeless gem in the school district's tiara.

• • •

I scribe this a day short of 9/11/03, and note that it was two years ago that I added the closing line of our column. I've been asked how long I plan to close with it. My response? Quite a while.

Have a good week, Let's Roll, and God bless America.

We strayed from downtown retail stores...

AN EARLY START AT SHOPPING

Keystone Square and Shoppers Square, ca. 1970

Following a couple of "Walking" columns, I received an interesting email: "I've lived here for thirty years and I don't know what you're talking about." I have a flash for this writer: There's people who've lived here twice as long who don't know what I'm talking about either, and I occasionally include myself.

So to appease him (her?); we'll only go back thirty years this morning to 1970 – there's only ten shopping days until Christmas, the Pinto's warmed up in the driveway so we'll drive to a couple of shopping areas. Park Lane Center, the granddaddy of local shopping has been open for four years now but we'll start elsewhere and wind up there next week.

We like the Keystone area, as do so many people who moved into that booming area when Sproul Contractors started building homes in the first one-third of the 1960s. A mini-town sprang up with its own banks, cleaners, service stations, even its own disk jockey on KOLO radio – live from the El Cortez Hotel – Pete Carrothers, who romanced the so-called "Sproul" (northwest Reno) trade on the air, asserting that he woke up next to every woman in northwest Reno (leaving out the "if she had her radio tuned to 920 AM. Lucky them.) The hot spot became the Keystone Center, built by Al Caton, the owner of Keystone Fuel/Reno Press Brick, committing land formerly occupied by the brickyard's quarry. It had a movie theater, and the hot spot we'll hit this morning, Uncle Happy's Toy Store, the best in the West. Sir Loin's Steak House was a favorite, operated by a couple of young guys named Nat Caraseli and Bill Paganetti, who later opened a little coffee shop called the Peppermill in 1971. We might go back there for lunch, there or the Chocolate Pit, later to become the Coffee Grinder that fed a generation of local folks.

Across Keystone was the greatest drug store in Reno, the big Keystone Owl Rexall Drug, Jim Henderson and Frank Desmond, your genial pill-pushers. Jim has passed away; Frank is an occasional contributor to this column, both good friends to many. Many remember Jim doing TV commercials occasionally with two guys he met playing golf at Hidden Valley, whose names were Dan Rowan and Dick Martin. While it was occasionally difficult to ascertain what product they were selling on TV, if any, they were having fun, and we at home enjoyed their own localized *Laugh-In*. We'll stop in there this morning on our shopping spree and pick up some gift wrap and stocking stuffers.

Traveling down Keystone Avenue, we can go over the fairly-new Keystone Bridge, through an intersection that pits motorists from Booth Street, Keystone and California Avenues together to the amazement of all when it opened. In the venerable Village Shopping Center by Reno High School were a number of old friends, like Safeway, Sprouse Reitz sundries, the Village Drug – a great complement to the Keystone Owl Rexall. The Mirabelli family had a record store there, later to move to Park Lane. A fabric shop that was there seemingly forever finally closed; the present shoe repair shop was probably an original tenant. P&S Hardware had a branch at the Village; Gene Parvin and Bill Spiersch making it easy for the burst of homeowner/fixit guys springing up in southwest Reno's new homes. A Pioneer Citizens Bank branch. We can't forget the Chinese Village restaurant, which had a number of names in years to follow, notably a Dick Graves chicken store, and would finally become the original Truckee River Bar & Grill. A lot of good grub has gone through that corner in forty-plus years.

The Village is a Reno fixture.

• • •

We're still stumped with a few gifts so let's keep moving; as I said, next weekend we'll poke around Park Lane a little in a column that's kind of an encore. Many people enjoyed that Park Lane column that's run several times in the past seven years, but we *Homefinder* columnists don't get the big bucks for resubmitting old retreaded columns. (Plus, I can't find it on my computer's disk.) *[I still can't.]* Next week we'll update it to the early 1970s.

But now, it's approaching noon on a December 1970 Saturday so we'll park at Shoppers Square on Plumb Lane (I wish that Security Bank on the corner had an ATM – I could use a little cash.) Like Park Lane across the street, Shoppers Square was open then between the stores; the roof came later. (What's with shopping center owners covering their malls? We Nevadans are a hardy lot.)

Silver State Camera held forth in the Square, probably the largest camera store in Reno at the time. I got an Instamatic there; still have it. But nowhere to buy film for it anymore. Hobby Towne was head-to-head in competition with Park Lane's hobby store, both good places to shop. There was a Spudnut shop, nothing like the original on West Fourth Street, not quite as crowded as Krispy Kreme would be thirty years later.

You can call it Savon, you can call it Osco, but you doesn't has ta call it Skagg's, the Square's big anchor's earliest incarnation. And my favorite store, two great merchants Hal Codding and Jerry Wetzel, who moved their ski-oriented sporting goods store Codding & Wetzel from Pine Street downtown (I wrote about it in conjunction with the Olympic A-Frame.) Both owners were fixtures in local skiing and the 1960 Squaw Olympics; Jerry would die a few years later in a skiing accident, while Hal brightened our town for many years to follow. I'd be derelict if I didn't point out that Hal's daughter Cindi married a good friend to many of my contemporaries – Joe Murin – who recently was named by the RSCVA as Sterling the Butler, and if he can be half as dashing as his late father-in-law was, he'll be a dynamite rep for our town. We're betting he will be.

The hour draws late. Nod at Santa in the plaza, but don't call him "George" and confuse the kid on his lap who thinks he's really Santa. Maybe he is. (George Randolph, the Square's perennial elf and Hartford Insurance retiree)Let's walk across Virginia to the Central Park lounge in the Continental Lodge for a hot-buttered-rum.

Cheers to 10 shopping days, 342 safe-days at Ralston Foods, and God Bless America!

• • •

The end of an era

This item hurts: The RGJ last week bore the news that Mirabelli's Music City in Park Lane Center is closing.

The article noted that the store moved to Park Lane as an original tenant in 1967 from the Village Shopping Center, where it opened in 1956. The Village was Reno High turf, and we sent two of our finest, Gary Bullis, now a local attorney and RSCVA board member, and Gary Machabee, local office furniture mogul, to be DJs at Mirabelli's live from the Village. They

weren't bad; Gary's even keeping it as a fallback career. What the article didn't say was that the store actually had tenuous roots even prior to that in Savier's Appliances on West Second and West Streets, where it was the "Record Room."

Good luck to Betty Mirabelli and to Buddy and Lori Lehman and their families, and our thanks for six decades of good tunes.

Epilogue: When Park Lane was opened by a bunch of local guys in the mid-'60s, the detractors wagged "How could a doctor and a car dealer [among others] possibly run a shopping center?" Who knows, but they did, and it was a great, successful center. Now it sits dying, even while standing on the confluence of two well-traveled Reno streets, with acres of parking and easy access, thanks to some out-of-town experts who came to show us local yokels how it's done. "Reno's demographics changed," they say.

Baloney. Any number of local commercial Realtor firms could fill it up again.

- 30

The Donner Ridge Fire

On a bucolic late-summer day, a small plume of smoke was spotted against an overcast cloud ceiling, emanating from a ridge high above Truckee, somewhere near the new Interstate 80 freeway. It was a Sunday afternoon, August the 21st of 1960, and countless Tahoe vacationers were loading up the family wagons for the trek back to the Bay Area and home. If they'd gassed their cars up by that hour, they stood a chance, but a slim one. If not, they were probably still sitting at Kings Beach or Tahoe City or South Shore on the following Tuesday morning.

The small smoke column above Truckee and Donner Lake grew with phenomenal intensity, spreading at its base and moving to the east at a speed fast enough to "crown" across the treetops over the earliest firemen on the scene, forcing them to retreat at a virtual dead-run, in some cases leaving their tools, and at least one Caterpillar dozer behind. The new freeway was closed almost immediately to preserve it for fire equipment – most of which were the on-road variety with few brush trucks capable of getting to the gnarly terrain of the fire's perimeter, which was enlarging exponentially above the highway toward the hamlet of Verdi. I recall leaving Kings Beach with a truckload of diesel fuel drums and being slowed to 15 miles an hour five miles south of Truckee by the heavy smoke lying over the Brockway Shortcut (Highway 267.) The smoke soon engulfed the Lake Tahoe basin.

At 4:15 p.m. the power went out, and not just in Truckee and Donner Lake; the outage reached from the state line as far east as Carlin and Battle Mountain, to Yerington and Hawthorne, and naturally, Sparks, Carson City, Minden, Gardnerville and Reno. Basically, the northern half of Nevada was in darkness as evening fell that Sunday.

• • •

The fire effort was legendary, with firefighters arriving hourly from distant points in the west, cutting lines similar to the effort last week on the Martis fire but without modern protective clothing, the heavy-lift helicopters and air tankers overhead, the handheld communications and on-site meteorological advances. Few were spared; gawkers stopping along the adjoining roads found themselves with a shovel in their hands conscripted to building a line.

Cloaked in darkness, we all fumbled our way through grocery stores with no refrigeration for provisions – in the store or at home – unsure how long the outage would continue. Harrah's cancelled Jack Benny's show at Stateline. We conserved fuel in our cars, as the service stations were out of business, the fire agencies all raising cain about some operators' efforts to pump by hand from underground tanks. This newspaper, actually two papers then, the *Gazette* and the *Journal*, relied on a heavy on-site generator at their building on West Second Street, and got newspapers onto the street almost on schedule, keeping residents and the tourists held hostage by the fuel shortage apprised of information about the fire and the future. (A major problem was created by the huge population of tourists who would normally have left for home, but were now left stranded in Reno, Sparks and the Lake Tahoe basin and requiring food and housing.)

One radio station in Sparks and another in Reno were able to stay on the air, their audience confined to listeners with battery radios or those willing to run their cars. The Reno airport continued to function, albeit hampered by the smoke that darkened the city to virtual nighttime visibility – the airport managers mustered up smoke pots, used liberally as warning devices in the late 1950s around construction sites, and lined them up to form approach lanes and runway and taxiway lighting. *Oceans Eleven* fell dark at the Majestic Theater.

The Wednesday morning Journal reported that power had been restored to almost all Sierra Pacific customers all over Nevada (the paper had carried the news the day before that a 120,000 kilovolt line in the Truckee/Donner Lake vicinity had been an early casualty of the embryonic fire on that Sunday afternoon, almost immediately followed by 13 poles burning out from under a 60,000 KV line nearby.) Few, if any, other significant structures were damaged by the fire.

After a long week, the fire was controlled, later confined, and then out, at least to the casual observer. California, Nevada, Arizona, Utah and federal agencies had been on the fire line for the week it took to control it, then remained in the burn area until the first snows fell in 1960, searching for hot spots, still finding some even in the cooling fall temperatures.

It was named the Donner Ridge fire – August 21st, 1960. Was it bigger than Martis Creek fire? Possibly not in terms of acreage, but in terms of disruption to a huge number of residents, tourists and the economy – and the heartbreak of ravaging the natural beauty and creating a scar that's still visible forty years later – it was certainly one of our area's major forest fires. And how was it caused?

Man…

• • •

[The cause was eventually determined to be a spark off the blade of a bulldozer working high on the mountain above Truckee. This column appeared the Saturday following the nearly-disastrous Martis Creek Fire, starting on Fathers Day, 2001.]

The mural, and the men who created it in 1949

THE HAROLDS CLUB MURAL, AND MORE

What a timely civic opportunity we have, to punctuate the modernistic planned downtown events center with a point of exclamation from Reno's past, while satisfying the legal requirement expending one per cent of a building's cost for the incorporation of art into the design of a public building à la the wind machine at the Convention Center and the Thompson Federal Courthouse's fish.

Astute art collectors and galleries have held the creators of the Harolds Club mural in high regard for many years since it was placed in 1949, both nationally recognized in their own right and medium. Theodore McFall was the artist who painted the original concept of the mural for the Smith family's approval, depicting astonishing detail within a palette to be 38 feet high and 78 feet wide – pioneers at a campsite that could be Crystal Peak to the west or the shore of the Truckee to the east – a campfire burning, azure-blue water falling in the background. Older Reno residents can remember a rattler sizing up a nourishing but unsuspecting camper's fanny – the snake concealed in years to follow by signage added near the bottom of the mural. The focal point of the mural is from anywhere the observer is standing, for McFall knew that one couldn't get far enough away from the scene to appreciate it fully so he scaled it for short range viewing (how sweet it will be to enjoy it from a distance in full sunlight!)*

McFall made his artistic mark in New Mexico where his work still appears liberally in the New Mexico Museum of Natural History and Science, and later by sea-life themed works seen in galleries in Monterey, Carmel, and Pacific Grove, where he passed away.

His accepted artwork was crafted into a sculpture in metal by Sargent Claude Johnson, who hung out in San Francisco's Bohemian North Beach sculpting commissions in wood and metal – mosaics for the grand staircases of Matson Navigation's cruise liners, the Monterey, Mariposa, and Lurline; statuary and mosaics seen in many parks around the Bay Area, notably Aquatic Park, and the Court of Pacifica for the 1939 World's Fair at Treasure Island, and in dozens of private homes. He later created and fired a work similar to the Harolds mural for the bygone Western Club in Las Vegas – that piece is now a focal point of the Salt Palace in Salt Lake City. *[Was – it's in storage at this writing.]* Johnson sculpted the steel and fired the colors at the Paine-Mahoney Company in Oakland. The mural's many porcelain panels –

their large number and relatively small size due to the great weight of each panel – were trucked to Reno in the summer of 1949 and hung on a beefy steel framework attached to Harolds Club's two buildings. Illumination came by tubes concealed on the perimeter. 'Twas a grand night indeed when it was unveiled with great ado, to the voices of the Sons of the Pioneers – as I recall, it was during Rodeo Week. *[The Fourth of July back then, unveiled but not completed until September of that year.]*

The dancing flame in the campfire and the cascading waterfall, both borrowing an animation process from early Wurlitzer jukebox' "bubbling" color columns, fell into disrepair and died soon after the casino was acquired by the Hughes interests. I'm told they're an easy fix. The heavy bronze border surrounding the mural was necessarily but irreparably damaged when the mural was otherwise tenderly removed in 1999, in preparation for demolition of the buildings. The panels are now stored in Styrofoam in the city's obsidian tower at the corner of Walk-and-Don't-Walk. *[at press time]*

Our city fathers and mothers have been handed a no-brainer choice: Civic artwork depicting our pioneer heritage, that once adorned *the* post-war destination epitomizing Reno the world around; the work product of two nationally-acclaimed artisans and now sitting bought-and-paid-for in the municipal basement; a snazzy brand-new auditorium to place it on, and all the while satisfying a requirement to embody public art into that building. How can they go wrong? Even a drive-by columnist could figure that out.

They might even add some catchy caption like *Dedicated in all humility to those who blazed the trail* above the artwork, the original legend generally credited to Tom Wilson, the creative genius of Thomas C. Wilson Advertising, who put Harolds on the map.

And ask any geezer of your acquaintance about the Sons of the Pioneers.

Have a good week, Cool Water, Tumbling Tumbleweeds, and God bless America.

• • •

**[Epilogue to the no-brainer council decision I predicted above: The mural won't go on the new downtown events center after all; but the city fathers and mothers have given approval to a Livestock Events Center location. Curiously, some of their reticence was the contra-PC appearance of Indians in the artwork; Tribal Leader Alan Melendez stated publicly that the Indians weren't concerned about the artwork. As you read this, we'll see where it wound up, or if it's still stored...*

Tom Wilson, who commissioned the mural, was an advertising genius, the statewide chairman of the 1964 Nevada Centennial observance, a rec-

ognized authority on northern Nevada's history and lore, and was a friend. And, what was to be in a readers' note, I'll put here: Tom, early in the development of Harolds Club with the Smith family, made the election not to use the apostrophe where it would normally be, and readers over the years have noted that. While it appeared on-and-off in early ads, it's customary to forego it.]

Early business on a street that once was "outlying" downtown Reno...

Walkin' California Avenue, ca. 1955

Had the foremothers and fathers who laid out this neck of the woods 120 years ago known that the Homefinders were going to be touring it this morning, they'd have paid more mind to get the north/south streets aligned a little better. Granite, Hill, and Flint Streets from the north, and Forest, Plumas, Humboldt and Lander Streets to the south resulted in seven dead-ends, totally botching up street numbers and frustrating the continuity of a narration of a mid-50s walk. But, as hardy sorts, we'll just amble along the south side of California Avenue this Saturday morning. A century ago, our path would be the first step on a journey to California, which is how the street got its name.

Westward from the Signal Oil station once on the southwest corner at Virginia Street, the Faulstich family's Magic Cleaners, heralded as the most modern in Reno when it opened in the early 1950s. Then past a couple of private homes, and on to Forest Street, then two-way, resulting in a number of interesting vehicular get-togethers when it was one-wayed, and spell-check that dandy for me. Across Forest Street is what was originally known as the New Carano Building, the longtime head-shed of the powerhouse – then and now – Kafoury & Armstrong CPA firm. Next a little building that housed Dr. Roland Stahr, who it would seem treated every infirm soul in Reno during a period after the war; it's now an optometry office. That building was at the direct dead-end of Sierra Street (which by that time had been re-named from Granite), and it is here on the walk that things get a little perplexing. Because, our city fathers in the mid-1970s elected to realign Sierra into Plumas Street, condemning the building that housed the Williams family's Liberty Drugs and the fabled Eagle Bar, safe-harbor to all manner of mankind; from the suits from the neighboring insurance and law firms settling hefty insurance claims out of court, to drop-dead gorgeous neighborhood secretaries on Friday afternoons, or cowboys playing C&W records backwards until their girlfriends reconciled, their dogs sprang back to life, their Bibles were returned and their pickups started up again. A man was murdered in the Eagle the wee hours of a 1964 Friday night and it took a little time to even determine that a crime had maybe occurred, and should we maybe call someone? The Eagle never flew again. Many think that it was in the two-story block building between present-Plumas and the little service street that was the original Plumas Street to the west. Nope – that building was built on the triangle resulting from the street realignment.

Continuing on shank's-mare across the original Plumas – I guess we have two 500-blocks and intersections of Plumas and California – a medical office, and the then-Ballet Arts, through a number of metamorphoses to the Yoga Shack; next the former local HQ of Fireman's Fund insurance and Lucini-Parish Insurance and Realty, later Feutsch-Argeres Realty. Next, the building housing a myriad of businesses, presently the Blue Plate Special, no connection to my old newsletter. Powell Drugs on the Humboldt corner – what a classic building, with a shake mansard roof and ornate brickwork, built by the Lee Brothers in the early 1950s, a great addition to the street. Dozens of local now-dominant law, insurance, and real estate firms opened as one- and two-man shops on Powell's second floor. And, a soda fountain right out of *American Graffiti* on the main level

Across westward Humboldt Street, the Humboldt Apartments, been around for 70 years, and never had a vacancy. West of the Humboldts and across from the Hardy House, a small building with a gaudy red, white and blue fascia that would make the original owner turn over in his grave, if his elder son hasn't forced that already on multiple occasions. Built in 1951 on the front lawn of the Larsen home, it housed Joselle's Fashions, the Victor Cleaners (my Realtor buddy Hank Garell's family), and a real estate and insurance office – Breckenridge Realty, I think it was called. Across the alley, one of Reno's premium apartments, the Jameson Arms, typically small for the luxury apartments of its time at only six two-bedroom units, built by the builder of the Christian Science Church, a year or so after the church. Then, a private home and next the California Avenue Market, about which I'd plagiarize an excellent account that appeared in the RGJ a score of years ago, but the Homes real estate editor (who wrote the piece) might recognize it, so I'll just say it was one of Reno's finest groceries until well into the 1970s, phone 3714 for home delivery (maybe not – now it's My Favorite Muffin). George Minor originally owned it, later sold it to his butcher Charlie Bradley, and I can't leave out another popular butcher, Fred Antoniazzi. (In an earlier incarnation it was the South Side Market.)

Crossing Lander Street, the Reno Business College in a brick-veneered building moved in from Stead AFB, later to become the studio of KOLO-radio, showcasing present-KSRN's Gutenberger, Slawthower, Carroll, and the late Pete Carrothers who claimed on the air to wake up next to every woman in northwest Reno (as long as her radio was set to 920 AM) – lucky them. Pete was not bashful. Meandering westward, Ferris & Erskine Architects (I opined to a reader recently that there *were* fine architects in Reno other that Frederic Delongchamps – maybe I'd better write about them someday). I was asked once, regarding Creek Place, where was the creek? The Creek *family*, it was, who owned the land by that little alley – Ellen Creek would one day become the bride of the late federal judge Bruce Thompson. Karen Hilary had an antique shop for many years in the old Creek home east of the alley, maybe one of the earliest shops in Reno, and I'll hear about that. *[In space-hungry columns, we write things like "became the bride of the late Bruce Thompson." I got called on that by a reader. Actually he was a very-much-alive attorney, a partner in Springmeyer &Thompson, when he and Ellen wed.]*

Two guys from Ely, Horace Bath and Dale Bell, fine men both, emigrated to Reno in 1957 and hired their college friend Mel Hancock to build them a two-story building on the west side of Creek Place, where they ran a real estate and appraisal office and rented the east side to Burge-Lloyd Surgical (limbs and braces). Harold Lloyd's son-in-law Walt Bennecke would later move the operation to the old Powell Drug, when Powell's closed in the mid-1970s. *[The Two Guys from Ely brought some mail following the column: Yes, Dale was popular "Skosh" Bell's dad, and Horace the father of Ron Bath, now keeping watch at the Pentagon after his air guard flying days.]*

Ahhh, yes, now the Wells Fargo Bank, then FNB, our "Four Hundred Million Dollar Partner" when it was built in the early 1960s on the Arlington corner, the domain of its late manager Walt Mitchell, an affable friend to many column readers and a great banker in days when you knew your banker and vice-versa.

Next week, we'll meet at 533 California Avenue, once the State Farm Insurance company office, later the Louis T. Mastos Insurance Brokers world headquarters, to then head eastward along the little north-side *boites* and shoppés. Have a good week, and God bless America.

Clowning around on California Avenue, II

We parted last week at the FNB/Wells Fargo California Avenue branch at Arlington, agreeing to stroll east along California's north side to South Virginia Street on this spring Saturday in the mid-1950s. A block to the west is the storied William Graham home (Graham as in half the Graham/McKay consortium) – we're saving that tale for a later column. Across Arlington we see the Russell Mills-designed Pincolini medical building, then glance towards the Lutheran Church of the Good Shepherd on the northwest corner.

The original edifice was hand-built during many weekends by the parishioners, stout Garrison Keillor-sorts all, under the watchful tutelage of the churches first pastor, Jim Oslund, to be replaced eventually by Reverend Vernon Kotter, whose popular daughter Marilyn was my Reno High classmate – Reverend Kotter was always there for a lot of us in school, denomination not a consideration.An early choir director at the church was Tennessee Ernie Ford, accounting for the congregation's signature hymn, *Sixteen Tons. [I caught a little hell for that line, but it was worth it.]* The same men would later build, from the ground up, the Kotter's family home at 923 University Terrace, at the corner of Sunnyside Drive. *Mrs.* Kotter oversaw that job.We'll cross *Belmont* Street now, for that was the name of Arlington Avenue from California to the Truckee River back then. The handsome brick 18-unit Belmont Apartments that loom before us is, in my mind, the building most under-appreciated by local preservationists, and the most evocative rendition of period urban luxury apartment living in Reno – the interior, mimicking a Moorish theatre like the old Majestic, is as opulent as the exterior is refined and dignified. We'll get back to the Belmonts in greater depth on another Saturday.

We see a few old homes next, in this 1950s time frame being converted to retail and medical offices – note the popular Dr. Sonderegger's '58 Mercedes 300SL ragtop in front of his office (can one call a classic Mercedes roadster a *ragtop*? Where is my mind…?). *[This dream car brought three or four queries: "Wasn't the 300SL the* Gullwing*?" Mercedes built both, Sandy had the only one I ever saw in Reno, or anywhere else.]* At 445 California, the Linn Litho Lettershop, flourishing in an era long before Xerox copiers and Adobe PhotoShop. Owner Otto Linnecke originally opened the print shop only to take care of his Reno Business College across the street, but soon began serving the public and did so for many years to follow. The old house on the Flint Street corner was owned by a mother/daughter combination best described in this family column as eccentric (they also owned the two adjacent houses northward on Flint Street.) In that corner house was an array of tenants, notably a furniture store, which did quite well, and a contract bridge studio that lasted for many years. The two southern-most houses were later razed for barrister offices, now housing Lane, Fahrendorf, Valoria and Oliphant (hey, Mills – we're thinkin' of ya, Bubba.)

We'll cross Flint Street, and before us is the Hardy's house, or the Hardy House in later years (although actually built by a family named Giraud). On this bright morning 1950's walk Roy Hardy himself might greet us, for he loved his sunporch and frequently vegged there on nice days. An early elevation of the home's plans shows a *porte-cochere* and carriage-go-round to the south, but Delongchamp's final execution of the original home dumped the cover in favor of an open porch centered on the south side. Later owners Marvin Gruilli, Leon Hernandez and Max Evans, who opened the Hardy House as a watering hole in the mid-70s, enclosed the porch. Many of us still miss the old Hardy on Friday afternoons.

Careful, don't bump your hip on one of those hewn granite hitching posts in the parkway by the street. (I'd like to know who got away with those beauties...)

Crossing the alley, Ramos Drug, the fiefdom of Bill Ramos, an El Salvadoran who relocated his drug store from Second and Virginia Street to California Avenue in 1952, and was a part of many readers' families for many years like a TV sitcom – the avuncular Bill, pharmacist Hugh Allen, the ever-perplexed saleslady Vi, and the irascible Anna, who ran the fountain with an iron hand (best burgers in town, ask any Reno High grad). Teutonic Anna was a dead shot with a spatula at four meters, and no one ever complained about her cooking. Twice. Bill hired us all for after-school jobs; Debbie Bramby (longtime owner of the Cheese Board and Wine Cellar that occupies the building now), and I agreed that in 1950s Reno if you didn't deliver pills for Bill Ramos, pump gas for Walker & Melarkey's Flying A or Traynor's Shell, or stock shelves at Mt. Rose Sporting Goods, you probably grew up to be a derelict. *[I might have gone all weekend without writing that line, incurring the wrath of friends who never worked at any of them. And my classmate/frat brother Lynn Gerow, Jr., delivering pills one night, was robbed of his cargo one night on deliveries. That was a shot heard 'round the town, for things like that just didn't happen in 1957. Today it wouldn't make the news. Lynn recovered, married another classmate Ann (Prida) and made it through med school in spite of the knot in his head he received that night.]*

Bill Ramos lived upstairs in the drug store before he moved to Hidden Valley; his quarters later opened as the quirky Deux Gros Ne in 1985. Jess Brooks owned the Texaco Station, when service stations had air hoses and stuff, in the present parking lot on the corner. His pretty daughter Patsy was our classmate; she passed away a score of years ago.

Ted Schroeder – whose efforts (with his wife Sue and others) saved Mt. Rose School – and David Sinai now pitch law in the neat white two-story frame house on the northeast corner of Hill and California – the popular Howell family's residence on our '50s stroll. A slick little gathering spot, HIGHsocieTEA, caps stet, please, now occupies the once-private home next east, leading to the Levy Mansion. I've written in columns past about the mansion being rotated in 1940 from facing Sierra (then Granite) Street, to face north. Its former front yard was leased to Lyons & Maffi originally, the final one the Chevron station operated by California Avenue legend O.B. (Obie) Dunn until the street realignment shaved the parcel in half to swoop Sierra Street west to meet Plumas and swooping Obie's Chevron away forever.

I don't know and can't learn if anything of consequence ever occupied the northeast corner of Sierra and California – the busy Eagle Thrifty market building to the north is still visible from that corner. The last building of significance now is the 12-unit California Apartments, a sturdy granite fortress that should last forever. In the 1950s we would have concluded our walk this morning at the Myron Lake home, which has risen in status and awe to the Lake Mansion since it was removed to the convention center in 1971. And that's a good place for it to stay.

• • •

[The tail end of this chapter was deleted as irrelevant, but in light of the column's head, I'd better paraphrase it: The two circus clowns, Cuddles and Canoli, who were canned from Circus Circus had just been hired by the Silver Club in Sparks as this column came to print. The endline was a bulletin that all of their local fellow clowns had attended their inaugural show at the Silver Club; all twelve of them arriving in one car.]

Then again, maybe I should have left it deleted…

Father Bob's Car, and a 1959 newspaper

Just as 500 Reno and Sparks kids vowed 50 years ago to return to the Tower Theater on the next Saturday morning, with 14 cents and the top of an Old Home Dairy milk bottle as admission, to find out if the swamp creature would really munch on the fair maiden as it was starting to do when the episode came to an end, Homefinders flock to page 8 for little other motivation other than to find out what personalized license plate FRBSKR on the late Monsignor Robert Bowling's plain-vanilla Chevy Caprice stood for, as promised in a recent column. You read it above: Father Bob's Kar. Such was the wit of Father Bowling.

You have also read here that columnists who write about architects, churches, banks and railroads should have their heads examined, and I will now add "irrigation ditches" to that list. A literary house of cards built upon ditches just floated downstream due to conflicting information and will be rebuilt.

Therefore, the column for this Saturday morning will be taken from the text in a newspaper I was researching for ditch info, this a *Nevada State Journal [precursor of that paper merging with the* Reno Evening Gazette*]* of a day or two before the Fourth of July of 1959. (The hardest part of newspaper-microfilm research is sticking to the topic while ignoring the news of the day!)

On that day Topic A, aside from the Reno Rodeo in progress and Fred MacMurray winning the Silver Spurs award, was the upcoming bond issue for a convention center somewhere in Reno and a site search team headed up by warehouseman Frank Bender, and a beef already going on over room taxes (repetition herein of "imagine that" and "dayja-voo" could become frequent, as some things never seem to change.) *[We did eventually build the Centennial Coliseum, now convention center.]* Some old friends and column readers were the flag girls for the rodeo, chicks like LeeAnn Zimmerman, Anne-Louise Cantlon, Georgia Teskey, Karry Devincenzi, Susie Wedge and the Wilson twins, Marilyn and Kay. Cindi Codding, later the bride of Sterling the Butler and Joe Murin, same guy, won a city parks art contest.

A "freeway" down Third Street, along the railroad tracks? Who the hell thought of that? Let's put it somewhere else, maybe north of the University campus, screamed the editorial. Walter Baring introduced a bill to compensate homeowners along a downtown "freeway" route. The Reno city dump closed on June 30 – up on the end of what would later be Sutro Street – and Reno, Sparks and Washoe County officials had their heads together on where to put a replacement facility, great timing to address that issue. Roger Brander was named by the city council as coordinator for the upcoming 1960 Olympics – he died in the East Bay as a passenger on the first aircraft hijacking, three years later on a hijacked airplane, a full column about that somewhere in this tome. The Lancer restaurant opened on the bluff across from present Galena High School (it would burn to the ground on July 30, 1971.)

In our 1959 newspaper we read that Ted Patrick, a fixture at Nevada Bell and father of our classmates Mimi and Nancy, husband of Billie, passes away, too young. Businessman's lunch at Newt Crumley's Holiday Hotel this day was seafood and rice – crab legs, shrimp, lobster and scallops in the Shore Room, a buck ninety-five with a beverage. The Governor's Mansion got a dishwasher and garbage disposal. The 1959 Hot August Nights are only a month away? Get thee by Lee Bros. for a used '56 Ford, $845, or a '57 Chevy $1,395 (with a heater).Realtor Mat Gibbons has a starter home for sale in Sparks, $12,000 for three bedrooms, a one car garage and asbestos siding (ouch).

A two-bit union agent named Jimmy Hoffa told a congressional committee that he was "no damned angel," and look where it got him. *Romance of Scarlet Gulch,* a corny Comstock melodrama – he ties her to the railroad tracks, as the audience gasps – with an all-Reno amateur cast moves to Piper's Opera House for the summer; for many summers to follow it played at the Liberty Belle in July, at Piper's in August – great times, music and laughs. The Bud Connell Trio played Vista Gardens, two miles east of Sparks on Hwy. 40, Bud and the Gardens now long gone. Carl Ravazza played at Harolds seventh-floor Fun Room, Jimmy Durante at the Tahoe Cal-Neva, and Ish Kabibble at the new Harrah's South Shore (before the showroom was built.) First National Bank, with 19 offices statewide, elevates E.H. (Bud) Fitz to VP-Operations and Harold Gorman to First VP, announced by FNB president Eddie Questa. *[Ravazza and his bride Marcie would eventually buy a ranch south of town – now Ravazza Road – and became popular folks in the community. Carl gave up singing Vieni Su to become a Realtor, worked with my dad for 22 years, and never sold a house – which was exactly the way he and Sr. wanted it.]*

There were 174 motorcycle license plates issued throughout the state, an out-of-town trucker was taken to the Reno city limits and thrown out of town for fighting at Mac's Club on South Virginia Street, and Nevada's entry to the Miss Universe Pageant in Long Beach was 5'7" tall and 36-23-36 back when ladies had measurements in newspapers. Like to meet her today…

The sports page? A great one in the old *Journal* – the night before this paper ran, the Cleveland Indian's legendary pitcher Herb Score fanned 14 Kansas City Athletics (that's right, *Kansas City*.)There was an article about the start of a third major league, with interest from Montreal, Toronto, Miami and Buffalo. No league divisions then, just Boston alone at 9? games out in the American League's cellar, no All-Star Break in 1959, and the Dodgers and Giants tied up for the National League lead, (and yes, both teams by then were on the west coast.) Locally, a bunch of hotshot young golfers were tuning up for the National Chamber of Commerce Junior Tournament, my contemporaries Skosh Bell, Skip Meeks, Harry Massoth and Rudy Semenza, all mentored by popular pro Pete Marich. Cam Solari was the lead caddy. (Just kidding – Cam, my childhood neighbor, was first alternate to the delegation.) Good guys, all.

And that's the way it was on the eve of the 1959 Fourth of July – a rather impromptu collection of notes for a Saturday morning. Have a good weekend and a safe short week ahead – let's see some flags flying this Friday, and God bless America.

The first airline hijacking's Reno origin...

The Flight of PAL 773

A month ago, while traipsing hastily through a July 3, 1959 *Nevada State Journal* seeking something beside real estate to report on, I noted that adman Roger Brander had been named the Reno City Council's liaison to the 1960 Winter Olympic Organizing Committee. In what could have proven to be a moment of irresponsibility by lacking confirmation, I wrote that Brander would die a few years later in an airplane crash in the rolling hills of San Francisco's East Bay.

Old friend and column reader Bill Buck confirmed that my recollection was correct, that I hadn't killed someone again. His call rekindled my interest in this crash when I had the luxury of time to do a little more scratching around. I vividly recall that it had overtones that forever changed air travel in America with our wild-west town receiving major attention in the news datelines across the nation.

Our Saturday morning yarn begins in midweek at the San Francisco airport almost 40 years ago, where a man, described later by acquaintances and family as debt-ridden and erratic, purchased two life insurance policies with a value of over $160,000 from an airport vending machine, naming his wife as the beneficiary. To add relevance to that figure, I'd guess that 80 per cent of the homes in Reno could then be bought for under $25,000. He flew Pacific Air Lines to Reno and knocked around most of the night in the casinos. And, in the *laissez-faire* world of the early 1960s, he was able to both purchase a Colt .357 on-the-spot from a downtown Reno hock shop, and to board San Francisco-bound PAL flight #773 in Reno early the next morning, carrying the gun aboard. *[Followup unconfirmed correspondence speculates that he bought the gun not in Reno, but in his Bay Area home town. From that we could surmise that he boarded an airliner* twice *with a gun, not once.]*

PAL 773 was under the hand of Captain Ernest Clark, a 22,000-hour commercial and Army Air Corps pilot with 3,000 of those hours in the Fairchild F-27 in use that day – the plane a twin-turboprop favorite workhorse of short- and medium-range regional carriers. The flight stopped briefly in Stockton, and passengers who deplaned in Stockton recalled the man seated in the front row, behind the open cockpit door.

Departing Stockton, the flight was on schedule over the East Bay on a long final approach into San Francisco International Airport when a frantic voice broke over the SFO arrival traffic frequency *"PAL seven-seven-three, Skipper's shot...we've been shot...trying to help"* – the voice of 6,000-hour co-pilot Raymond Andress. One account suggested the phrase *"...passenger in the cockpit"* followed by a gunshot. Medical examiners would find the pilot and co-pilot shot in the back of their heads, and all six rounds of the revolver fired.

Investigators speculated that the F-27, trimmed for landing, would, if left unattended, maintain level flight for a while, and that the hijacker must have exerted considerable pressure on the yolk to start the plane into the near-vertical dive that eyewitnesses on the ground reported seeing. The plane impacted on a grassy hill near San Ramon, which on that early hour of May 7th of 1964 was just a wide spot in the road in Contra Costa County.

The incident had worldwide repercussions, inasmuch as it was the first intrusion by an armed passenger into a commercial airliner cockpit. And the PAL 773 hijacking became even more heinous by the catastrophic loss of life. Living in San Francisco, I was amazed and amused, but saddened to see my 'lil ol' hometown making the news so often for days and weeks – the *"Reno hijacking"* this and *"Gamblers' Special"* that – (which it wasn't). The flight originated in Reno with only one Nevadan aboard, with an intervening stop in Stockton and ended in San Ramon, all by a plan premeditated by a San Francisco resident, but around the nation's newsrooms the unheard-of first-ever hijacking had to be an only-in-sin-city-divorcin' and gamblin'-Reno occurrence. The siege of take-me-to-Cuba diversions and D. B. Cooper's stunt would come in years to follow. (And none originated in Reno.)

The fatal flight's occupant manifest listed 44 souls, inclusive of the pilot and co-pilot, 30-year-old stewardess Marjorie Schafer, the skyjacker (thanks, Herb Caen, for that slang), 39 mostly-Bay Area residents, and *...Roger Brander, 34, gnrl. mgr. KBUB-AM radio, Reno, Nev*

And according to Bill Buck, he was a hell of a nice guy.

Epilogue: Slain pilot Ernest Clark's daughter, Julie Clark, who was 15 at the time of the tragedy, went on to buy an ex-Navy T-34 trainer (think Beechcraft Bonanza with tandem seats and a conventional tail) that she flew to numerous international aerobatic championships and demonstrated at the Reno Air Races in the late 1990s.

[Brander's family still resides in Reno.]

No computer timing, helmet cameras or Kevlar bobsleds at Squaw Valley in 1960...

Written February 7, 2002

Let The Games Begin!

Some readers may have watched NBC's Olympic Opening Ceremony coverage from Salt Lake City last night.

CBS carried an earlier opening a little differently 42 years ago at Squaw Valley. I quote from the official VIII Winter Games' brochure, published – writer unattributed – prior to the opening ceremony: "...A fanfare of trumpets, crisp against the mountain snow...2,000 doves of peace flutter skyward...and all eyes are on Little Papoose Peak as Andrea Mead Lawrence bears the Olympic torch down the hill on the final leg of its journey from Norway.

"She passes the torch to a speed skater who circles the speed skating oval once, then holds the flame aloft and lights the Olympic torch...the Olympic prayer is preceded by chimes high in the mountains... the 2,645 voices and a band of 1,285 pieces render an impressive *God of our Fathers.*"

A nice prediction, but the real drama preceded the event. What the writer didn't foresee was that there was no snow at all until a day before the Games' opening on February 18th, 1960. Fallback plans were being made to use Slide Mountain for the downhill events. Then on the 17th it snowed – boy, did it ever. It was cloudy and still snowing an hour before the Opening Ceremony. And windy and bitter cold – the musicians' trumpet valves and trombone slides froze. The 2,000 doves, caged in two flatbed trucks brought by Walt Disney Productions (who staged the opening ceremony) chirped "no way" and stayed perched, waiting for the trucks to haul them back to balmy Anaheim.

Then – and I kid you not: As the chorus started to sing through the gloom, the clouds parted and a brilliant sun – which we hadn't seen for three days – glowed above Little Papoose then eventually lit up the valley as Lawrence descended the slope with the torch. She did hand it off to the skater, who took it around the track. (One glitch: As he lit the flame, it flared as high as the nearby pine trees, scared the hell out of him and he fell off the tower. That's show biz...)

The program writer mentioned chimes and the chorus, maybe not knowing of the yodelers and the Alpenhorns – a half-dozen of these ungodly loud instruments, surely the Swiss' revenge to the Scots' bagpipes, waited high above the valley and began at once to play (you don't *hear* an

Alpenhorn – you *feel* it under your boots!) The sky by then was fully bright and blue, the pine trees green, the new-fallen snow pure white. The five Olympic rings hung above Blythe Arena, framing the Tower of Nations and the burning cauldron (a replica of this peristyle had been built in Newt Crumley's Holiday Hotel – now the Siena – parking lot.)

From a valley bereft of snow two days before, to a breath-taking winter scene, filled with that ethereal, incredible Alpine sound. *River and plain, and mighty peak – and who could stand unawed? As the summits blazed, you could stand half dazed, at the foot of the throne of God."*

I wish I had written that, but poet Robert Service beat me to it in his *Spell of the Yukon*. And this Disney fellow was good, breaking that sunshine through like he did. But his doves never did leave their cages.

• • •

The Games were underway in Squaw Valley and the eyes of the world were upon us. Bill Harrah had opened up a brand new casino at Lake Tahoe's south end, and Red Skelton inaugurated the South Shore Room just before midnight on New Years Eve of 1959 and continued into the newyear. (Liberace and Marlene Dietrich would play the room during the Olympics.) Lee Frankovich had renamed the Riverside Hotel's showroom the Olympic Room; the Will Mastin Trio with a new fellow named Sammy Davis Jr. would head up the Mapes Sky Room. A leggy local fashion model named Bobbie Bender wrote a segment in a ski magazine about appropriate dress for snow, and another fashion article told of the new ski-pant style called "Bogners," described as an ankle-length bikini. A guy named Don Dondero was taking a lot of pictures for the world press, of racers Penny Pitou, Heidi Biebl, Betsy Snite and Joan Hannah. Knowing Don, he's still got the negatives, and weirder yet, he can still locate 'em. *[Don passed away, but his family can still locate them...]*

(Before proceeding, I should thank my friends Don and Jolene Stockwell of Sparks for loaning me a box of Olympic memorabilia, which enabled a lot of honest research on this piece.) It develops that Olympic hype is not new. Be advised that Absorbine was the Official Liniment of the VIII Winter Olympics, while Listerine, the Official Mouthwash, kept Carol Heiss and Toni Sailer from buffalo breath on the high Sierra mornings. (An older person can tell you of those Olympic idols.) The Renault Dauphine, sold at Retzloff Motors on South Wells Avenue, was the Official Car of the Olympic Games. Skater/commentator Dick Button had hair. And he was already annoying. The Bavarian Inn was on Fulton Alley downtown and catered to the Nordic oom-pah crowd. Double rooms were 12 bucks at the

Holiday Hotel, no vacancy though. Long-forgotten facts: The cross-country and biathlon events were held at Lake Tahoe's McKinney Creek. And, there was no bobsled or luge in these VIII Olympics.

Luce & Son of Reno, the liquor wholesaler to the local establishments for many decades, pushed the Tahoe Toddy, the official drink of the 1960 Winter Olympics. I have the recipe and I'll include it here next week. I owe it to *Homefinder* readers to test it first before endorsing it.

The Twilight Zone: Leaving the 1960 Olympics just for a moment – I write this an hour after the Super Bowl broadcast, where John Madden bid Pat Summerall into a happy retirement. One of the resources in the Stockwells' Olympic memorabilia box is a January 4th, 1960 *Sports Illustrated*, its lead story an account of the famous Colts-Giants football game, the game where a young Giant place kicker named Pat Summerall kicked three field goals…

They're having no more fun in Park City and Salt Lake City right now than we had working up at Squaw Valley so we'll probably go back to Squaw Valley next weekend. I'm on a roll.

Have a good week, and God Bless America.

• • •

The View from KT-22, 1960

President George W. Bush's invitation to the children of the world to convene in Salt Lake City, extended in that magical Olympic opening telecast last Friday night on NBC, must have put *Homefinder* readers in the mood to reminisce about the 1960 Squaw Valley Winter Olympics. The e-mails and phone calls with your recollections following last Saturday's piece were welcome and wonderful.

A favorite Squaw Valley moment came from a favorite Reno High sweetie of mine, a comely lass named Sherry (Cannon) Butler, now a Southern California denizen who picks this column up off the internet. Sherry, using her considerable feminine wiles, scored a ticket for the semifinal hockey match, the U.S.A. versus the U.S.S.R. Remember now, relations between these two superpowers were plumbing new depths in 1960 and the whole hockey match was seen as a metaphor of world politics, but that wasn't what Sherry remembered most: It was the slightly disoriented inebriate seated next to her who spent the entire match rooting for "Stanford." Apparently the Russians' jerseys looked a little like the Cardinal. At least to Sherry's bleacher mate. Many of you remembered that contest, on the closing day of the Games – a real thriller – and the final score, 3-2, (the U.S.A. won.) That score remained on the scoreboard at Blythe Arena until the arena collapsed in

1981, a "maintenance accident" that should have landed Squaw's management in the hoosegow. Did a Russian skater die in that match? One of you resurrected that rumor that flourished for a decade following the Games. Their goalie got slammed into the wall with a crash you could hear on top of KT-22, and many thought he died. Don't know myself, but if he was alive, he was damn sure counting birdies on his stretcher ride out of the arena.

And just who was Andrea Mead Lawrence, the skier who carried the torch down Little Papoose? Sorry, I should have fleshed that in for the younger readers: Lawrence won the Slalom and Giant Slalom at the Oslo games in 1952 and was the 27-year old darling of the American skiing scene in 1960. One anonymous caller corrected me, rudely, that it was Tenley Albright who skied the torch down the hill. Not likely; Albright was the ladies figure skating Gold medalist in the 1956 Games at Cortina (Italy). Maybe this caller is a Stanford alum.

The reigning jumper during many prior Winter Olympics was the Finn Juhani Karkinen, a star jumper in the Oslo and Cortina (1952 and 1956) Games. USA's Gene Kotlarek, who won the Gold in Squaw and Innsbruck (1964) jumping wore classic, as in baggy, Nordic-style ski apparel and hit the 80-meter jump like a herd of turtles with his arms out in front of him, his knickers rattling in his own 50 mile-an-hour breeze. Imagine his surprise, (and jump hill steward/judge Jerry Wetzel's), when the Japanese jumpers hit the inrun wearing new skin-tight Spandex flight suits, their hands at their waists. And they glided like silent birds… Not enough good can be said about Wetzel, the late Reno ski-store co-owner (with partner Hal Codding). And, as some old 1960 newspapers remind me, the local employees of Nevada Bell, then a local company, donated their time generously, and Bell made time available to them. They basically ran the communications for the Olympics, with few portable radios back then that I recall. One volunteer who has to be included, although I haven't permission to use his name, was a college guy from the Midwest who came to Squaw as the operator of the brand-new Zamboni. He lovingly tended the ice rink and speed skating oval and now lives in Lakeridge. Truly, the hero of every American male (a Zamboni's a guy thing.) I should probably do a stand-alone column about Squaw Olympic volunteers. Virtually the whole town of Reno and certainly the University of Nevada came to a standstill, providing labor to the Games. White Stag ski wear donated the officials' nylon parkas with the Games' logo, probably a thousand of them, color-coded by work assignment (Nordic, Alpine, Ski Patrol, Gatekeepers, Communications – things were pretty well organized.) I recently dug my red (Press) parka out, and pulled a "Sparks Nugget – Two Fine Restaurants" matchbook from a pocket. I'm donating it to John.

I mentioned "Bogners" last week – a reader pointed out that the namesake for these ski-pants (Willi Bogner) competed in the Squaw Olympics (Downhill, 8th place). Another reader reminds us that Vuarnet sunglasses got their name from the gold medalist in Downhill (Jean). Several of your recollections were of the Indian snow-dances in the valley – the Shoshone tribe sending a team of their best dancers. They did well – it snowed beyond belief for twenty-four hours preceding the opening. And the valley "parking lot" – many remembered that fiasco: Sawdust was mixed with snow and compacted, to make a solid, non-slip surface to park on. Worked great for the Games' chilly first week, then it warmed up and thawed the second week, and, well, there's probably a couple of heavy DeSotos and Packards still out in that valley somewhere. Yikes, what a mess!

Last week we promised to reveal the Tahoe Toddy, the Official Warmer of the Olympic Games, according to Esquire magazine, March 1960 edition. Here goes: garnish a glass with lemon twist, pour in four ounces of very hot water, add a level tablespoon of batter. (That's batter, not butter.) Batter up: 4 teaspoons brown sugar; 2 teaspoons butter (that's butter, not batter.) 2 dashes of cinnamon, a pinch of nutmeg, a pinch of allspice, and 2 teaspoons Bols Orange Curacao. Serves four. (Oh, and did I mention one ounce of Early Times per drink.) Have three and the butter and batter won't matter.

Of course, as we learned in a column last summer, it would be easier go to Eugene's restaurant on the way home from Squaw Valley, where bartender Cliff Challender could make us a Toddy from memory. And, we might see Eugene's owner Gilbert Vasserot entertaining the athletes from his native Switzerland, notably favored skater Madaleine Chamot. (Eugene's hosted the prestigious International Olympic Committee at a luncheon prior to the games, a feather in Reno's cap.)

Have a Toddy, go buy a couple houses – or vice versa – and God Bless America.

Wrapping up Squaw Valley

The original plan for this Saturday morning was another *Homefinder* walk, probably taking a couple of Saturdays, along South Wells Avenue. While we usually walk downtown in 1950, we'll walk Wells in the 1970s, to try to bring a little clarity into its metamorphosis; to watch a street go from a post-war residential street, gradually flourishing with businesses and shops, then to a street that everyone traverses daily but never shops on, then a dying street, finally to a street attracting a new culture and neighbors, and tardy attention from the city fathers, slowly waking up to the fact that there's more to Reno than downtown. This is going to be a great walk.

But wait! An email and a phone call arrive into our lonely writer's garret in the God-forsaken desert, regarding our visits to Squaw Valley during the 1960 Winter Olympics. One's from an old friend, the other from an Incline Village resident who called me a male chauvinist for the way I worded a passage. Imagine that.

What offended her was that I identified by name the 27-year old darling of the 1960s slopes, Andrea Mead Lawrence, the twice-Gold medallist skier who brought the torch down the hill during the Olympic opening ceremony, but then left the male speed skater that Mead Lawrence handed the torch off to to remain in obscurity.

Frankly, I skipped over a whole bunch of people in that description of the opening ceremony, including Richard Milhous Nixon, who declared the Games open, and Karl Malden, who recited the Olympic prayer. But the skater? He fell into relative obscurity, and only after uncharacteristic and tedious research can I offer that his name was Kenneth Henry, which should make Henry's mother and the Incline Village reader happy.

Karl Malden???

• • •

The phone call came from my old buddy Buddy Sorensen, who helped me with a couple of names: Gene Kotlarek and Juhe Karkinen. I'm glad he called, because it prompted me to write what many of us know: When local skiers gather in the warming hut to speak of the golden days of 1950s-skiing, Buddy's name comes up prominently with Dick Buek, Jack Bosta, Dick Dorworth, Harry Ericson, Lynette Gotchy, Rusty Crook and a bunch of other guys, as a Far West Ski Association official and coach, Nordic Director, sometime Falcon coach and a mentor to a hundred local skiers that went on to regional and national prominence. Our area and our sport are indebted to him.

Another name and anecdote that came up in the past few weeks was that of George Kerr, known by many as Harolds Club's photographer/host, when mighty Harolds and Harrah's ruled Reno. George clicked thousands of golf tournament and celebrity photographs, many going 'round the world on wire services, and was known as a linguist:

Just prior to the Games, he was asked to be available as an interpreter. "You speak several languages, don't you?" George was asked. "Actually, I speak only two: the King's English, and Nevadan."

In truth, George could say "Say Cheese" in seven languages, not counting the King's Nevadan after a Tahoe Toddy at Eugene's. He did Yeoman duty during the Games.

• • •

A week ago I wrote of my red Olympic parka, the color assigned to the Press whereupon a friend accused me of posturing as a hotshot. In truth, I was a grunt, working with five other University of Nevada grunts who could ski, backpack and snowshoe, and we were assigned "Weasels" – open Jeep-sized tracked vehicles built by Studebaker, loaned to the Olympics by the marines at Pickel Meadows Winter Training Center. We ran all over the valley, typical cargo being endless paperwork, clipboards full of race results, times, schedules, a dead Longines timing clock, an urn of coffee destined for a CBS camera crew at the jump tower, somebody's glove that was left in a limousine, a pair of snowshoes, three reels of communication cable, box lunches for the slalom timers and a very important person needing to be somewhere else (a very important person being almost anyone in Squaw Valley beside us.) We mentioned earlier that CBS carried the Games, but in 1960 only 15 to 30 minutes each day – taped – in reality not even videotape, but movie film with sound on a different recorder, the big tanks of film and huge batteries somewhere in the back of the Weasels, to be processed in the Bay Area and aired that night.

I'm waxing (skier-term) sentimentally toward the close of the 1960 and 2002 Games, with an observation about how things have changed in 42 years, as we watch on NBC tonight – a production not filmed, but digitized, sent not to Sacramento by courier for processing, but to a satellite for instant broadcast. The clocks, timing, and standings are instantaneous, not delayed hours by the lag between the start house and the finish line and virtual longhand computation. A tiny camera gives us a real-time pilot's view from a bobsleigh (the sleigh built from materials developed by NASA). Ice dancing and the half-pipe. How the sport, and the way we view it, has changed in 42 years…

• • •

They were wonderful weeks in our towns' heritage, and we wish the children of the world now convening at Park City the fun, success and memories that we continue to enjoy.

A peek under the hood of Hot August Nights...

Happy birthday sweet 16

How far has Hot August Nights come since the first cruise in 1986? I'll start a roundabout answer by stating that in 17 years, HAN has had 19 posters. *[This appeared August 2002.]*

Why, you ask, were there two extra posters? Harry Parsons, HAN Director Emeritus and local CPA – Cruisin' Public Accountant – explains: In the second year of the show, 1987, the show's organizers fashioned a poster with a Mel's Drive-In waitress on skates waiting on a James Dean-lookalike dude slouching in a hot-pink '57 Chevy convertible. They took the poster back to Detroit, arrived on the steps of GM's Chevrolet division and told the Chevy execs how lucky Chevrolet was to be chosen the prime sponsor of such a primo car show.

The Chevy guys told them, through their security staff, for the local entrepreneurs never made it past the lobby, how lucky they were to be able to just leave, take their poster with them, and get back to the divorce capital of the world – that, the view of our town held by most people east of Denver back then

So how far have we come? This year, 2002, General Motors came to Hot August Nights, to ask if GM could unveil the all-new 50-Year Anniversary Corvette during the celebration. HAN Director David Saville, always the showman, met with the HAN committee, and after seven nanoseconds of consideration, said yes. And so it shall be done next week at the Hilton, Wednesday morning at 10 AM – under the watchful eye of the nation's automotive press – what a feather in our area's cap!

Several thoughts linger – why was there a second poster that year? Because our early organizers took the 1987 poster, reshot it with the same waitress serving James Dean, this version in a hot pink '56 Thunderbird, and marched to Dearborn, where T-Birds are built, told the Ford folks how lucky they were that…well, you know the rest. Ford also had bouncers in their lobby, so the organizers again returned to Reno. (That's one extra poster. The second extra poster, to round out the thought, was the '92 edition, a '58 Buick – they shot one clean poster and another with tire tracks and an oil drip across it – purposely.) The clean version was adopted, but a few of the dirty ones survived and are collected. I like the oil-stained edition – it's cool.

And I'll pose a final question and some speculation: Chevrolet historically named their post-war cars after beach towns – Del Ray, Bel Air,

Biscayne – where did they come up with "Corvette," a smallish warship? No answer here; as I recall the working name of the American dream roadster in the early 1950s was the "Laguna" or the "Cerro." Nor do I know how Pontiac took "Catalina" away from Chevy, should you ask…

I dropped in on David in the Hot August Nights office on East Greg Street a few days ago – on the eve of the incredible HAN volunteer team welcoming a couple of hundred thousand guests to our valley and the show. I took more notes than I'll ever get into one column, so I'm opting for the good ol' Herb Caen three-dot journalism to conserve the verbiage:

From now until the time you read next week's column the show will have brought 88 million dollars into our towns and the surrounding area…the HAN committee goes out of their way to avoid displacing the locals by tying up all the parks and facilities…the event is by some measure in its 37th year, inasmuch as it was a continuation of the wonderful old Harrah's Auto Collection annual swap meets…HAN was originally an Easter Seal benefit; the event now benefits the Hot August Nights Children's Charities Funds…the limit of 5,000 cars has been long-since registered and HAN expects to pre-register 2,000 cars for 2003 even prior to the end of this event…registration buys two tickets, with a package of goodies worth about double the registration fee, and extra passes are available, including kid passes (HAN stresses family participation)…the cars must be American or European built, 1972s or older (extended from the original 1968 to take in the end of the muscle-car era.)...

Some car owners are purists, and for example won't put a modern radio into their dashboard, but opt to stay with the factory tube-set with the ConElRad triangles (I'll explain all that to the younger set on a slower week)…to accommodate them, Dave ensures that AM as well as FM radio stations are kept in the loop broadcasting during the event…HAN 2002 President Dave Roundtree explains that this is the HAN "Sweet Sixteen" because it's the seventeenth event, 1986's being Year Zero... I mentioned the Big Bopper last week; two callers confused him with Wolfman Jack, the 1950s Southern California disk jockey who defined the Hot August Nights ethos…those of us who lived in Reno and Sparks could only get the Wolfman's Los Angeles AM station – XEAK Mighty Six Ninety – in the evening hours…Wolfman was prominent at some of the early Hot August Nights – what a voice! The Big Bopper died with Richie Valens and Buddy Holly when Miss American Pie – a twin Beech – crashed in February of 1959…Wolfman's news intro of that event, spoken in an uncharacteristically sobered voice was "tonight the music died," and inspired the title of Don McLean' enduring and cryptic *Bye, Bye Miss American Pie*…you'll hear it a lot this week.

Where did you go during the original hot August nights in the fifties? How about the Friday night dances at the American Legion Hall at South Tahoe? (Harrah's hadn't opened the South Shore Room then; it was still Sahati's Stateline Club.) The fireworks on the Tahoe Commons? Or the Limelighters or Peter, Paul & Mary at Blythe Arena in Squaw Valley after the Olympics – a great night out, two bucks admission, one end of the arena open to the stars.

One last note for this week is of David's plans for a "teardrop" category in 2003 – before Airstreams crowded the Interstate, teardrop-shaped trailers, little more than a double bed with a streamlined aluminum bedspread, let the Highway 40 traveler avoid "motor courts" – motels. There's a resurgence of these tiny trailers taking place, and some are beauties. We're far from done writing about this party – have a good week, make our towns' guests welcome, and God Bless America.

•••

This appeared August 10th, 2002

Fun fun fun 'til your daddy takes the T-Bird away

Hot August Nights continues. And it should be said that following 17 Hot August Night celebrations, a solemn truth fell over me: We didn't own the cars that evoke our long-gone hot August nights; our parents did. We were cool, cruisin' the Big-Y in Jon Key's robin's egg-blue '57 Chev, but in truth his mother Kay loaned it to us. The Beach Boys should write a song about that forgotten aspect of youth…

Last week I mentioned a ConElRad radio and received a spate of welcome "how-about this accessory" mail. I like nothing more than just assembling a column that readers write, so here we go:

Fuzzy dice need no introduction here, but I'm challenged to find anyone who ever had them in 1960; a churchkey was more prevalent, 'cuz we were wild and crazy guys who could make a 4-pack of Colt 45 from the Ralston Market go all night. Air conditioning was a novelty in the '50s – a GM car with factory air had a little air intake bubble on each side behind the rear doors. Windwings, by federal law, should be restored. All of us had "4-40" air conditioning; four windows down, 40 miles an hour. Or, if it's a really hot Friday night downtown, put one of the old swamp coolers in your back window and fill it with water, plug it in to your cigarette lighter, and be cool, even while looking like a complete nerd, or "square," the pre-nerd term. (But, the evaporative coolers are still in the J.C.Whitney catalogue, and they worked like crazy – a salvation for our family on a 1952 summer ride across the nation in a '50 Buick straight-8.)

Safety was not a big deal – look at some old show cars downtown today with chrome bullets on the steering wheel hub, knobs and dials that stick out everywhere on the dashboard, and door handles and hood ornaments to impale errant pedestrians (the spear on the front of the aforementioned Buick could shish-kebab one average *Homefinder* reader or three second-graders.) Lincoln led the pack in the late '50s with a Dolly Partonesque-doodad on either side of the radio that would disembowel both the driver and passenger long before the windshield glass filleted them. Seat belts? "They'll never last," pooh-poohed Mechanix Illustrated auto writer Tom McCahill in about 1952. " The 'Mer'can public will never accept 'em." Should we tell Tom about the Ziploc baggie that would snap out of the dashboard 30 years later and plant him against the seat while the engine of the oncoming car he just had a head-on with was heading for his trunk? Nawww...

"I'll never pay two hundred dollars for a gadget that does this, and this, and this," I vividly remember a friend of my dad's saying about 1950, moving his right hand in the pattern of low, second and high gears on the shift column. He later became a District Judge, and no doubt went to his reward in a stick shift, $200 the richer. Acceptance was slow, of Hydramatic, Dynaflow, FordoMatic, Fluid Drive and Powerglide – "slush," we called them, or PNDLR. In fact the earlier units didn't even have a Park gear. *[In later years we'd pay a premium for four-on-the-floor. Go figure.]*

Anyone who worked in a service station, emphasis on "service," which was almost all of us, learned where to find hood latches and gas fill caps. If you're downtown later today, have a proud owner of a '57 Chev show you the gas fill door, or neater yet, a '56 Chevy or the many Cadillacs from '49 on, where you twisted here or pushed the reflector to raise the taillight lens – sheer poetry in engineering. Ford and Chrysler leaned toward fills behind a spring-loaded license plate in the center, another feature that should be mandated by federal law. Handy as hell...

The beat goes on: Dashboard prisms to see the stoplight, when intersections only had one, directly over the center of the traffic lane. Dimmer switches on the floorboard, where they belong. An Incline Village reader e-mailed about push-button starter buttons and two-position day-night inside mirrors, a big deal when they came out (early 1950s); I have one on my pickup; never switched it in 62,000 miles. Automatic headlight dimmers, first one I remember was on a neighbor's '51 Caddy. Didn't work then, they still don't in 2002.

Several of you wrote about what we really called Hot Pink cars (last week's column). While we all know what my heart was writing, this is a family column. They're Hot *Homefinder* Pink. And the family aspect also precludes writing about chrome plating the glove box doors on '49 through '54 Chevys – ask your dad or hubby about that – he'll know.

• • •

Tomorrow the cats and chicks take their cars home, Jan and Dean go back into the record album jacket for a year, and we're back to business. Have a good week, go buy a house, and God Bless America.

• • •

[Loose ends]: "Some car owners are purists," I wrote during Hot August Nights, "and for example won't put a modern radio into their dashboards, but stay with the factory tube-sets with the ConElRad triangles (I'll explain all that to the younger set on a slower week)."

This is a slower week. "CONtrol of ELectronic RADiation," it was, a cold war Civil Defense technique to get all of America to tune to just two radio frequencies, at 640 and 1240 megacycles – now megahertz – while the Russian bombers were approaching to nuke us, homing in on individual radio stations as localizers for their targets. Radios all had little triangles on their dials at 640 and 1240, and those, boys and girls, were the hallmark of a truly pure 1950s classic car's dashboard. Now, I assume you all know what "dials" are…

One of Reno's Big Three hotels burns to the ground...

THE GOLDEN HOTEL FIRE

I sat in my school bus at a red light on the corner of East Second and Center Streets, a hair past seven o'clock on a Tuesday morning. It was 40 years ago this week. *[The column appeared March 30, 2002]*

Smoke – or maybe steam? – was coming out of a sidewalk freight elevator door in front of the Golden Hotel, on the west side of Center between Second and Commercial Row. It was smoke. I drove through the intersection, parked and pulled the handle on the fire alarm pedestal in front of Parker's Mens Store. I had no option than to leave for Stead airbase and collect my high school kids, and as I drove north on Center Street I saw one fire truck come around the corner off West Second Street from the old main station on Commercial Row at West Street, then another. A plume of smoke steadily grew in my mirrors by the time I reached the hill above the U of N, where I would normally be in class by 9 AM.

But not on April 3rd, 1962...

• • •

Frank Golden – a Tonopah miner and banker – built the opulent four-story Golden Hotel in 1906. Golden died shortly after it was completed, and the hotel was operated by the Wingfield clan for two decades, then finally the Tomerlin brothers, who bought it in 1956. They remodeled it, including long rows of aluminum louvers on each row of windows facing the street; louvers that City Building Inspector Ronald Coleman would later say were in compliance with city code. The "New Golden" was a Reno icon of excellence.

• • •

On that fateful morning, a welder's acetylene tank had exploded in the basement, while most of the 142 hotel guests were still asleep. The fire spread quickly, and ignited a Nash Metro – a little car, for the younger readers – that was positioned above the acetylene tank on the first floor, displayed as a prize. The heat from the tank and the car was intense, and traveled straight up in a matter of a very few minutes, filling all the hallways with dense smoke and exploding through the roof hard enough to blow roofing material all over the block.

Guests and hotel employees did a commendable job of running throughout the building spreading the word to evacuate, which many were able to do through stairwells. Others, however, were trapped in their rooms and the fire department was having one hell of a time trying to evacuate them through the aluminum trim that had been placed over the windows in the 1956 effort to modernize the hotel.

Fire Chief Wagner Sorensen recognized early on that this was a fire of major proportion and pulled out all the stops, mustering help from Sparks, who sent a pumper and fifteen men, Stead Air Force Base, another pumper; Washoe County Fire – later Truckee Meadows Fire Protection District, now incorporated into Reno – an engine, and Warren Engine Company from Carson City, who sent their brand new "Snorkel" unit. Reno even put their little 1926 American LaFrance, which had long been in reserve, into service and it performed yeoman duty as a pumper. Bell Telephone and Sierra Pacific Power sent high-lift equipment, as did several contracting firms and Reno Iron Works, who sent a crane that lifted a bucket carrying several firemen with hoses. Newspaper photos clearly show hoses playing water off the fire escapes of Harolds Club's seven-story tower to cool them down.

Some horror stories of trapped hotel guests were beginning to hit the street – one of a dancer named Carol Maye, line captain of the Barry Ashton "Playmates of Paris Review" that was playing at the Golden. Carol was last seen overcome in a smoky corridor. Jimmy Nuzzo, one of Sam Butera's Witnesses, playing at the Mapes with Louis Prima and Keely Smith, was nowhere to be found. Reno police Lieutenant Ray Cavallo was credited with one of the brightest deeds of the day – entering the hotel at the outset of the fire and grabbing the hotel's guest register, enabling rescue crews to account for guests. The register was already singed when Ray brought it out of the building.

But the smoke continued to billow relentlessly hours later, even with the incredible amount of water being dumped into the fire. (Sierra Pacific Power boosted their Idlewild Park and High Street pumps up to summer output.) In Carson City, State Forester George Zappettini offered the services of the state on behalf of Governor Grant Sawyer, who was enroute to Japan. State pilot Chuck Destree, a native Hawthorne boy, hopped the State's Beechcraft C-45 – a D-18 to you civilians – from Carson City to the Reno airport and took on plain Truckee River H_20, not Borate, as many people thought. Chuck made two passes over the carcass of the Golden, still churning out black smoke, and on each pass dumped half his cargo on the fire.

Playing hooky from class – as was the rest of the campus and everyone else in Reno – I watched from the roof of Harolds Club's tower as Chuck came in from the south and made the first dump, smack-into the cavity of the fire, and *voila*, the smoke abated considerably. He climbed and circled to the west and flew over again, dumping the second chamber, and the smoke turned white and let up even more. The will of the fire was broken and the firemen were then able to see where to best play their streams of water. Soon it was under control, if far from out.

And I got pictures for the University's *Sagebrush* newspaper of the *top* of a Twin Beech airplane – about 75 feet above the parapets of the Golden. I asked Chuck last week what he remembered the most about the mission, and he said it was the University of Nevada looming up in front of him as he looked back at his work.

One victim was taken from the Golden that day, the only known fatality that day. It would be a full month before the sixth victim was found.

Next Saturday, the saga continues…

• • •

Mopping Up the Golden Hotel Fire

In the last column we gawked as the four-story downtown Golden Hotel burned to the ground in a spectacular inferno on April 3, 1962, a Tuesday. This Saturday morning, we have a few facts, reader questions, and anecdotes about the 40-year old fire, which defy being put into any particular order:

How many people died? Good question. While most assumed the count to be seven, I'm able to verify only six, that last one a hotel employee found in the basement debris a full month after the fire. Hospitalized? Forty people, give or take a few. Five firefighters hospitalized briefly were Leonard Howard, 27 at the time and William (OB) O'Brien, both still with us, and three late firemen, Bob Kerns, then 31, John Henderson, 39, and Garvel (Ace) Acres. Heroes? Hotel employee Paul Gallo and fireman Smokey (Lloyd) Davison, who carried, down two flights of stairs and out the front door, a woman – Margaret McCollum – self-described in an April 4th Nevada State *Journal* interview as weighing 200 pounds, by a Gazette reporter as "stout" and by fireman Davison as 300 pounds. No ballerina, by anybody's account, but she sent them thank-you cards for many years to follow.

How much water did the airplane drop? Twelve hundred gallons, according to the *Reno Evening Gazette,* 200 gallons according to State Forestry pilot Chuck Destree (1,200 gallons – five tons – might slightly overgross a Twin Beech!) Did it help? The firefighters said not much, the Pacific Fire Rating Bureau (whose records I had access to) in their final report said yes. Either way it was cool to watch. From several readers: Didn't the hotel burn once before? No, the Grand Hotel, to the south of the Golden (on the corner), burned on March 4th of 1959 and two top floors had to be removed, "top" quoted straight from a 1959 REG story. (Can't be too explicit; might have been the two *middle* floors!) And the Golden Eagle hotel, a block away, burned on May 6, 1929 (NSJ). How many people worked at the Golden? 513 on April 3, 1962. (And 143 guests on that day.)

What did surrounding businesses do? Officials of First National Bank – now the Planet Hollywood *[and now struggling]* – doused their roof with a garden hose. Harrah's and Harolds did finally close, briefly. Harold Smith Sr. walked around Harolds casino floor playing his violin, and no, I don't know if he was fiddling "Nearer My God to Thee."

From a reader: "What was the name of the malt shop in the basement?" The Malt Shop. And a dandy it was, right off of a Hot August Nights poster – white wrought-iron furniture, a checkerboard floor, candy-striped awnings and real malts. No one asked, but many will remember Art Conde and Joe De Rosa, who owned the hotel barbershop. They relocated to the Ryland Barber Shop on South Virginia and were clippin' again by Saturday. Didn't (Justice of the Peace) Bill Beemer pull one body out of the debris? That story's another only-Bill Beemer local legend, but one best left unchronicled. I'll leave it at "yes."

What happened to the money and chips on the gaming tables when the fire broke out? My personal guess would be that at that midweek early hour (7 AM) in the off-season there probably weren't too many tables open. The April 4th REG details Golden exec Phil Downey running around trying to salvage what he could until the heat of the fire drove him out onto the street. Grifall Construction ultimately took the Golden Hotel's carcass to the Isbell pit – near the bluff by the Hilton Hotel's south main floor entrance – where the debris was rechecked for bodies. And, according to Don Stockwell, he of the photographic memory, guards finally had to be posted to keep treasure hunters from scavenging for souvenir chips and the silver melted into the slot machines.

Former Golden employee Susan Marler tells a couple of stories. First, a Thornton Wilder-like tale of a sixty-ish Golden Hotel resident, whose name was Lucia Pedlar according to both papers if it's the same person Susan spoke of. Lucia was confined to a wheelchair following a surgery, and able, more each passing day, to leave her room for meals and remain on the ground floor for an ever-lengthening period of time. The whole Golden staff was pulling for her and sustaining her courage to pump up her rehabilitation. Lucia was doing well.

She died in the fire.

The second Susan Marler story is happier, of Marilyn Monroe, who resided in the Mapes, natch, during the filming of *The Misfits* a couple years before the fire. Following the completion of the movie, Marilyn moved into the Golden for a time, by one account. Susan recalls seeing her shopping for a magazine at the gift store one day, and watched to see what the starlet liked to read.

Marilyn left for the elevator and her room with the latest copy of *Sunshine and Health* – an *aù naturel* sunbathing magazine. OK, OK – a nudie mag. *[The report that Marilyn ever stayed at the Golden was questioned by several readers.]*

And off track from our fire topic, I'm compelled to report that the April 5th *Gazette* included a sports piece about pro rassler Don Manoukian's State Building bout with twin midgets, named Lord Littlebrook and Little Beaver. Ask 'Nouk about that night. I'd rather not.

I'm grateful to Janyce Bentley and Mary Florentz for offering me some old *Reno Evening-Gazette*s and *Nevada State Journal*s – coincidentally just as I was planning this piece for the fire's 40th anniversary. I'm also indebted to the Nevada Historical Society, retired Reno Fire Captains Joe Granata and the late Jim Arlin, Reno Fire Department archives, and the Pacific Fire Rating Bureau (now Insurance Service Office/ISO) – and to you readers for your input.

This firefighter's silence speaks volumes...

The Guy on the Bench

He looked dog-tired. He sat alone, wearing heavy turnouts, all bunched up at the boots. His head fell to his chest, left hand resting on his knee holding a helmet with *SFD* on the crown. A couple of teenagers took turns sitting by him and taking pictures of each other, and then they walked away, leaving him alone again. I sat down next to him on the park bench in a shady setting on Pyramid Way, right behind the Sparks Heritage Museum on Victorian Avenue.

I'd seen him before, while he was directing traffic at a wreck on Rock Boulevard and Prater. Or maybe dragging a cotton hose into the burning garage at an old house on D Street where the barbecue coals got away from the homeowner, or earlier that same day inspecting an office in the Ribeiro complex on Stanford Way. Once I saw one of Sparks' Snorkel trucks in the Disc Drive Scolari's parking lot, the truck's operator keeping watch like a quail on a rooftop while his buddies joked around inside the store about whether to get chicken or burgers for their Sunday dinner. The quail in the Snorkel called them all back to work, pronto, on the walkie-talkie; 15 minutes later they were pulling an unconscious teenager out of an abandoned mine shaft. Dinner would have to wait this Sunday. Maybe the guy on the bench was one of the crew on the Snorkel.

But I was sure that there was a hint of a smile on his countenance, so I might have seem him at a happier time – like when he was cooking at the Fire Prevention Week pancake feed at the main station last October, best in the west, or slinging weenies at the SFD booth on a Thursday night Farmers' Market on Victorian Square. Or showing an elementary school kid how to "Stop, Drop and Roll" at the department's training trailer, or taking a rebuilt bicycle to a needy tyke in west Sparks on Christmas day.

Whoever he was, he was a Sparks firefighter. Maybe he was a she – in the turnouts I couldn't tell. She might have been the EMT on the Water Rescue Team that fished the kayaker out of the river by old Manogue High School, or the tillerman on the aerial truck when Sparks still had one (and political correctness be damned; in this column the operator steering the back wheels of a hook-and-ladder will always be a tillerman!) Sure, that's where I saw her. Or him.

Or it might have been a while back that I saw this firefighter. Maybe as far back as 1905 when Sparks' first firehouse opened at 12th and C

Streets, or 1917 when the town got their first motorized apparatus, or in 1960 hosing down Kleppe's Pond by wintry day so the Railroaders could go ice-skating by night, (the Reno Fire Department did this favor for us Huskies, flooding Idlewild Park and Lake Park in the northwest.) Sparks' firefighters have covered Reno's many times when the RFD got bogged down, like the 1957 Sierra Street fire we read about here a while ago or the 1962 Golden Hotel fire we've chronicled in the past few weekends that partially inspired this yarn. Or when the Galaxy Airlines propjet crashed on South Virginia Street, killing 62 passengers. Sparks' apparatus sat in a few Reno firehouses in case anything else got loose on that chilly night in January of 1985.

The Sparks Fire Department aided Reno in the August 1948 Lake Street fire, a nasty one. Sparks' chief Frank Hobson was overcome and died a hero's death rescuing someone in a building. I vividly remember standing in front of my dad's office on A Street, watching a flag-draped coffin being escorted down B Street in the hose bay of a Sparks pumper. Maybe the firefighter sitting next to me was one of the honor guardsmen that slowly marched alongside the pumper. Or maybe it's Hobson himself? Or Fred Steiner Sr., the other Sparks firefighter who died in the line of duty responding to a fire in 1953. Mutual aid between Reno and Sparks has always been the standard, and firehouse camaraderie transcends the shields of SFD or RFD, or FDNY or PAFD. This firefighter next to me could have had any one of those stenciled on the helmet in his/her hand.

A few other visitors visited the little park while I sat there. They saw seven bronze footprints in the walkway leading to the bench. They studied the life-size bronze figure in a moment of reverence, then took a few pictures and left.

• • •

The Sparks Fire Department Monument project was quarterbacked by SFD Apparatus Operator Barry Hagen, who, with help from Councilman Phil Salerno and SFD chief Lee Leighton *[retired 2004]*, made a successful request to the Sparks Redevelopment Agency for approval and funding of the project.Many Sparks businesses donated material, and 95 per cent of the labor was done by off-duty Sparks firefighters. Hagen contacted Colorado sculptor Gary Coulter, who had created a Fallen Firefighter memorial for Colorado Springs. That town released the right to replicate their statue, altering only the helmet to read *SFD,* and the monument was cast. Coulter passed away from cancer during the casting, so his wife Debbie completed it, and fashioned the axe in the Sparks firefighter's hand and the brass footprints leading to the bench. Three flagpoles fly the United States, Nevada, and City of Sparks flags 24 hours a day – and at half-staff on each September 11th. Bronze plaques descriptive of the department's history, the dedication of the monument, and the Firefighters' Prayer are emplaced on the three flagpoles' bases.

The monument will be dedicated on April 20th – next Saturday *[2002]* – at 11 a.m.; once again, it's right behind the Sparks Heritage Museum at Victorian and Pyramid. Easy parking.

And after the crowd leaves, hang around. Take a seat next to the firefighter, who might be on the quiet side, but the countenance at rest in this pastoral setting speaks volumes…

• • •

[I was proud of this column, and somewhat humbled to learn that it found its way into many firehouses across the country.]

Wherein your faithful reporter tangles with a loyal school's alumni, and matters relating thereto...

Leave the driving to us, and other school stuff

A fortnight ago in a treatise about Stead AFB I noted that "...there was only one high school in Reno until 1961" and proceeded to recall that all the high school students in town could fit into two 66-passenger school buses.

The remark endeared me to many a Manogue High School graduate, who called en masse to remind me that there was indeed a second high school in Reno in 1961 – their alma mater, then as now on a site just east of the University of Nevada campus. The thrust of what I was writing was that Reno High was the only school in Reno with a bus program. But, when life hands you a lemonade, a writer makes lemonade: In talking with one of the Manogue alums who was kidding me about my gaffe, Nancy Howell Spina, the topic of school buses inadvertently arose.

Starting closer to the beginning, a word about Manogue, formally Bishop Manogue High School. The school's name came from Bishop Patrick Manogue, who contributed to the education of miners' children during the Comstock gold rush and was later the first bishop of the Sacramento Catholic diocese.The school opened in 1947, in a couple of old barracks in a beautiful meadow at the old Flick ranch by the Truckee River near the present southeast McCarran Boulevard (it's now utilized by SageWinds school). Within a decade it had grown and was relocated to its present campus in 1957. I should say parenthetically that the present site will become part of the University campus when Manogue's new campus is completed south of town by Zolezzi Lane. (Arrowcreek Drive, to the newcomers.) *[And it's open, fall of 2004 – a beauty.]*

Nancy told me that a bus made the loop around Reno picking up Manogue students to transport to the school's original location, which back then you had to pack a lantern and a lunch to drive to. "A bus, you say?" I asked. "A bus," she replied. There I was prepared to get myself off a hook by saying that Manogue never had a school bus system and get myself into yet-another jam. But you read it here first: Bishop Manogue High School indeed had a school bus system, in the 1940s. There were two high schools in Reno in 1960. Finally, we wish Manogue's leadership well in completing their new campus. *[They did it!]*

• • •

Still on the topic of schools, Reno High School Alumni Club honcho Joe Granata tells of a bit of school apparatus that has been around longer that it might appear. There's a strong probability that the flagpole at Wooster High, which spoiled Reno High's place as the only *public!* High school in Reno when it opened in 1961, was the same pole that was originally installed in the front courtyard of the Reno High School on West Fifth and West Streets in 1923. (I almost wrote "Reno's original high school," which it wasn't.) Take a look at the flagpole next time you're traveling down East Plumb Lane past Wooster – that baby's been around for a long time.

Now, I'll solicit some reader help, maybe from Dale Sanderson, Washoe County School District's great facilities manager: I think, but have never been able to prove, that the scoreboard that originally clocked basketball games in the old Reno High (later serving as Central Junior High) gymnasium, was later relocated to Vaughn Middle School on Vassar Street near Kietzke. It's a classic scoreboard/timer with a revolving hand, not the contemporary 00:00 electric numerals – the words I'm groping for might be analog and digital. Last I saw it it was hanging unused in the Vaughn gym, alongside a modern digital scoreboard. It might be nice – if it is indeed the old West Street Reno High gym clock – to relocate it to the Reno High Alum Center on Booth Street someday, or at the least be aware of its heritage and not trash it as pre-WWII junk.

[Some responses came in, but no definitive word thus far.]

Often response to a column flummoxes me...

The El Reno Apartments

[One dark night three hours from the column's deadline, and with a trove of conflicting information for two columns in progress, the words of two old friends hearkened back: "Why don't you write about the little metal houses that started on South Virginia Street and were later moved all over town?"

The two friends are Carolyn Darney and Marilyn (Burkham) Bell – Ma Bell, my kindergarten classmate. I thank them for this tip, as the column I wrote that night, basically from my own recollection that I anticipated would be no more than a ho-hum column at best, evolved into one of the most popular topics of the column over a four-year period and still going.

You can read the maturation of information about the units as you read through the text. We've identified 14 now at production time. The addresses of existing homes and disposition of two others are included at the end of the chapter.]

Those little steel homes

So – you want to escape the hustle and bustle of downtown but stay close to shopping, to live where the air is fresh, the neighbors some distance away, shady trees, a garage, yard maintenance and walking distance to a new lake and park? Lakeridge Shores? Or Alum Creek? The Villas? The Cottages? Tavo Valera, in Sparks maybe? Expand your horizons: How about near the 1200 block of South Virginia Street by the Antique Mall and Statewide Lighting, your groceries from the AM/PM at Arroyo Street, and a fine meal at Landrum's. Or whatever they call it now.

Did I mention that this is the mid-1930s? The block where the El Reno Apartments were located at Arroyo and two-lane South Virginia Street is near the south edge of town, 'most anything south of there pretty rural. The Old Orchard Trailer Park and grocery was down there, Plumb Lane ended five blocks to the west and didn't cross Virginia Street, most homes to the south of that were summer homes, out by the Moana plunge. On the plus side, there was a country club by the new golf course now that they got rid of those damn noisy mail planes that flew out of Blanch Field on Urban Road. And there was a brand new lake being built, Virginia Lake they'd call it when it filled in 1940. You could walk from the El Reno Apartments on Arroyo and South Virginia to Virginia Lake. Pretty neat.

They were the hot place to live from the mid-1930s until well after World War II. A former El Reno resident I spoke with recalled that they had pleasant, private little yards and were very quiet, and a building with a few of those new-fangled automatic washing machines – no Bendixes with rollers here. The developer/landlord, whose name was Roland Giroux, also known as Joe, was handy, cordial and friendly (his wife Nora and son Louis would die years later in a small plane in a collision with a military plane somewhere by Independence Lake.) My own mother recalls returning to Reno after World War II and learning of the El Renos – the cachet attributed to residing there as comparable to living in the highest-end townhouse of today.

The El Reno's, we'll call them for short, were unique: They were prefabricated of metal. Cute little units, very stylish with board-and-batten metal sides and well-proportioned at 900 square feet. Reno steelman Fred Schwamb's father Martin owned Martin Iron Works, and Fred thinks they came by rail from Los Angeles, told me to check the 'web for U.S. Steel's site, because they might have built them. *[researched to no avail]* The other guru of steel in Reno, Andrea Pelter, recalled that her father John Ginocchio (Reno Iron Works) supplied some of the pinnings to hold them down, and Andy recalls his comment that they had some good alloy in them, more than just sheet metal, maybe some titanium.

Facts come hard about the El Renos; three that stump me are when they were built, which seems to be about 1935. And, how many there were, which seems to be somewhere between 11 and 14. Romolo Bevilacqua, whose house-moving business relocated them, recalls two semi-circular crescents of six homes each facing each other (the garages, later moved out on Del Monte Lane and now long gone, were on the west side of the property along Tonopah Street, accessed from the apartments.) The tenant list in 1939 shows 13 residents, but two with the same surname, a 1946 list lists ten. Go figure.

Finally, when did they close? They fell off any radar I can find between 1949 to 1951, which is not conclusive – soon I'll research when Sewell's opened on the El Reno site, which should be a little easier (Buster Sewell, you out there???!) *[Sewell's opened in 1955 per a Sanborn map.]*

I'm not done with this yet, but space is limited this Saturday morning. I do want to thank Andy Pelter, Carolyn Darney, Fred Schwamb, Romolo Bevilacqua, the Recorder's office, the phone company, and the library, but I'm still going.

Now – take a ride in southwest Reno.By Virginia Lake, at 236 Bonnie Briar, a classic little El Reno. Across from the 7-11 on Mount Rose, appropriately 711 Mount Rose Street. Clean, needs weeding. 1425 Plumas. Two at 1461 Lander, on one lot. Note, some porches are to the left, others to the right *[the porches were always on the Virginia Street/east sides whether the units faced north or south.]* 1409 Tonopah, just across from the original site, connected to another unit at 100 West Pueblo (my real estate buddies Skip Hansen and Ron Allen work in those.)A professional office at 115 Ridge Street. Up now to the University, on the southeast corner of College Drive and North Sierra Streets; an El Reno was set on top of another structure to form what was once an elegant private two-story home with a great view. Sierra has been widened and the trees now obscure the view, but the little home is still visible among the add-ons and vegetation.

There's more – where'd they go? Two reported at Sharon at Skyline (vicinity), joined together. Find 'em, I can't (yet). *[never did]* I think I have found it, but feel a little sheepish about roaming around someone's house with a magnet. One supposedly on East Liberty Street by City Hall. Another by the University, near Center. *[no]* Where? (Some are pretty well disguised by time...!)

• • •

From a later column:

A fortnight ago we credited reader Debbie Hinman with finding another relocated metal El Reno Apartment – at 326 West 11th Street. This prompted some calls; veteran Homefinders wondering how our quest for the homes, believed to number 16 originally, was going. Newer readers simply wondered what the hell we were talking about, steel houses indeed? I'll not rewrite here what took three columns to explore, but if you're really excited about them, contact me and I'll get an old column to you. The columns received national interest on my website; owners of these little steel homes, made in the 1930s by an outfit that made porcelain-clad service stations and diners, are faithful to them. Example: the owner of the home at 326 West 11th spent considerable time and money to restore the bearings on his home's trademark turbine attic ventilator.We'll update the original El Reno story someday, or you can read more about them in the column collection I'm trying to get under your Christmas trees. *[OK, so it took three more years.]* In the meantime, here are the El Renos we've found so far:

Out by Virginia Lake, find 400 Country Club Drive and 310 Bonnie Briar with an El Reno steel garage behind it (each unit had its own steel garage, with a turbine on their roofs also.) Then go to 711 Mt. Rose Street, two around the corner at 1401 and 1403 Lander Street, and another close by at 1425 Plumas Street. Then two across Tonopah Street from the original El

Reno Apartment location on South Virginia Street, both converted into offices at 1409 Tonopah Street and 100 Pueblo (I think that the building at 121 Pueblo – a different configuration – was the laundry area/office for the apartments. Check out the roof vents.) *[Never confirmed that.]* Closer to downtown, a law office at 115 Ridge Street. Proving that they could be moved across the bridges, we know of the one at College Drive and North Sierra Street, hard to see but it's there, and the one on West 11th. By Washoe Golf Course, 545 Skyline Drive, found by sharp-eyed Annette Mortimer. I've always thought there was another El Reno about six lots west of that and have asked a few neighbors, to no avail. Some think it was demolished…

In closing the El Reno thought, I'll include that a faithful but anonymous reader recently sent me a newspaper account of a dozen little all-steel homes currently being removed from the Marine base at Quantico, Virginia, and being sold to collectors.

The saga continues...

A piece ran a couple weeks ago, detailing the little prefabricated 900 square-foot all-metal homes – a dozen of them, we speculated; maybe 15 – that were put up before World War II on the 1200 block on South Virginia where Statewide Lighting now sits. They were moved off the site after the war, to all over town, and we gave the present locations of nine of them. In a first, I put some pictures on my website, with some additional narrative. *[I've since discontinued the website.]*

Information came via phone, mail and e-mail, from all over the country; Reno, of course, the southern states, a bunch from the midwest. Our sleepy little story probably got more feedback than I've ever received from any one topic, disregarding my account of the tunnel that led from the Hancock Mansion on Lakeside Drive to the island on Virginia Lake, dug before the lake filled in 1940 (a colossal fib but an urban legend that I'm afraid stuck.)

Curiously, our Reno version of the all-steel homes may not the same as the ones I received the mail on, which were known as "Lustron" homes, popularized by a company that made all-steel service stations and diners in the years following WWII. They were close in size, similar in appearance, but did not get into the marketplace until 1946 – our Reno units were in place during the 1930s, and the many websites about the Lustrons make no mention of post-war production. But there must be a link: The Lustrons were metal sheathed in porcelain, and two readers (not having permission I won't use their names) reminded me that the El Renos were also called the

"El Porcelains," a detail I had forgotten. The Lustron website is fascinating, accounts of many, many homeowners writing in about their homes in present-day settings, their dilemma in keeping the home's combination dish-clothes washer-sink working (yes, after the war, that was tried, and some still work.) They have an owner's club, like '57 Chevys with two bedrooms and a bath-and-a-half, and they e-mail each other telling where to find the serial numbers of a Model 3 home. They're all over the nation, many concentrated around Ohio and the midwest, where they were built in an old Navy plant. One of the names frequently mentioned as a principal in the company was Carl Strandlund, the father of the modern Stran-Steel industrial buildings that we see all over the valley. Another principal was named Tucker, ostensibly from the Tucker auto family. (The Lustron website is still on the Web at production time.)

There has been quite a bit of interest nationally in our Reno units, even although they are not Lustrons. The fact that we had twelve (fourteen, sixteen, fifteen and a laundry building, fill in the blank) interests other Lustron owners, many of whom feel strongly enough about the homes as a lifestyle that some have been included in various states' registers of historical structures, with some national mention. My pictures of nine on one website blew a few web watchers' minds.

I'll let a reader write the rest of this Saturday morning's column; her name is Jill and she lives in the Bay Area. (The [bracketed] additions are mine.)

"...I grew up in Reno. From 1946 to 1948 I lived with my parents in the El Reno Apartments. We moved in in the spring of 1946. I think there were 14 or 15 units; I know for sure there were four units on each of the side streets [Pueblo and Arroyo] and a crescent of maybe six units facing South Virginia.

"The units were way ahead of their time. They had a bath-and-a-half and all-metal kitchen cabinets and a great floor plan. Our family loved living there.

"Shortly after the Second World War ended, Louis Giroux [the apartment's owner] wanted to raise the rents. As I remember it, all of the residents agreed, but the rent control board refused. This made him so angry that he chose to sell the units off and be finished with it.

"My parents [Homer Forrester, an IRS agent, and Virginia Forrester, manager of the Riverside Hotel and later the Mapes Hotel] planned to purchase one of the units and move it to other land. For some reason they chose the first unit facing South Virginia, so we moved into that unit with the plan of purchasing it. The person that moved out was Bill Harrah's first wife

[Thelma], and I think that he had also lived there at one time.

"Before the planned purchase was completed [the Forresters' plans changed] and we moved to northwest Reno on Melba Drive in 1948, and the El Reno units started to be moved out shortly after that.

"I think that the Sewell's [grocery] store was already in place when lived at the El Reno. I remember shopping there the whole time we lived there. The land that El Reno stood on was vacant for a long time... *[Washoe Market existed; Sewell's came later.]*

"Hope this information helps."

It does, Jill...immensely. It's people like you who take the time to type a letter and draw a map that enable us to keep track of how our valley came to be. *[The map Jill sent of the apartment site was very close to the Reno Sanborn fire map diagram, sheet 41.]*

• • •

[A few El Reno notes from within other columns:]

Speaking of El Reno units, my childhood buddy and Sigma Nu frat brother Dr. Lynn Gerow the Younger told me while we were blocking an aisle at Albertson's that his father, Dr. Gerow the Elder paid $800 for the El Reno unit that Bevilaqua Movers then moved to 115 Ridge Street to use as his medical office. (Lynn Jr. later used it also for his practice.) Bill Harrah and his first wife, Thelma, had occupied the unit.

• • •

Hide the children: A naked El Reno metal apartment unit on the loose, last seen on Plumas just north of Mt. Rose Street. The thing was skinned so that stucco could be and at this writing one can see the metal studs, surprisingly none of which are close to any uniform interval – and the diagonal metal sheer bracing. What's interesting is the number of Homefinders who drive by it and the resulting contacts I received regarding this public skinning, all about a bit of Reno nostalgia that I first wrote of four years ago almost as an aside. Our Dynamic Diva Pat Klos and the Historic Reno Preservation Society are actually going to anoint these little tin boxes, influenced by architect Paul Revere Williams (architect of the Christian Science Church on the river), by giving a tour of the 13 we've found so far, sometime in September. We'll try to get you inside one – they're nifty. Stay tuned.

I have never confirmed that Williams designed them; I speculated in the original El Reno column that ran a few years ago that they were a Williams design only because while browsing through a coffee-table edition of Hollywood mansions a swimming pool lanai, pictured behind a Beverly

Hills, Williams-designed mansion, jumped off the page at me, as being identical to an El Reno unit. Williams' hallmark bay window and the lacy ironwork on the little poolhouse mimicked those of the mansion (the mansion owners' name was Paley, if you locate the book.)

In other Saturday morning news, Debbie Hinman – or "eagle eye," as her Nevada Bell co-workers call her – has found another relocated El Reno Apartment for us, this her second discovery, the earlier in the 300 block of West Eleventh Street. It's embarrassing for me to divulge the location of this newest one because I have driven past it 8,000 times: It's at 1698 Plumas Street, east side, just north of Glenmanor between Mt. Rose Street and West Plumb Lane. It's been set onto a high concrete foundation to create a half-basement, there's an addition on the rear (east) side, and it's pretty well covered by foliage, but it's an El Reno, for sure. And an original El Reno steel garage sits to the north of it. This puts us at 14 located out of a probably 15 original units. Thanks, eagle eye.

And no El Renos went to Sparks – that the wisdom of Romolo Bevelacqua, Reno's premier house mover, who in his seven-decade career has moved hundreds of homes in the local area. I congratulate Rom on being recognized by the City of Reno's Historical Resources Commission as the 2002 Recipient of the Distinguished Service Award for his insight into a bygone Reno. He has always been a prime contributor and resource to this *Homefinder* column, with his recollection of relocations, like the El Reno units and our Levy Mansion story of last summer – (his firm turned the mansion to face California Avenue.) *[Romolo passed away late in 2002.]*

There's more El Reno buildings out there somewhere, folks – let's go find them.

• • •

The following are the addresses or locations of the 14 units we've located:

545 Skyline Drive (1)
400 Country Club Drive
711 Mount Rose Street (2)
1425 Plumas Street (3)
1698 Plumas Street
236 Bonnie Briar (4)
Two at 1461 Lander, on one lot
1409 Tonopah Street
100 West Pueblo Street
115 Ridge Street (5)

College Drive and North Sierra Streets
326 West 11th Street
Byars Const. (6)

(1) demolished, site rebuilt

(2) Paul Revere William would be proud; compare the colors to Raphael Herman home in Rancho San Rafael

(3) stuccoed, per text

(4) owned for many years by Bevilacqua family who moved the units from South Virginia Street, repairs being effected at production time

(5) Medical office for many years; was originally the apartment of Bill and Thelma Harrah

(6) This unit was called to my attention by Terry Markwell, an original principal in Byars Construction, as was Roland Giroux, who developed the El Reno Apartments on their original South Virginia Street location. We believe now that this unit was originally built on Giroux' property on Del Monte Lane, not the El Reno site, and when Byars Construction was formed in the early 1960s the unit was moved to this location. It has been demolished, but its slab and corresponding anchors remain visible in the concrete slab.

Endowed by a yeast magnate, and designed by a mayonnaise scion...

INSULTING TO THE MAX

On a recent morn, talk at the Seven-Ayem Senior Moment Krispy Kreme BS and Coffee Klatch turned to the Fleischmann Atmospherium-Planetarium and the man who endowed it, and the voices around the table agreed, "He had polo ponies, yachts, an airplane before Lindbergh, played pro baseball for the Cincinnati Red Stockings in 1900, damn near got himself killed as a balloon pilot in the first World War and eventually plowed most of his fortune back into northern Nevada." Another voice, from a recent transplant from the Bay Area: "Yeah, and I used to swim at the plunge he donated to San Francisco, the biggest pool ever built." Whoops – I felt a column coming on.

That legendary saltwater pool where the lifeguards used rowboats, and for that matter the zoo nearby it in San Francisco, were endowed by Herbert *Fleischhacker*. Our Nevada philanthropist was Max C. *Fleischmann*. Similar names, both rich, but different guys. (The Fleischhacker Pool closed in 1971, the once-Fleischhacker Zoo is now the San Francisco Zoo.)

While much ado has been made recently of razing the Fleischmann Planetarium on the University of Nevada campus, little seems to be known by many locals of the man who endowed the building. Max C. Fleischmann was born in 1877, to parents who had already made their fortune in yeast production, and in yeast's natural extension – gin. He was once president of Nabisco, eventually inherited the family yeast business, and sold it to the J. P. Morgan interests in 1920. What follows is the tale of a man who started with 20 million dollars and ran it into a fortune.

He moved to Nevada with his wife Sarah in 1930 – tax advantages, natch – bought ranches near Yerington and Carson City, and built a grand home in Glenbrook on Tahoe's east shore. He lost little time in starting to enhance northern Nevada for the next half-century. Early on came the conversion of the Carson City Mint to the Nevada State Museum, the purchase-then-donation of the sprawling 264-acre Ladino Dairy Ranch to the University, help to the Boy Scouts, Ducks Unlimited, libraries, the hospitals and public schools. After WWII came the endowment of the Max C. Fleischmann College of Agriculture and the Sarah H. Fleischmann College of Home Economics. Regarding accolades, according to a vintage Rollan Melton column Fleischmann once said, "Rich men don't deserve a damn bit of praise for helping others, only criticism if they fail to help out!" Right on.

In 1952 he endowed the Fleischmann Foundation, to the tune of 63 million dollars, give or take a mil and rising with accruing interest like the yeast that created it, charged with continuing grants for 20 years past the time of his demise. Pillars of Forbes-500 companies served as trustees – Julius Bergen, the chairman, plus local members Judge Clark Guild Sr., attorneys Lester Summerfield and Fran Breen, stockbroker Tom Little and author/RHS teacher Sessions (Buck) Wheeler. Veteran Homefinders will recognize this as an all-star cast. (Wheeler's biography of Fleischmann *Gentleman in the Outdoors* was published by the University Press in 1985.)

Max died by his own hand on October 16, 1951 in Santa Barbara, where he maintained another ranch, very shortly after being diagnosed with cancer. The foundation continued his philanthropic work; two major benefactors in the years shortly following his death were the new National Judicial College and the Desert Research Institute, both University adjuncts. Sarah passed away in July of 1960. The corpus of the trust grew almost as fast as it could be distributed, requiring an extension beyond its decreed sundown date. Its final reconciliation was made in 1978 as required in the public record, revealing 192 million dollars in grants, with 47 per cent of them staying in northern Nevada, the University the biggest benefactor. Its smallest single grant was 250 dollars; the largest, 19.3 million dollars, to the University. Remember those numbers for a couple of paragraphs.

The Fleischmann Atmospherium-Planetarium was named not for himself and Sarah, but for his parents, at his request. It was designed by local architect Ray Hellman, who in the same time frame had designed the graceful Sierra Pacific Power headquarters at Moana Lane and South Virginia Street. The hyperbolic paraboloid Planetarium was built by McKenzie Construction, and dedicated on November 14, 1963. Its primary sky projector (the second, kicked-up one still in service) was a donation from the Gannett Foundation, an independent adjunct of Gannett Corp. – owner of the RGJ and recognized for its benevolence and great real estate columnists.

The specter of demolition of the facility recently met with commendable community outrage. Curiously, the building was not universally welcomed in 1962, viewed by some as yet another space age freaky-looking building in an era when Sputnik, solid rockets, Astroturf, weightless flying monkeys, splashdowns, Tang, "A-OK"-techspeak and garish auto tail fins bespoke America's moonstruck obsession. With time, its once-lonely location on a barren bluff above the bustling campus has grown verdant and pastoral, and the "space-place," as it was known – at that time a pejorative nickname – has matured into the University's signature landmark.

The University has magnanimously given the Planetarium structure a new lease on life, some say – others speculate that somebody on the Hill got their head out of their asteroid, researched some documentation, and realized that trustees from national corporate boardrooms – many of them attorneys and damn good ones at that – weren't quite so dumb as to commit the Fleischmann Foundation's assets to a building bearing Fleischmann's name that might be demolished for a parking lot 40 years hence. If I'm permitted an opinion, those who dreamed up putting a parking lot on the site should take another look at the Aggie and Home Ec buildings, the Judicial College, DRI on Red Mountain, the dairy farm on East McCarran, do the math on 47 per cent of the Fleischmann Foundation's 192 million bucks distributed within our state and most of that on campus, and then become genuinely ashamed of themselves.

The rest of you have a good week, go buy a house, and God bless America and the Columbia Seven

I thank docent Richard Critz at the Nevada Historical Society for his research help.

• • •

The e-mailman always knocks twice

Most works of art have a theme that holds them together; this column is not that disciplined so it's easy to just prance barefoot through the e-mail folder and some Post-It notes.

Here's one: Our Realtor Sharon Quinn reminds me that it was John and Dorothy Benson, longtime owners of the Arlington Nursery – Reno's first garden shop – who installed and endowed the maintenance of the Benson Gardens adjoining the Fleischmann Planetarium. The Bensons were wonderful people; John my shirttail relative, a burly 1940s Wolf Pack football player with a heart of gold, and Dorothy, who always had – for young Nevada coeds far from home – a bed, a shoulder or a job at the nursery where West Plumb Lane dead-ended into Arlington Avenue. (Until 1955). *[Read of the Arlington Nursery, elsewhere in this book]*

Where did the rest of the Fleischmann Foundation's grants go? (Forty-seven per cent of 130-some million dollars stayed in northern Nevada.) A great deal went to education throughout Southern California and specifically Santa Barbara, and some major endowments to schools in the Rockies heavy into mining and agriculture, including a wing on the University of Colorado's planetarium. We'd like to think he just frittered a few mil away (his airplane mentioned in the column was a Lockheed Vega, similar to

Amelia Earhart's Electra.) One reader, a Daughter of Italy, didn't recall the Ladino family in Reno – (I wrote that Fleischmann bought the Ladino Dairy Farm to donate to the University.) Following more research than I care to put into this column for mere trivia, I determined that Ladino is a strain of clover, not a family surname. We know that Fleischmann also manufactured gin, but no, Max was not the first to utter the words "Keep your cotton-pickin' hands off my gin"; that honor goes to Eli Whitney. I cited Ray Hellman as the architect of the Planetarium, and a reader's note reinforced a recollection I've harbored for many years but have been unable to prove: That Ray was brought to Reno by Fleischmann to act as the architect for Fleischmann buildings, and further, that their relationship actually went back to Hellman's family ties. (*Jeopardy!* fans know Best Foods Mayonnaise is known as "Hellman's" west of the Rockies.) This reader suggested a link between producing yeast and mayonnaise. Now if we could work the gin angle into all this somehow, we'd have a real scoop, shaken, not stirred. *[Keep reading.]*

That Hellman/Fleischmann connection and some other Fleischmann and Planetarium info is in the works, but I've left it in *Homefinder* researcher Carmine Ghia's hands, so we can get it right.

• • •

[And RGJ real estate editor Tom McGuire reminded me that in an emergency one could substitute mayonnaise for egg-whites in a gin fizz, proving that there is a connection. And providing yet another reason not to party with your editor.]

Go East and West, Young Readers...

Walkin' the Side Streets, ca. 1955

"When you walked downtown in the columns, you missed Hatton's." Or, "How 'come you didn't mention the Grand Café?" Such were the messages before Christmas. I wrote them down, one-by-one, to address them, and then the pattern formed: The shops I "missed" on our walks downtown were on the side streets – First, Second and Commercial Row or Plaza Streets, not Virginia or Sierra, where we walked.

So, this fine first Saturday of the new year, we'll turn back the clock to 1950, the era when we took our Saturday walks in the past, lock our bikes by Grey Reids at West First and Sierra, and criss-cross the side streets. Walking west along West First, an area we should mention that would get hammered by a major flood this coming winter, we walk past the Granada Theater and Town & Country Furs, then Brundidge's Art Store. Looking across West First, the Vanity ladies store, the Town House Bar; actually we mentioned that before, with Al Vario behind the plank. Morgan Smith was a popular jeweler, next to Mitzi's Flowers, then east to the Virginia Street corner Woolworth's five-and-dime. In an older building than the long-closed present structure. Great fountain in there, on the squeaky floors. A surprising number of people who sent in recollections mentioned the squeaky floors in all the downtown stores we visited. Another recollection that came up in several e-mails and calls was of the sidewalk freight elevators that would rise out of buildings' basements to street level – many buildings back then were built out under the sidewalk. OK, that popped up one memory of mine: the thick round glass cylinders set into the concrete sidewalks to enable daylight to pass into basements.

Crossing South Virginia, we walk past the Mapes, then by a hole in the ground where the beautiful Delongchamps-designed YMCA stood until a boiler in the basement blew three years ago and it burned to the ground. *[Neill West and Les Conklin Jr. reminded me it was still there in 1950 – try 1952 as the right year.]* The Y was a close match, design-wise, to the Nevada State Journal newspaper building just around the corner and north on Center Street.At the East First and Center Street corner stood the mighty Majestic theatre on the southwest, across East First from the old city hall. On a slow day both Reno police cars and Patrolman Karl Broberg's Harley would be parked there, Karl having a doughnut at the Log Cabin Café next to City Hall. Washoe Title was in that block on the north side. A reader asked about the "Button Shop" – I found that near there, but in a pre-war era (remember this is the early 1950s!).

Northward up Center Street we go to West Second Street and the brand-new Cal Neva, and turn to the right. Looking across the street, from the Center Street corner working west, were a Hales Drug, Jacobs Men's Store – top-of-the-line only – and the Grand Café, a downtown Reno institution where much of the heavy-hitting business and government decisions of the day were made. West of the Grand, Semenza's grocery, then the Smart Shop, spelled Shoppe in one resource, your choice, then First National Bank's "main," read *power* branch. On the south side of East Second Street walking west from Center was Leon & Eddies popular bar, then Modern Photo, where the late owner Jerry Cobb catalogued a huge fount of local historical photos. Cobb's son, Neal, has a superb job of getting the photos out to be seen and enjoyed by all, sharing with the them with the Nevada Historical Society, and adding to the collection. And, wrapping up that block of East Second Street, the Orchid Florist, between Modern Photo and Skeel's drug store on the corner at North Virginia Street.

We'll stop here for this week, because writing of Neal Cobb and Modern Photo triggered a great old Reno story that I'll use space to recount herein. Meet me at West Second and Virginia next Saturday and we'll Go West, Young Homefinders.

The story goes, that in the 1950s local artist Eddie Starr publicly took on Neal Cobb's mother Mildred, regarded by most as an excellent painter. He did so because she painted from photos, which Starr asserted lacked originality because they looked like photographs. In a pique, Mildred set up an easel in Modern Photo's display window on Second Street. On the canvas, in public view, over a span of many weeks she painted an intricate representation of a human skeleton, from memory. Time marched on, and when the skeleton was completed, she fleshed in the bones with muscles and tendons, veins and arteries – from memory *a la* Leonardo Da Vinci. A growing crowd gathered each day. Next came skin, covering the muscles, until a drop-dead gorgeous life-size nude eventually graced the window at 28 East Second Street. All from memory.

Neal recalls that Mildred only grudgingly omitted the middle finger of one of the Modern Photo lady's hands, daintily extending from the proximal interphalangeal joint as a public greeting to her detractor Eddie Starr.

Where's the portrait now?? It's around, maybe coming to my website. Stay tuned.

• • •

The Side Streets, continued

Last week we stopped at the corner of West Second and North Virginia

Streets on a brisk 1950s day, our stamina stretched thin from our walk criss-crossing Reno's east/west streets downtown. 'Cept for the First National Bank on the northeast corner – now a Planet Hollywood *[that died on the vine]* – the other three corners were drug stores – Walgreen to the northwest, Skeel's to the southeast, and Ramos' on the southwest – Ramos' would move in the next two years to California Avenue by Hill Street.

Our walk takes us now west to North Sierra Street, to a one-block section of 1950s Reno that was metaphoric for every little town in America. If one were filming *Peggy Sue Got Married in Reno*, this is the block they'd pick. Walking west on the south side of West Second, after Ramos', a Security Bank of Nevada branch, soon to be relocated to the river on West First Street. Wilson Jewelers. The Merry-Go-Round bar. On the alley, Pay-Less Drugs, provoking a heartwarming story of a local youth's shoplifting excursion (not mine!) and 1950s-style justice; we'll spin the tale in the next few columns. *[see the* Real Neal *chapter]* Still on the south side of Second, a Mode O'Day ladies store, followed by a Reeves and Leed's store to the corner of Sierra.

Crossing West Second to the north, it wouldn't be a *Homefinder* walk downtown if we didn't stop at Les Lerude's Wigwam Café on the northeast corner for some hot apple pie and the special sauce, which in the ensuing 50 years everybody in the world claims to have the secret recipe for (kind of like John Ascauga's French dressing recipe.) Don't believe it; part of Les' recipe for hot apple pie was the ambiance of the little joint, which will never be replicated. How we took the Wigwam for granted, before it closed forever! Next door to the east, the Crest Theater, a venue with the steepest aisles we ever saw, and loges! What a wonderful concept – loge seating! E-mail me if you need an explanation. The Majestic had them; the Tower and Granada never did. *[I was reminded that the Granada had loges before it burned in 1953.]* We should point out that the Crest is still remembered by many readers as the "Nevada" theater in the early 1940s – prior to that it was the Wigwam theater. But never the Teepee.

A great candy store was next to the Crest – fresh candy was a treat in 1950, as no one could get it over Donner Summit intact. It would be years later before See's left the Bay Area, and Blum's, another San Francisco favorite, went out of business before ever coming to Reno. Eddy Floral came next on West Second past the candy store: Reno icon George Hamilton relocated his optician shop from across the street (it later became Lear-Higdon opticians, see the Wells Avenue Walk.) Folk & Campbell Shoes, where every kid in town got his Buster Browns – except for the guys that went to the Sparks Bootery – we'll walk B Street soon and stop in the Bootery. (Does anyone remember the X-ray fluoroscopes we could stand on to look through the shoes to see where our toes were?? How'd you like to see what the FDA, AEC and the Cancer Society would say about those babies 50 years later!) Hatton's, a fine old Reno store and one of the power-dressing shops for men's clothes followed Hamilton's to the east. *[And not a few readers wrote to remind of Buster Brown's sponsorship of* No School Today *with Big John and Sparky on KOH radio on Saturday mornings – a must-listen show before the movies at the Tower Theater. Homefinder question: Who led the band?]**

• • •

A while back I alluded to the Harolds Club pigeonhole parking garage. We'll park our bikes on Plaza Street now, just north of the tracks, and study this bit of engineering which we offered as proof-positive that grown-ups often weren't much brighter that us kids. The structure was 16 cars wide on Plaza Street. The unwitting driver would leave his car, and a forklift, for want of a better term, that rolled east and west on tracks, would stop even with the car, hopefully, and slide two rails under the car. Cars, you're reminded, at that time had frames and differentials and predictable stuff under them for the rails to engage, hopefully. The rails would lift the car slightly, then retract the car into the garage structure, then roll left or right to align with a vacant pigeonhole, hopefully, lift the car up to one of the seven levels, then extend the rails into the pigeonhole, and set the car down. With any luck at all the front of the car wouldn't get smashed into the steel wall of the garage – the dings on the steel wall visible from south of the tracks foretold frequent collisions between blue license plates and the wall. The lift would then travel to another parked car on the ground, or go to retract an already-parked car to set it onto the ground. The thing had a nasty habit of hanging up a car being retrieved, the car becoming stuck in the pigeonhole. Or on a couple of occasions, just flat dropping the car onto the ground. Need I point out that while those messes were being sorted out, if you had a car in the garage you might as well go have a cold one at the Turf Club or the Stag Inn on Commercial Row for an hour or so.

For a generation of kids deprived of PlayStation and XboX, the Harolds Club pigeonhole parking supplied a wealth of free entertainment following the Tower Theater Saturday movie matinee. And we learned some cool words.

• • •

**[re No School Today: Remember Gilhooley Mahoney and the Leprechaun Marching Band?]*

Do not touch your dial; the difficulties are with the columnist...

[This column appeared September 21, 2003]

The Team You Knew and Trusted

Ahh, it's five o'clock on any weekday, time to squeeze the remote and bring the tube to life, Tad and Terri in living color, weird creepers running under their elaborate newsdesk, a picture-in-picture image of a news-making scene above their heads, a white contrail trailing under weatherman Dick Stoddard's pinkie as he explains what some phenomena somewhere is doing for the first of four times he'll explain it in the next hour, and replays of sports from around the nation, all in stereo sound, slo-mo, and right here in your media room.

No, that's not how it happened, 50 years ago this week, as the Donald W. Reynolds Media Company (Donrey) put Reno's first TV station – "KZTV," it was called, onto the air on channel 8 of the 13 possible notches on the early sets. And you didn't sit on your Barcalounger with a remote – you walked over to your Philco television set, turned on the black ceramic panther lamp on the top of your set (for we were told we'd go blind or sterile or something if we didn't have a light on in the room), then turned the set on. In a moment or five it would warm up, and the sound might be OK, but the flipping image forced another walk to the set to adjust the vertical hold.

Instead of Tad and Terri and Dick, we'd see KZTV news anchor Frank Lawrence in black-and-white, with very little, if any, on-the-scene news coverage (on the early staff was Jimmy Nichols, the 16-millimeter movie cinematographer.) The weather came, maybe, from June Osborne – no fancy props and maps in 1953, and if a change wasn't in the wings, maybe no weathercast at all (a novel idea someone might resurrect.) Sports updates came from Leila Brown (yup, Gene's wife). *[Leila passed away in early 2004]* After the news – maybe the 17th re-showing of Liberace, Groucho Marx, Hopalong Cassidy (sponsored by Sewell's Market), Dragnet, or maybe a infomercial for Vegomatics. "Please Stand By," incessantly. Maybe a movie – all this stuff was on 16-millimeter film, as were any commercials filmed locally. Some of the daytime shows, all live, were Uncle Happy, Carol Guild's "Clean Plate Club" (possibly what whetted Dunbar's early appetite for TV), Betty Stoddard's "Be My Guest," Chet and Link's "Sportsman's Corner," Vicky & Jim Johnson's afternoon local guest show and Mighty Mite Wrestling. And a sign-off, the flag waving and the National Anthem playing.

The station's facilities were at 770 East Fifth Street, which I visited as an electronics geek before the term was originated. Station manager Harry Huey had been transferred here from Donrey's head shed in Arkansas and was anxious to show off the facility; ex-Navy SNJ jock Dick Colon was the general sales manager – key advertisers were Sierra Pacific Power, First National Bank, Savier's (who sold TV sets, natch), Osborne & Dermody (ditto), and the Nevada Club. The studio originally had one camera, black-and-white, need I remind you, and a dozen sets for the different shows, all made be Durward Yasmer, a great guy with a great voice that you've heard for 50 years on commercial voice-overs, and still volunteering as a computer teacher with the school district.

Heat was the byword inside the station as I recall it; heat from the myriad Kleig lights necessary to make the lone low-tech Westinghouse camera work, heat from the vacuum-tube electronics at the other end of the thick cable connecting the camera to the control booth, the booth to the amplifiers, and the amplifier to the four-story antenna on the station's premises (their Slide Mountain "big-stick" and countless repeaters would come in later years.) And heat, it was, that ended the life of the building at 770 East Fifth Street, causing a spectacular fire on March 31st of 1977 that took the station off the air for a few days while it was relocated with rudimentary equipment.

Where, you ask, did the current call letters come from? KOLO radio, the brainchild of early radioman Hy Wells, was bought by Donrey a couple of years following KZTV's debut, and the television station renamed "KOLO-TV." The radio outlet was moved to the El Cortez Hotel in 1955, and some of the names associated with the two Donrey media outlets are legendary in our town – Fred Davis, later to spend three decades at the Nugget; Howie Doyle and Gene McKenna, who later operated one of Reno's major advertising agencies for many years, and Mark Curtis Sr., who did a popular daytime show "Mark Time."

The years were kind to KOLO-TV, and the station still puts immense good back into our community. One of my favorite memories of the early years were in the late 1960s and early 1970s – I was a part-time (night) cameraman, and the station, which had been broadcasting color only from network shows for several years, finally got color cameras and videotape recorders. I did a few "Be My Guest" shows, but the best comedy acts in town, albeit acts that never hit Harrah's or the Nugget's showrooms, came from two stars: The first was the Carson Five, five Carson City auto dealers who took the scenic route from the Capital City periodically and loosened up a bit for their stint in front of the cameras (KOLO had two by then), and we were lucky if we could get four complete usable commercials in two hours of taping.

Ditto, the late druggist Jim Henderson of the Big Keystone Owl Rexall Drug, who by chance befriended Dan Rowan and Dick Martin (of TV's Laugh-In) when they were performing at Harrah's. "We'll help you make a few commercials," one of them proclaimed at the 19th hole after a round. I can vouch that after four hours of taping we had five useable 30-second spots, none of which included a clue of what they were advertising, but to this day are still the funniest commercials that ever hit the local market and packed shoppers into the drug store. Rowan and Martin returned to Harrah's for a number of years, and always made a few more spots for Henderson. If someone located the tapes with the outtakes of Keystone Owl's or the Carson City Five's spots today, they'd be priceless entertainment. Yet every one still un-airable.

I have a feeling that the saga of KOLO's 50th anniversary is far from over, and look forward to some e-mails and calls with anecdotes and old-timers' names and stories. We'll probably revisit this in a couple of weeks.Until then we wish all the present Team That We Know and Trust, and the earlier team that brought them to where they are today, a Happy Anniversary and 50 more years of success.

Have a good week, film at eleven, and God bless America.

Send in the clowns

Last week's tale of KZTV/KOLO-TV's 50th anniversary resulted in some wonderful correspondence and recollections, which we'll weave into this space during the coming weeks. One such note came from Wilma Sheldon, and her words are impossible to improve upon so I'm just including it as written:

"In regards to the column about KZTV and KOLO-TV, you mentioned my late husband, Russ Sheldon, and 'Uncle Happy,' among others. Russ was the sportscaster on both the early and late sportscasts starting on Oct. 15, 1955 until April 15, 1960, for seven days a week. This included broadcasting the 1960 Winter Olympics, and numerous other sports interview shows over all those interesting years. Russ really enjoyed the sports shows as he was a natural athlete himself.

"Perhaps you did not realize it, but in those 'olden days' the person doing those shows got paid by how many commercials you had. In fact, you had to go out and sell the spots and service the account as well.

"In order to support our family of four children, Russ started 'Uncle Happy's Playhouse' on Saturdays on June 21, 1958 with our costumed children as helpers and then the weekday cartoon show 'Uncle Happy's Snootrac.' In order to change his personality for this, he had to change into the wig and other attire. This lasted until July 8, 1967. We started our 'Uncle Happy's Toy Shop' Oct. 1, 1960 *[in Keystone Square]* and retired (because of his ill health) June 15, 1985. He passed away Feb. 7, 1991."

Thanks, Wilma – Russ and Uncle Happy remain on as Reno legends. And while in Uncle Happy's Keystone Square area, I can report to have on the best authority how Jim Henderson of the Keystone Owl Rexall Drugs came to know Dan Rowan and Dick Martin, an element in our KOLO column last weekend. The three met initially all over chapped lips. Dick Martin had 'em. Had 'em bad, real bad, especially in the dry air of the high desert. And Martin simply could not find any Chapstick, which worked wonders for him, in Reno. Henderson became Martin's supplier. By the case. Shipped it to him wherever and whenever he needed more

Returning to KOLO-TV for our final episode for this edition, several readers noted that I had omitted "Frank Greco's Revue," a popular weekly live accordion concert that was on the air almost from KZTV's Day One. Sorry – I remember the revue vividly, as many old-timers remember the revue's Nilsine Nilsson, now Nilsine Hansen (the better half of my Realtor buddy Skip Hansen) as "the girl in the back row with the happy, dancing eyes." After 50 years it can be revealed that Nilsine went on to join a traveling topless accordion band and her bright dancing eyes were a direct result of getting acclimated to her new costume.

[Little here needs embellishment other than several readers who looked for a typo in Uncle Happy's "Snootrac." It's Yiddish, folks – read it backwards.]

It rolled across the Great Divide, to Vallejo and stopped in Idlewild...

The Little Engine That Could

In 1942 the movie *Iron Horse* opened in the little Colorado mining town of Trinidad, and movie ticket holders were offered a free ride on a miniature train that was operating behind the theater. That short ride was just the beginning of the train's journey that would eventually take it for thousands of miles, hauling probably a couple of hundred thousand passengers on a ride that's lasted sixty years and is still running this morning, right here in Idlewild Park. *[during the warm season...]*

The engine – a coal-burning, steam replica of a Pacific-class steam locomotive – was fashioned by a Trinidad ironworker to pull the four open passenger cars, each holding four adults or three dozen kids. The lash-up soon caught the eye of John and Joe Cihura, sons of Polish immigrants who followed the rails and coalmines from Pennsylvania to Colorado. They acquired the train equipment and relocated it to Walsenburg, Colorado, and set it up after the war as an attraction behind a little restaurant, selling rides at a dime a pop to the kids in the diner.

In 1949, they again moved it, this time to Vallejo, and in 1952 negotiated a contract with the City of Vallejo to operate the train – and a few kiddie cars, a merry-go-round and "airplane" rides – in Blue Rock Springs Park in Vallejo. Joe and John traveled to Virginia City in their pickup and bought some old ore cart rails that were being salvaged from the mines. The present railbed in Idlewild Park came down from the Comstock, via Vallejo. (For the train nuts, er, aficionados, like my favorite railroad expert/reader Richard C. Datin, the rail is set at live-steam gauge of 11-1/2 inches. And the loco is a 4-6-2 class; if you never saw it, it was about six feet long with a throaty brass bell, a real two-chime steam whistle, and towed a tender with coal, water and a seat for Joe. End of tech-talk.)

In 1961, the brothers moved to Reno and began negotiating for a site for their train and some rides, and zeroed in on a kiddie park in Idlewild Park. The Reno Arch Lions and the 20-30 Club shouldered the task of putting the park together, working with everyone's old buddy Duke Lindeman from the City of Reno, toward a grand opening in 1963. (Many old-timers remember the huge lion-head drinking fountain, which was eventually replaced because the smaller tykes were afraid to put their heads inside the lion's mouth for a gulp!)

• • •

Our town embraced the little park and the train for a decade, the pleasant scent of coal and steam wafting around the park near the California building and the real S.P. locomotives across the river blowing their whistles as they passed the park, and Joe, the only engineer the train ever had, returning a toot for the passengers in tow. Rusty Crook frequently brought the kids from his *This Is It Ranch* for a ride. Disabled citizens, young and old, were always welcomed as guests. Older children who rocked in their cars found themselves booted off the train in mid-ride. (Every now and then, Joe's daughter Carol recalls, a waif would show up without the price of a ride in his jeans. Joe would send him out into the park to find 10 scraps of paper or other junk and bring it back in return for a ticket to ride. John and Joe were the long-time *ex officio* custodians, guardians and champions of Idlewild Park.)

Change was coming. The US of A was coming up upon a Bicentennial celebration in 1976. In anticipation of all this gala, Joe and John began rebuilding the coal-black locomotive to replicate Southern Pacific's Daylight streamliner locomotive that the S.P. was repainting red, white and blue to tour the nation for the Bicentennial as the "Freedom Train." The miniature Pacific's boiler was shrouded and the cowcatcher was removed. The loco and cars were repainted. On June 7th of 1976 Joe appeared in a *Gazette* photo in the paper with the rebuilt engine, and on July 4th, 1976, the new line was inaugurated.

• • •

In 1980, Joe and John sold the operation, lock, stock and barrel, to Aldo Andrietta, and took their fifth-wheeler to Alaska for three months for a well-deserved vacation. Aldo ran the park very capably until about three years ago, *[1999]* when he sold it to a Sacramento-based amusement company that owns several other kiddie rides. The Cihura brothers kept the steam locomotive – it's still in John's garage. Aldo opted for another engine the brothers had built, this one a gasoline/propane powered replica of a 1957 General Motors passenger diesel (a steam powered loco was nifty, but firing it up and bringing it up to steam was a chore that only Joe enjoyed.)

Joe passed away in 1986, and on Arbor Day of 1987 a sequoia was planted near the train's right-of-way in his honor. The families' contribution to the children of all ages of our town was feted in a ceremony near the park's railroad station, led by then-Governor Dick Bryan and -Mayor Pete Sferrazza. Joe's wife Harriet was later memorialized with a Colorado Blue Spruce across the street by the California Building. Bronze plaques mark each tree.

The Lions Kiddie Park and the Cihura brothers' train is a long-standing asset of our town, and this would not be a bad morning to take a couple of kids, of any age, out to enjoy it. As I wrote above, I'd welcome more info about other service clubs that contributed to the Kiddie Park, for a future follow-up column. *[None came in; the clubs included did it all.]*

I am grateful to my old friend and retired State Farm Insurance executive Carol Brown – (Joe Cihura's daughter) – for her extensive input into the column, and, as always, the resources of the Nevada Historical Society and the RGJ archives.

Go ride a train today. 474 Safe Days at Ralston Foods. God bless America.

The mystic Orient and movers-and-shakers meet on the Truckee River...

THE BUNDOX

Word reached me last weekend that yet another Reno landmark will bite the dust – the once-intimate Bundox restaurant and the adjoining River House motel on Lake Street at the river will soon feel the wrecker's ball.

I was working on a column of the oldest, first, longest running whatever's, but found myself musing about the Bundox and the popular Reno couple that built it. The longest running column can wait for a week. What follows is one of my famous stay-with-me, we'll-get-to-a-point-eventually examples of how not to let your child write on an SAT exam. Hang on:

We'll turn back the clock to about 1910 when a photographer of national renown named Loomis*, who with his wife, the former Anna Frandsen, was working in Argentina for a number of American newspapers. Anna was the daughter of Andrew Frandsen, a pioneer Reno sheep man who had emigrated from Denmark. In Buenos Aires, the Loomis' only son would be born and named Eugene Frandsen Loomis. One day he would become known simply as "Bud." (Bud's older sister, Inez, would marry Scoop Johnson in later years; his younger sister, Mary

Alice, would marry Bill Blakely.) *[All, and Cebe below, have passed away.]*

Bud grew up and went to law school, then journeyed to mysterious pre-war China, where he acted as an envoy for American people and companies doing business in that inscrutable land. He acquired – legally – many artifacts, shipping them home periodically to Reno, where his mother was by then teaching Spanish at Reno High School. When the Chinese closed their borders and excluded foreign nationals in the 1930s, Bud returned to America and Reno. He met and wed his wife Cebe – say "Seeb." He opened a law practice, and maintained an interest in his father's vocation – photography. Bud and Cebe moved into a home on the Frandsen family property at the west end of Wingfield Park, that originally served as a carriage house for the Gray mansion above it on the Court Street bluff, that burned in 1939. Across the river was the Christian Science Church, on a site donated to the church by Anna Frandsen Loomis – as kids, we called her "Dosh." Anna commissioned architect Paul Revere Williams to design the church and the Loomis Manor Apartments to the west of the church on Riverside Drive. The Frandsen Apartments on West Fourth Street bounded the family's property holdings to the north.

• • •

But the Loomis's' home was not large enough to display their art collection. Bud at that time was serving as an advocate to the Chinese community in Reno, and the Chinese owned a piece of property on the north bank of the Truckee River – there was still a joss house operating on it even into the 1950s.

Loomis negotiated with whatever entity owned the site, and eventually acquired it. He and Cebe built, on its eastern end, the headquarters for Ben Dasher's Universe Life Insurance Company. On the East First Street corner they built a smallish restaurant, cocktail lounge, and the River House motel, all with a Chinese motif. Into this restaurant and bar, and with the hearty approval of the local Chinese community, who were grateful to have their story told, went the Loomises' collection of artifacts. Cebe told me years ago that there was at least one artifact from China in every room of the motel.

The name? Bundox. It was frequently mispronounced *bun,* as in "cheek," but always by the cognoscenti as *boondocks*. Bud told me years ago that the origin of the name was the Tagalog – (Filipino) – word *bundoc* anglicized by pre-World War II American soldiers to connote a remote, forgotten, and somewhat romantic place, somewhat like Xanadu.

At least I think that's what he said – better than 20 *[30!]* years ago. Or then again, maybe it's taken from Kipling or Coleridge – who knows?

But it was never remote to many movers and shakers in Reno, and the little bar was a favorite watering hole for the rich and the famous for several decades, or at least for civic leaders in the days when civic leaders actually got something done from start to finish. (I remember my own father laboring there into the wee hours in the nascent days of acquiring land south of town for a big building to be called the Centennial Coliseum in 1962.) *[the present Reno/Sparks Convention Center.]*

At least, that's what he told my mother…

Maybe the civic leaders should have acquired a little restaurant called the Liberty Belle back then, which had already been open for three years, but that's for another column – the Belle lives.

Straying back now to the Bundox story: Bud died about 20 years ago; Cebe kept the place hopping for another ten years, and then sold the property. (Cebe too passed away, last June *[2003]* in southern California.)

The corner's buildings are now abandoned and boarded up, an ongoing insult to the by-gone revelry and that certain je nè cais quà that the Bundox and the Loomises once brought to our fair city and the Truckee's shore. *[And now they're gone altogether. The question on everyone's mind: Who got the brass door handles…?]*

• • •

Two footnotes form an epilogue to this yarn: The wrecker's ball is not Earl Games Construction's Christmas party, and "je nè cais quà" is dedicated to the lady who questioned "ethos" last week. We're introducing a new feature: the *Homefinder* word of the week – use it correctly and the duck'll drop down and bring you 25 bucks. *[And as you read that, I hope you watched the old Groucho Marx* You Bet Your Life *on KZTV, or you won't know what I'm writing about.]*

Have a good week, and God bless America.

• • •

**[The rest of that story, that might have been inappropriate for the column: I am close enough to the Blakely family that some use me as a tax deduction, and one night I asked "What was Dosh's husband's given name?" (The photographer of "national renown" in my column.) No one knew – he was always "Mr. Loomis" when they were growing up. Dosh and Mr. parted after their youngest child (Mary Alice) was born, and Dosh came back to Reno and taught Spanish for many years at Reno High School.]*

Tom Swart sets the brakes on a million-pound SUV at the railyard...

Report from the Rail City

We've all left the family SUV idling while we stopped at the mailbox, and then turned to see the ol' Explorer bucking inexorably off through the boxwood hedge then into the tree beyond. Picture in your mind's eye one of S.P.'s legendary cab-forward locomotives walking itself slowly off the track into the roundhouse pit, or crashing through the brick walls of the big railroad shop east of the Sparks Nugget – after a drowsy engineer left the behemoth "in gear" with the boiler fire down, yet slowly building up steam and finally creeping unattended in the wee small hours of the morning when Sparks was fast asleep. Ugly spectres indeed, but they've both occurred.

Tom Swart entered the world in 1912 in his family's home on B Street behind the livery stable we all remember between 11th and 12th Streets and now the Silver Club's parking lot. He attended Mary Ann Nichols, Robert Mitchell, and Sparks High Schools, Procter Hug Sr. his bookkeeping teacher; he then took a job with the mighty Southern Pacific Railroad in the locomotive shop for eighteen and a half cents an hour.

One of his shop duties was as a chainman – placing lengths of chains between the driver wheels of the big malleys and the track, to keep them where they belonged in the yard (*malley*, eponymous with Swiss mechanical engineer Anatole Mallet, a descriptor of the cab-forward locos accurate only through the 1920s but surviving to this day as a term of endearment.) Tom's recollections of life in the SP roundhouse and shops could make a book – or a chapter in one coming out later this year. He speaks of the massive overhead-rolling crane in the shop – lifting the boilers and fireboxes off the axles and cylinders, all to go in different directions for maintenance, then be rejoined and repainted. The flue box area, airbrake shop, the huge vat of boiling water laced with carbolic acid that locomotive parts and the employees' tools could be lowered into for cleaning, then cooled and drained periodically to retrieve the stuff. (Maybe we don't even want to know where the wastewater wound up.) Tom recalls a mechanic falling into the vat and arriving instantly at the Great Beyond, his soul and bibb overalls cleansed. The flue rattler? All 2,500 residents of Sparks knew when the flue rattler was running – the giant vibrator the only way to shake the built-up crud out of the locomotives' fireboxes and flues.

Tom recalls life in Sparks vividly – in his early youth an Indian reservation occupied the area now the site of City Hall on 4th and Prater Way.

The U. S. Air Mail's deHavilland biplane pilots that navigated by following SP trackage from Elko enroute to their daily arrival at Blanch Field on the site of the present Washoe Golf Course, rocking their wings to the railyard workers below. Conductor Heights south of B Street and west of the train yard (near then-17th Street, now Rock Boulevard), the preferred lair of railroaders and their families.

He worked at the Pacific Fruit Express icehouse for a time, bunking in nearby railroad-owned dormitories, on-call around the clock for refilling the ice bunkers of UP/SP produce trains. And, the good stuff you can only get by hanging out with guys like Tom Swart: After two-score and seven years of assuming that all the produce trains ran eastbound from California's agricultural fields, lo and behold I learn that the hottest trains on the line were those hauling precious strawberries *westbound* – those cargoes superior to the passenger trains that were switched to a sidetrack as the strawberries highballed through to California.

A gnarly railroad strike broke out in 1922 that would continue for two years, pitting S.P.'s management against the train operations and maintenance employees. Tom, as a ten-year old, recalls a powerful spotlight, placed on the roof of the roundhouse by management to ensure security in the yard, but also finding use as a tool of harassment, its powerful beam trained at union members' homes and into bedrooms through the night. And railroad timekeeping? Once a pride and priority with the S.P., less so in the Amtrak days, time was set by the yard whistle sounded precisely at 8 a.m., noon, and 4 p.m., or available in the railroad's clock in the window of W. R. Adams & Son Jewelers on B Street to set your Hamilton pocket watch with a railroad dial to.

We'll revisit Tom again, for many more invaluable Swart yarns remain.

• • •

The *Homefinder* factoid for the week is that *bookkeeper*, seen on page 8, is the only word in the English language with three consecutive double letters. You're welcome. Have a good week, 1,252 Accident-Free Days @ Ralston Foods, and God bless America.

Even a columnist has to have fun once in a while...

A FEW LOCAL MERGERS

Writing about old Reno businesses as we occasionally do becomes cumbersome, so my researcher Carmine Ghia and I have struck upon a brainstorm to speed it up by combining a few. We could write of the Flaming Wok & Wait CPA and stir-fry house, or Second Hand Rose-Glenn, used furniture and new public relations. Chicks-with-Stix 'n Bricks, a premier restaurant with a distaff golf school, and another restaurant at Lakeridge, The 19th Hohl Motors, fine food plus Caddys, Buicks and a side of GMCs. Old timers will remember the Franco-Armanko sourdough and stationery store. Visit the Jay Sourwine and Cheese Board in the old Ramos Drug on California Avenue, for an interlude of law and lunch. Realtor Dan Rider teams with barrister Keegan Low for Low-Rider Enterprises; and a big merger between Realtors Skip Zink, Norma Fink, Morton Link, Phil Klink and Brick Tenk – the firm of Zink, Tenk, Link, Klink and Fink (Inc.). Realtors George Peek and George Hatjakes bought out Meeks Lumber in Carson City, forming Peek, Meek and the Greek's Teak.

It gets worse. Jon Key and Bill Locke, too easy: Locke & Key pharmacy and subpoenas (they deliver); Bible & Hoy's-R-Us, for quality writs and Barbie Dolls. A modeling agency (Strolling Fashions, anyone remember them?) opened a restaurant, called Eve-Lynn Suiter's Hooters. Soon we'll write of J.R. Bradley & Drendel's hardware/law shop. Butch (Bobo) Sheehan and Dan Earl, as quietly as Mogul Mice, are teaming for the Butch and Sundance bookstore and patio furniture in Keystone Square.

And the friend mentioned in last week's column who got me started down this pathetic path, Cheryl Yee, joined forces with Realtor Maureen Haw to form Yee Haw Realty, just in time for the World's Richest Rodeo. Here's one to cover a lot of businesses quick: The Reel Fast Reliable Peerless Quality Smart & Final Construction, Glass, Fencing, Laundry, Linen and Sundries Company. (And hats blocked.) You'll recall the Sister Seraphine Mother Superior Tax Service. An aging SAE Realtor Joe Mayer and likewise Sigma Nu stockbroker Herb Nichols helped their wives open a stable, called Penny & Nichols' Quarter horses. (Susie Nichols, that would be.) Up now to Virginia City, for the Bucket of Blood Services of Reno for a pint and a brew – a brew in and a pint out, of you, that is. Still in VC: No discouraging word here, the cowpoke from The Team You Know and Trust hitches his cayuse at the legendary Buffalo Bar in Sparks to palaver over the name Tyson's Bisons for his Virginia City dude ranch. Nothing escapes us.

Michelle Barry's husband – a stalwart of the University of Nevada's sports and alumni programs – opened an insurance office, Woody Barry Bonds. And another pair Carmine's interviewing is Sierra Pacific Power's Frame Shop, apologies to Roy, Jackie, and the ratepayers. Great old Reno construction and liquor distributor veterans join to form Luce and Titan (I tried to work in Mr. Goodwrench here but no-go.) We all know Sparks icon/office supplier Gordon Foote, but few know of his sullied nephew, the proprietor of Dirty Harry's Business Machines.

Happy Birthday #XXXIII on June first to our airport's Minister of Propaganda, Adam Mayberry RFD – I felt quite old one night having to decipher RFD to a group of folks Adam's age. (It's *Rural Free Delivery*, Aunt Bea.) *[Adam has since left us to be Congressman Porter's spokesman in Washington.]* Close your escrow at an old downtown bar, Paradise Lost & Founders Title. The patio cover experts and an attorney, or judge, could merge into a catchy Sunkist & Hug, your honor, and Mail Flower Boxes Etc. would combine into a column about postage and petals.

I've victims left over, but a deadline beckons, the dead-still night that started at 85 degrees has hit 90 and my laptop's screen is making less and less sense – it couldn't be me – so we're heading for the gate. No local firms are off the hook just yet.

A local rummage sale lasts for over 30 years...

TOMBOLA DAY

There was a time in this great land when a function that was vital to the populace would find itself on the ropes, financially in this Saturday morning's yarn, and rather than crying to state legislatures and selling out to the federal system, or hyping up a shaky stock offering or pruning down their loyal employees' wages, they would roll up their sleeves and do something about it – with dignity, honor, and a little bit of fun.

And that's the way it was in the late 1940s at a little business down at the corner of Mill and Kirman Streets – the original brick building built in 1904 can still be seen amid the sprawl. The Washoe County Hospital has roots back to 1876, when 40 acres of the Hatch ranch were purchased for a hospital and a poor farm. At mid-century its fiscal pulse, respiration and temperature were approaching Code Blue – the (three, then) County Commissioners were noodling with the eventuality of closing the whole thing down.

A knight in shining scrubs rode into town from Arizona – his name was Clyde Fox – and he took over as the hospital's administrator. One of his first acts was to create a body that had been successful for him in other hospitals: an auxiliary, composed of community ladies and doctors' wives. His auxiliary rapidly grew to 500 members and old newspaper clips include the movers-and-shakers of our towns. I was surprised to see my own grandmother in a newsclip, shaking her ancient booty in some hen party at the Twentieth Century Club, all in support of the Washoe Hospital Ladies Auxiliary.

"We shall raise money," they decreed, and in the year fuzzily identified as 1951 they gathered on a sunny Saturday in Pickett Park across from the hospital, and held a rummage sale. The name was "Tombola Day" – I've references to tombola as some sort of salsa bingo game, and/or a Central American fiesta. Tents were set up for the merchandise, the hospital brought some grub over and they had a few booths for kiddies – a "Wheel of Fortune" sort of thing, a Fortune Teller and a Wishing Well.They went all day, sold out, made a few bucks for the hospital and had a ball.

Well, next year, it's going to be a little different, someone said, and it was. The rummage had a little greater variety, the children's games were expanded a bit, and a school and a church were brought in to provide a few tunes. Someone brought a barbecue, and recall if you will an outdoor grill was not an amenity in everyone's home in the early 1950s – most were homemade from 55-gallon drums with little ostentation. But – they had hot food. And here I'll run a few years together from newspaper accounts: Each year brought a little more entertainment – for the kids and the adults. At some point a barbecued lamb became a fixture at the event and remained so for many years – John Iratcabal arriving the night before, digging a pit and starting the little creature's journey to between two slices of bread the following afternoon (the lambs on several occasions, maybe more, were courtesy of John Ascuaga or Bill Harrah.) And, the *piece de resistance* of every Tombola Day was a raffle for a little house, an A-Frame of about 10 by 10 feet square and 10 feet to the roof peak, complete with plumbing and electricity, ready to be occupied as a hunting cabin or backyard playhouse. Washoe Med's (its later name) maintenance crew, headed by superintendent Edin Sontag built the little houses and they're still collectors' items seen occasionally around town.

Tombola Day grew, few in town didn't visit it, and what a show – great parking, food, entertainment from schools, churches, the University, Tink's Municipal Band, an early Day with Lash Larue and the Singin' Cherokees, later whoever was playing downtown in an impromptu visit (a youthful Bill Cosby sticks out in my mind, I'd guess this in the early '70s, and no kid went home without a snapshot of him or herself and the Cos, often on his shoulders – what a terrific friend he is to kids of all ages.) A couple of Harrah's museum cars showed up one year including a fire truck with a Dixieland band; not to be outdone by all that was John Ascuaga, who dispatched Bertha & Tina, hoisting a few Nugget showgirls and some bolder volunteer celebrants with their trunks. Reno Fire Department parked a couple of engines for the kids to climb all over, and Bill and Moya Lear, who were among the strongest supporters of the hospital and the League, delighted all by landing a LearAvia medivac helicopter for ground tours. (This in 1974, a joint venture with Reno's Aids Ambulance. The semipublic Careflight air-evac service would come seven years later.) Some thought the helicopter looked a lot like a French Alouette III, but Bill Lear liked to put his own name on things.

Tombola was Reno's big summer show, akin to the Harrah Swap Meet with many similar attractions – both bespoke a great time in our town, when kids were safe riding bikes on their own to Pickett Park and none, rich or poor, went without a hot dog, coke, and cotton candy; a tour of a fire truck, touching the snoot of one of the Nevada White Hat riding team's palominos, ringing the bell at the Strongman Hammer booth and leaving with a Hartford Insurance fireman's helmet – local businesses' participation grew steadily over the years.

And for the adults? Lash Larue and the Singin' Cherokees, can't beat that. A fashion show. Great food and company; a late-afternoon hoedown, I think a cold brew or two might have found its way onto City property, and a sense of getting something done for the community.

Tombola Day went away about 1984. It was a point of municipal pride for three decades. Could we carry off another one in theses times? Maybe.

This note cannot go unpublished: On July the second of 1974, a bold step was taken at Washoe Med: Smoking was banned on the entire fourth floor, staff, visitors and patients alike, no exceptions. Have a good week, Remember D-Day, and God bless America.

Often called the Elks' Fire – we lost a considerable number of downtown businesses...

This appeared in the Reno Gazette-Journal *on October 6th, 2001*

The 1957 Sierra Street explosion and fire

A number of people noticed the odor of natural gas on South Sierra Street near the Truckee River during that bright Tuesday morning in 1957. Yet none called the fire department or the power company, initially.

The first two calls to the fire department came almost simultaneously at 12:53 p.m., from Spina's shoe store, and Paterson's Mens Store, next door to Spina's – both businesses on the west side of South Sierra Street between the Truckee and West First. While those calls were arriving, Elks Club manager J. C. Kumle – aware that something was amiss – was quickly breaking up card games and post-lunch chatter, marshaling members out of the Elks building across Sierra Street from Spina's, if necessary without their jackets – it was a relatively warm day for early February – February 5th, to be exact.

It was 12:59 p.m. as the first fire truck pulled up from the old firehouse on Commercial Row, a short four blocks away, and as it stopped in front of Spina's Nevada Shoe Factory, a violent explosion blew windows out of buildings for blocks around and scattered dust and wood and metal and bricks into the air, reverting the area into darkness. At the Reno High campus on Booth Street, we felt it before we heard it. The concussion that followed was unbelievable, a full mile up the river from the blast.

A second explosion followed, rivaling the first; a third was smaller. The smoke visible almost immediately over town and the wail of sirens signaled that this was no dress rehearsal. We didn't know what, but something big had blown higher than a kite.

• • •

Downtown workers and shoppers scattered, while emergency equipment from the Reno police and fire department and Sierra Pacific Power converged on the scene. Fire quickly broke out in the three-story Elks Home; by evening it would be reduced to a few partial brick walls and twisted steel beams and columns.

Across Sierra Street the three buildings lining the street from West First to the river – Paterson's on the corner, then the building housing Spina's Nevada Shoe Factory, Cambar Fabrics, Tait's Shoes and Slingerland Insurance Agency facing West First Street. Finally the Biltz building, housing the Sanford law firm, Realtor Ben Edwards, and the Kaylene clothing shop on the street level – all caught fire, almost simultaneously, and were gutted by late afternoon.

That's four buildings gone by a little past 5 p.m.– the fifth building involved was the Gray Reids department store on the southeast corner of West First and Sierra Street. That well-built old building put up a valiant battle, as did the firefighters struggling to save it. And so they did, although it was later necessary to remove the third (top) floor. The surviving structure later became part of the Granada Theater. And recalling the Granada, that building was spared, thanks to a deluge of water from Reno firemen, who were joined in mid-afternoon by the Sparks, Carson City and Virginia City fire departments, Nevada National Guard personnel to augment the Reno police, and the Red Cross, who set up canteens to feed emergency workers.

A point of confusion for the past 40 years has been the retail building on the northeast corner of Sierra and West First, that I identified in an earlier column as housing Murdock's, the Vanity, Morgan Smith Jewelers and the Town House, and a few more that I didn't include. Here's the straight scoop: That building had already been torn down and the new J.C. Penney's was being built on the corner at the time the blast occurred. The older building did not burn with its neighbors in the fire.

Two people died instantly that day. Adeline DuPratt was 57 years old and was struck by flying debris while crossing West First at Sierra. Frank Spina, 48, owned Nevada Shoe Factory at mid-block, and was found under a crushed automobile in front of his store several hours after the explosion. (A broken gas pipe attributed by some as the cause of the blast was discovered almost in front of that shoe store, three feet below the pavement.)

Over a hundred physicians grouped at Washoe Medical Center and St. Mary's Hospital, and dealt late into the night with scores of firemen, store employees and shoppers injured by flying glass, smoke and splinters. Kumle, the executive secretary of the Elks Club, was lauded in the papers for his efforts – somewhat assertive, according to some accounts – in getting the lunch-crowd diners out of the club, for that was the largest concentration of people in the vicinity of the blast. The Elks later named the street that their replacement building was built on for him (Kumle Lane, across from the Convention Center.)

• • •

I acknowledge reader Darla Potter's inspiration to get this story written, and archives of the Reno Fire Department and the Hartford Insurance Group; and February 6–13, 1957 issues of the *Reno Evening Gazette* and the *Nevada State Journal.*

• • •

Hark, a letter followed:

Of Parakeets, Fires, and High-school Architects…

The Homefinders' recollections about the 1957 fire/explosion column are still coming in and will doubtless result in a follow-up one of these weekends, but this one is too good to wait: Helen Teglia fondly tells the story of her father Joe Girola, who owned the building on the west side of Sierra Street that housed his business – American Credit – and Cambar Fabrics and the Nevada Shoe Factory. Seems that Joe, during the fateful morning we wrote of, February 5th of 1957, thought he smelled gas in his building. He went down to the basement, and lacking a tweety-bird like the Comstock miners used to warn of explosive gases, performed the next natural test for natural gas: he struck a match.

"So Joe blew up downtown??" I asked Helen. No, Helen replied, for whatever reason nothing happened, so he miraculously returned to street level and went outside. His brother Henry was not as lucky. Seconds later when the explosion finally hit, Henry was incapacitated in the now-burning building's office. Helen credits quickly-arriving Air National Guardsmen Pat Rippingham and guard chaplain father leo mcfadden – lower case intentional – for pulling Henry to safety. He was taken to a hospital and treated for burns and bruises.

Henry and Joe Girola have since passed away, as has Pat Rippingham, who drowned in a fishing accident at Pyramid Lake. leo mcfadden became a legendary columnist for the *reno gazette-journal*, without ever once using a capital letter.

[and father leo still writes once in a while, still in lower case]

A school principal who influenced most Reno residents during the mid-20th century

Ruffling Finch's Feathers

In a Gazoo column I wrote one time, the text turned toward the Frandsen Apartments. That saga leads to David Finch, a fixture in the legacy of Reno High School when it was Reno's only public secondary school (through 1961.)

Finch was an English teacher, and later the principal of enormous tenure at RHS, and many callers reminded me that he lived – using the term loosely – at the Frandsen Apartments, alone, for many decades. Very few residents of Reno in the mid-1900s were not touched by his influence – either themselves, or their children or parents. I'll let my friend and frequent correspondent Lenore Jordan, who lives in Santa Rosa, Calif., write the next segment of the column (Lenore left Reno in 1947 but has many friends here and reads my column weekly.) Lenore speaks of her childhood in a small mining camp called Rochester in the Humboldt Range east of Lovelock. Her father was a millwright for the silver mine, her mother the postmistress, teacher, seamstress and president of the school board. The family journeyed to Reno when Lenore was to be born in 1919 (sorry, Lenore! I needed that year for the story...). She writes:

"When I was about 5 years old a new teacher came to Rochester. He was fairly tall, carried himself straight as could be, had beautiful hair with a perfect wave in it and was, of all things, a Stanford graduate! He was looking for a place to live in and my folks owned a little cabin, which was vacant at the time, with its own outhouse. This new fellow was Mister Finch!

"I wanted to go to school but I was too young, however Mr. Finch would now and then let me sit in the schoolroom and look at books. By the time I was old enough to enroll he was off to some place else – maybe Reno – I don't know.

"Fast forward to about 1934 when I was going to Reno High School and guess who turned out to be my English teacher! He was truly a good teacher and seemed fond of kids, and I learned a great deal from him. He had dinner with us from time to time but never showed me any favoritism at school.

"By the way, Miss Singleton was my home room teacher! Great memories all."

What a great letter, one of many Lenore has sent me. (Two notes beg to be scribed: Mentioning David Finch and outhouse in the same paragraph defies responsible journalism, and Beulah Singleton was still around in the late 1950s as well. In an old column I misidentified her as the co-author of our Nevada history book with Effie Mona Mack. Mack's co-author was Byrd Sawyer, former Nevada Gov. Grant Sawyer's mother. Singleton later did a revision.

Lenore's description of Finch hit the nail on the head two decades later: tall, impeccable hair with a wave, ramrod-straight carriage, aloof, austere. He ran Reno High with an iron hand, teaching by the mid-1950s only one class a year – Human Relations – an honors, by-invitation-only course that was the only safe harbor on the then-new Booth Street campus where one could utter a horrid word like "inter..." well, you know, without being bounced off the baseball or debate team, in the stringent world of David Finch. He was an automaton that would stride home each night to the Frandsen Apartments – if he owned a car I don't recall it – to reappear, wraithlike, the next morning.

We did South Pacific as a senior class play (1959), and as one might imagine, Oscar Hammerstein's lyrics became by necessity "...There is nothing like a *girl*!" in the Finch libretto. No dames in our gym, no sirree. (That's during the final dress rehearsal, of course – at the Big Show, there was nothing like a dame…)

People I knew as teachers, administrators and coaches then, who in the last 40 years have become adult friends, agree that he retired without fanfare. He since passed away on the San Francisco Peninsula, in almost-embarrassing obscurity.

Only in recent years have a few of us begun to realize that maybe he did one hell of a job as a principal, in his own Victorian way – the proof was in the pudding: Reno High enjoyed national recognition in many areas. Lenore's letter infused a miniscule spark of affection in me for the man – the respect was always there – and who knows, if a new high school ever needs a name (it would have to be a high school), then "David Finch High" doesn't have a bad ring to it after all. We've named schools after a few a lot less deserving. And the team-name mascot's a snap: the Finch Finchies. *That suggestion ought to get the ol' phone a-ringing. ...*

• • •

[Footnote: this column brought a lot of response from all corners of the nation, from Reno High alums who came to respect the iconoclastic David Finch in the years following our graduation into later life.]

A finny-diner loose in Trader Dick's aquarium...

John meets Jaws

The locals have long since forgotten, and the tourists have no clue, that when you're sitting at the bar in Trader Dick's restaurant in the Sparks Nugget, Interstate 80 is only about 25 feet away. Straight up. A system of columns separates the little umbrella in your Mai Tai from the tires of one of Granite's big green three-dump-trailer rigs.

In a triumph of design, a massive aquarium of Ascuagan proportions was built around the three freeway columns behind the bar, those columns textured to appear as a Pacific atoll rock formation. And into this aquarium were placed hundreds of tropical fish, all content to aimlessly mill around the tank, with a wonderfully mesmerizing effect on the bar's patrons.

But there was an unseen malaise in this seemingly-placid lagoon when the present Trader Dick's opened in 1988, for the large school of fish was slowly, inexorably diminishing – the bartenders were the first to notice that it just *seemed* that there just weren't as many fish in the tank as there once were. More fish were introduced. And their number too also diminished over time. What was happening to the fish in the tank? Were the chefs at the Oyster Bar covertly raiding it on busy Friday nights when their fish lockers were becoming sparse? Unthinkable.

In yakking this story up, I've heard various accounts of how the mystery was solved; my own recollection is that an out-of-towner sitting at the plank, obviously a fish guy, looked toward the tank and muttered under his breath, "Who the hell would put that shark into an aquarium?"

A bartender overheard him, and lights began going on. Fish people on a grand scale (*sorry*) were called in and determined that yes indeed; a juvenile shark was in the tank and should be isolated, pronto, for the good of the remaining herd.

The press got wind of it, which created a problem for the Nugget's PR honchos: What do we do with this little beast now? The little guy *[gal]* was clearly In Harm's Way, trespassing in an establishment with eight fine restaurants – Shark Fin Soup at Trader Dick's and the Captain's Platter in the Oyster Bar come to mind – but Greenpeace would never let the Nugget off the hook for a stunt like that. So John did the only right, decent thing to do: He spoke with the folks at Steinhart Aquarium in Golden Gate Park in San Francisco, and when the arrangements were complete, he sent the errant shark, who after all really had no blame coming in the whole matter, *in a*

Nugget limousine, to the park, where it could eat a more seemly menu and frolic with its own species, maybe start a family someday.

Epilogue *[for this column]:* I called Steinhart in the days just before the July Fourth weekend when no one's mind was on business anyway, to inquire about the Nugget shark's welfare these 13 years later. I told my tale, and was rebuffed with "Sure, mister, we'll get right on it." I then asked my son Brent, who lives *[lived]* within three blocks of the Steinhart and was in town for the long weekend, if he and his friend *[now* wife*]* Laura could maybe pedal to the park and check out the shark for the Homefinders. He responded laconically, "Sure, dad, we're on it."

Detecting a note of Breckenridge sarcasm in his voice, I'm going to Plan C: I'm sending this column to the aquarium if it's published, with this sentence highlighted, hoping for a report. If it's not forthcoming, we'll assume that the aquarium's famous 855-pound Great Lakes goldfish, the largest in captivity, while in a mood for a Basque appetizer nailed our shark in a moment of poetic justice.

I thank my old U of N classmate Nancy Trabert, inside the walls of the Nugget's third-floor executive offices and who will probably disavow any knowledge of me, for helping me get the year of this fish-tale correct.

• • •

And then I wrote:

We get mail; one such note is of the shark that was devouring the other fish in John Ascuaga's Nugget's big aquarium behind Trader Dick's bar. We reported that the shark was inadvertently placed into the general population of fish, then apprehended and taken by Nugget limousine to the Steinhart Aquarium in San Francisco. And we promised a report on the young shark's welfare.

Well, Stephanie Greenman, Steinhart's Marketing and Communications Coordinator, and Tom Tucker, the Aquarium Curator, dove right in, so to speak, and filled me in on some background. Tom pleasantly recalled working with Tonis (Tony) Lubbers, the Nugget's general manager for many decades, on the transfer of the little creature and recalls it as a nurse shark, allaying my fear that maybe it was a card shark. Given the 25-year lifespan of a female nurse shark and the excellent care it's receiving at the Steinhart, it's a safe assumption that the little shark is 12 years older, alive, and well, a pleasant alternative to medium well as it might have become in John's Oyster Bar. I thank Stephanie and Tom, who made this an enjoyable feature to write about. They invited me to visit the shark, and so I will, soon. *[I did.]*

Speaking of which – (how's this for a writer's segue?: Watch closely, don't try it at home): The Steinhart Aquarium is part of the California Academy of Sciences in Golden Gate Park in San Francisco, a complex started around 1915. Italian architect Renzo Piano has been commissioned to design a replacement for the buildings, and said of the old Academy campus "…sometimes you love a building because she is an old hound. Not because she's beautiful, but because she's your old hound."

Mike Greenan, public information officer of Western Nevada Community College read Piano's quote in a recent S.F. Sunday *Chron*, and wrote a poignant Letter to the RGJ Editor equating the Academy to the Mapes Hotel – "Now that she's gone, I miss her…she was my old hound, a comfortable place where I had worked, eaten, partied, and slept…she was our old hound, and she's gone forever, replaced by nothing." Nice words from both Mike and Renzo.

A once-great Reno neighborhood, risin' like the Phoenix as we go to press...

Walkin' East Fourth Street, ca. 1955

"You've walked all over town in past columns, why don't the *Homefinder* readers walk East Fourth Street?" Or so a few readers wrote.

It's mostly because the RGJ recently carried an excellent three-issue overview of East Fourth with more ink and graphics than I could ever hope to squeeze out of the real estate editor. This morning's piece started as a commentary on old signs, but while riding around with a notepad some quirky thoughts of East Fourth in Reno and B Street – Victorian Way – in Sparks still beckoned to be heard, so we'll mix up the two themes this morning.

To my bride's ongoing horror, the two neon signs that most interest me while I'm enjoying an ale or three at the Great Basin in Sparks are first, the Pony Express Motel sign at the Prater/Victorian "Y," a late-1940s product of Pappy Smith's (Harolds Club) and Young Electric Sign's imaginations. I started to write that it was the first "motion" neon sign in town – (the arrows being shot from the Indians' bows) – but I now spell-check out any superlatives, like first, oldest, highest, etc. And "railroad," "church" or "architect" for that matter.

It's much too big to steal, but the second sign I lust after is more portable, in front of the old Park Motel on Prater Way; the Phillip Morris-type bellboy with the once-waving arm that used to beckon travelers into the "motor lodge." It's a creation that would blow the CC&Rs of the God-forsaken desert to smithereens if I lit it up in my backyard, waving at the architectural committee. No chance. Note the other remaining motor hotel signs on East Fourth – the Sandman, with the tires on the prewar sedan that once appeared to rotate. And the classic neon art style, with no name that I know of attributed to it other than post-war contemporary, on Everybody's Inn and Alejo's motels' signs, and a few others – hopefully they will all be saved, rehabilitated and displayed somewhere as signs of a bygone era, pun intended.

Check out the architecture on East Fourth – the brick patterns in the Alturas Hotel, J.R. Bradley Company, the buildings that flourished in the early postwar period like Siri's Restaurant, Reno Mattress and some of the retail stores. Replicating the rococo brickwork style in some of those buildings today would cost a fortune. And Ernie's Flying "A" truck stop, we called it then, now signed as RSC Something-or-other: The fluted column-tower signature of Flying "A" stations has long since been all but removed from this garage, but look close and you can easily detect a close resemblance to Landrum's Café architecture on South Virginia – a very prevalent commercial style of a prewar period. (Ernie's was, with McKinnon & Hubbard on West Fourth Street, the forerunner of Boomtown, the Alamo and Sierra Sid's to old U.S. Highway 40 truckers.) And, if I'm permitted to editorialize, hats off to my old buddy Steve Scolari, whose family business Ray Heating – now RHP – has been on East Fourth for 70-plus years. Faced with the need to expand, he turned the main office building facing East Fourth Street into a great-looking little office, retaining its pre-war nuance, then upgraded a half-dozen industrial buildings on the street and railroad land to the south into very serviceable first-class modern shops, preserving the workforce and tax base in the East Fourth corridor. A gutty move, but a lead that more property owners in areas like East Fourth and South Wells Avenue should follow. And progressive city management, now hell-bent on plowing two or three hundred million dollars into a hole in the ground for choo-choos, should offer tax incentives for this "infill" redevelopment like other cities do. End of tirade. *[They didn't, and they're digging.]*

Evidence of a bygone retail presence on East Fourth is Windy Moon Quilts on Morrill Avenue, the only quilt shop in town with a drive-up window. Why? 'Cuz it once was a busy and highly profitable branch of First National Bank, that's why. [And Windy Moon has moved to the Velvet Ice Cream building on Kuenzli Lane, at one time known as *North* Street.

We couldn't tour East Fourth without stopping at the architecturally resplendent Tap 'n Tavern Saloon, and then mosey on down Highway 40 to Casale's Halfway Club for world-class pizza. And if host Mama Stempeck ain't happy, ain't nobody happy. What a great lady…

Many notes remain and readers will kick in a few more, so we'll probably go back and finish this tour soon. I detected a slight deterrent to retail development on East Fourth while driving, starting, stopping, backing up, making notes and taking pictures, stopping again: On several occasions local ladies practicing the world's oldest profession invited themselves into my pickup for a good time, some of whom were probably undercover police. "Honest, officer, I'm researching a column for the *Homefinder*." (Good story, buddy, tell it to Judge Salcedo.)

• • •

And we walked some more…

We took a little stroll around East Fourth Street last week, and one observation that just wouldn't fit was of the arachnid – OK, scarab – atop the roof of the building visible best from the Wells Avenue overpass. The spider first appeared in the late 1970s, some say as a dare, others say a work of art, still others as the result of seven Sigma Nu frat-rats finding four cases of beer, a blowtorch, and an SAE's Volkswagen. As the sun rose over Lagomarsino Canyon the spider appeared on a field south of a Quonset hut-barn so far out South Virginia Street that you had to pack a lantern and a lunch to get there (but now the only Quonset hut in the South Meadows techie park.) Bug you a little? *[A column about the Scarab appears somewhere in this book.]*

The structure that the big bug sits on was Reno's most modern and largest fire station (Station 2, the first numbered station, replacing the former system, *Central*, *North*, etc.) when it was built after World War II. It replaced Reno's East fire station across East Fourth and west a few blocks, and was a twin of the now-gone Station 3 at the dead-end of California Avenue and South Virginia Street. Walker Boudwin Construction converted it into a construction office many years ago; it became an independent-living resource for the handicapped, and now it's a halfway house.

I had a call or two about the old Wells Avenue Bridge – this is the second modern one. Seven more frat rats (probably ATOs in this case) with a trunkful of Burgermeister might have built that earlier bridge – swayed in the breeze, it did; no trucks bigger than a Ford Excursion could use it and it ended in mid-lane on the north landing at Wells Avenue, creating basically a one-lane northbound affair. So much for the low bidder, railroad trench proponents take note.

Akert's Market? Right across from Hale's Drugs. Benny Akert – as in Ben's Discount Liquors in years to follow – and his sister Betty (Brown), later one of my favorite Realtors, worked Akert's for their parents, at the corner of East Fourth and then-Alameda Avenue – now North Wells. *[No it wasn't the first Ben's Discount Liquors – that was at Pine and Center Streets.]*

Did I tour East Fourth without even a whisper of Louis' Basque Corner? Did I do that? I owe you all a Piçon…

If it won't fit into a column the first time, force it...

Bits & Pieces

Hang on to your Stetsons – this morning were going all over the map with some old and new notes, mostly of reader inquiries. For openers,

"Why has the rodeo been moved from July 4th? Is there some type of July 4th parade down Virginia Street? I do believe the youth of today should all ride on a float in a strapless dress and have blisters on their sunburned shoulders for the following weeks. Their teenage years would not be complete without this experience...

"Why no Silver Spurs awards? Why no Model A Ford Black Maria, scooping up the unwary venturing downtown during Rodeo Week that weren't wearing cowboy duds, throwing them into the Kangaroo Kourt and making them sing a song to regain their freedom. Why not?"

So e-mails Sherry (Cannon) Butler, a favorite RHS classmate who was transplanted four decades ago to La-La Land in Southern California who picks this column up off the Web. Don't know, Sherry; the RGJ's Guy Clifton is the Rodeo guy at the paper, but you're right, those were good days.

• • •

"Does the marble, granite and limestone lining that architect Frederick Delongchamps used for the old YMCA swimming pool remain under the now-vacant lot that adjoined the Mapes?" (Pardon me; "10 North Virginia Street." Reno's cognoscenti don't call it the "Mapes" site…) Back to the question: I don't know. Maybe they'll blow it up also. Or tunnel a train through it. Most agree it's probably still there.

• • •

"Where was the Triune Building?" Still is, southwest corner of State and Center, south of the Pioneer Theater (the cognoscenti have a fancy name for that place too.) The Triune Building was built by attorney/author Clel Georgetta in the 1940s and named for the ranch he grew up on in eastern Nevada. His book *Wool, Beef and Gold* is still the best single resource about our state's past that's ever been written; runner-up, his *Golden Fleece*. In my humble opinion.

• • •

One of Neal Cobb's early aerial photos shows the roof of the bygone Reno Garage across Center from the Majestic Theater at East First Street.

The garage's roof had what several other large, flat roofs in Reno had at the time – two arrows, one pointing toward magnetic north, the other toward the airport (Hubbard Field), for barnstorming pilots arriving in RNO.

This photo recalls a yarn about the confusion apparently created for many who arrived into the valley and spotted the University's Block *N* painted northwest of the university campus, and Sparks High's Block *S* on the hill due east of B Street in Sparks. These flyboys were convinced the *N* was for North and the *S* was for South, got their bearings haywire by 90 degrees, then swooped off to land in Gerlach and ask Bruno for a lift to the Mapes Hotel.

This may not have happened, but it's a good – well, a mediocre – story, and at least touches on the big Block *N* for the Blue and Silver in Mackay Stadium today. *[Homecoming]*

• • •

"You should write about the San Francisco Men's Fishing Club up the river toward Truckee." Already have. And in the final stage of research I called their San Francisco office and was asked not to publicize the club, please – a request that writers have been honoring since 1904. As I will also.

• • •

I recently named some teachers that deserve to have a school named for them. (None were successful.) This prompted two variants of calls: one, "Please don't name me in the future; association with you is obviously an albatross about the neck." The second group asked, "Why didn't you name *me*?" This in turn prompted two responses from me: "I'm sorry I didn't include you"; or, "I didn't like you when you taught me and I still don't like you." Heading the category of the ones I revered could be Roberta Kirchner, my high school English teacher who gave me an A-minus that we've been wrangling over for 40 years. She's a treasure. And looking back, an A-minus was probably charitable. Don't like long, run-on sentences, Bert? (She wasn't one of the callers, by the way.) Roberta puts her English skills to work now on the Hidden Valley Country Club newsletter, when she's not out on the golf course.

• • •

We responded to a reader question following a lot of research – about the location of the USO during World War II – as being the Palms Club, on North Center Street. But it turns out there were other venues also; some remembered the lower level of the Elks' Home on Sierra Street at the river, others mentioned the El Patio Ballroom. Les Conklin the Younger, who himself could write a phenomenal nostalgia column weekly, semi-remembers a party or two (well after WWII) somewhere on South Sierra Street near Liberty. It sounds as if the USO did what Huskies' Haven did in later years – had their party wherever somebody would have them.

• • •

Inevitably, we must complete some Golden Hotel calls. Where did Marilyn Monroe stay during the filming? We can now confirm three hotels, from print: the Mapes, the Golden, (possibly after the filming was completed, it now appears), and the Holiday. And I recall that she spent quite a few days, if not numerous nights, at a private residence on Skyline Drive north of Moana Lane. The home's owners turned the place over to the cast, and invited local tennis players to hang out and give the stars a match.

Did I turn in the alarm for the Golden Hotel fire? The first the fire department heard of it was an incoherent phone call, *Fire!,* but no location, then two alarms on the Gamewell system from street boxes two blocks apart – one mine – those followed almost simultaneously with a useable phone call. The alarms got everybody's eyes open; the latter phone call told them where the fire was. (Provoking the old joke: *Fire Dispatcher*: "Wait, how do we get there?" *Rattled voice on 911*: "Don't you still have the big red trucks?") OK, OK…

And you thought your Saturday mornings were slow: Rancher Jim Bronson, who reads this column every Saturday morning over coffee at the Dew Drop Inn in Standish (California, a hoot and a holler from Susanville), calls to reminisce that he, I and a bunch of other Sigma Nus dined in the Golden a night or two before it burned, in the Malt Shop downstairs. We've spoken before of the classic hamburger joints of bygone days; the Golden's Malt Shop has to be on that list. (Jimmy wants a refund for buying an RGJ without this column last week – hey, even George Will gets a day off once in a while.)

• • •

No one asked, but a train, any train, approaching a crossing blows its whistle (railroaders know it isn't a horn) two long toots, then a short one, then a long one to the midpoint of the crossing. Something to do with enabling the conductor in the caboose, knowing the length of the train, to compute how fast the train is going. (The day is coming when I'll have to explain *caboose!)* If you Reno folks get your railroad trench, the only whistles you'll hear will be the one on the little train in the Lion's Kiddie Park in Idlewild Park, and the real locos who toot their whistles for the kids as they pass Idlewild. Sad.

• • •

We'll throw this out to get the pot boiling a little: Realtor Paul Crooks supplied a 1958 photo of Crooks Bros. Tractor Co. on two-lane Glendale Road, which he reported to be the first building ever built by real estate magnate John Dermody (and I suspect was actually constructed by McKenzie Construction.) It's still visible as the core building of mighty Cashman Equipment, your local Cat dealer.

• • •

Headline in last Sunday's RGJ: "…Alleged bomber fretted over guitar… ." Dumb luck, or journalistic brilliance?

• • •

Got Milk?: Reno resident Frank Gross speaking at a Reno Redevelopment Agency meeting, quoted in the RGJ on September 25th: "You're a big cash cow, an utter failure."

Frank's our kind of guy.

• • •

A couple of calls following our week hanging around East Fourth Street, about "East Street." We've covered this street in the past; it's now renamed, officially or otherwise, as Record Street, just west of Valley Road, once known as Surprise Valley Road, because it used to lead to Surprise Valley, just as Sierra Street lead to the Sierra Valley and California Avenue to California. Enough street talk.

• • •

In a column about bomb shelters, a fine Virginia Lake house, a few old Reno merchants and just a scintilla of political affairs brought the sort of reader responses that make writing worthwhile, with welcome recollections that are the stuff of future columns. But what flummoxed me were the five, count 'em, five, emails about the cultish Zenith Transoceanic I mentioned as being in the Hancock mansion's bomb shelter. Why all that driving around and time in the Gazoo's morgue and the Nevada Historical Society when I could just write about a nerdy radio!? (In truth, it was revealing to read about the things, for which there's actually a score of websites and even a Transoceanic Society. Their meetings are posted in Zulu time.)

• • •

In an unguarded moment I emailed a *Homefinder* advertiser, who advertised that their "…mantle was full of trophies," and asked if they were over their "mantle" or their "mantel"? The advertiser responded that the words were interchangeable. I guess it was just a matter of principal…

• • •

Real estate editor Tom McGuire thinks that my mother's downtown origami shop – mentioned during a downtown walk – folded because she failed to keep a good paper trail.

I've had trouble like this with him before. Following a reference to the chicken's brother Gregory peck, he called it poultry in motion.

• • •

I committed the sin of using the word "ethos" in a recent column, sending one reader to her Webster's. Sorry, I'll put that in the spellchecker alongside two other effete buzzwords of the 21st century, "paradigm" and "collaborative."

Yikes – now I'll hear about *effete*!

• • •

And – I left this thought off the end of the Sparks Firefighter Memorial column, and heard about it all last week: *God bless America.*

Thanks for noticing.

The early fountain, a buck-a-beak for a cormorant's beak, floating Jeeps and the time they drained it…

Thoughts on Virginia Lake

During a week of fumbling with two separate Greatest *Homefinder* Longest Running Business entries both in disarray, I drove by Virginia Lake, saw the new fountains and it dawned on me that a column about Virginia Lake is almost an autumn tradition in these pages.

I winced at the lake's island, devoid of its once-verdant vegetation, an embarrassment gone from bad to worse in what was not long ago the crown jewel in the Reno park system's tiara. A childhood recollection haunts me that the barren guano-covered island, together with the fish hatchery (now a puppy playground) south of Mountain View Drive and the long-gone protective sanctuary for migratory waterfowl on the northeast corner of the park east of Lakeside Drive were all requisites of the Department of Interior's funding of the lake as a WPA project in the mid-1930s. I think the island and its upkeep might still belong – technically – to the federal government.

I try to avoid research wherever possible, as fact usually just stands in the way of a good column, and the Nevada Historical Society's files on Virginia Lake only pulled me all over the map away from my quest, which was federal ownership of parts of the lake. For example, I learned that fish were first stocked in 1938, 100,000 of 'em, and Canada Geese later the same year. Probably a decision we'd like to have over again. In their defense, the Honkers all flew south in the winter until some morons started bulk-feeding them year 'round; now they think south is the fourth fairway at Lakeridge. Another note in the Society's files: Harolds Club's Pappy Smith was a major private sponsor of the lake. And the tufa rock was brought from Pyramid Lake to form the northeast mini-park's structures and benches.

Here's a good clip: In 1945, Lieutenant Hogan of the Army's vehicle maintenance facility out East Second Street by the present Washoe Med received permission from the Washoe County Commission, led by chairman Carl Shelly, to test an "amphibious Jeep" in Virginia Lake. The Army's bravest swimmers drove the Jeeps, basically Ford-built MB militaries enclosed in a hull, onto (into?!) the lake and several of them actually floated, one making it all the way to the island and back. As a kid I remember some of the Nevada National Guard's amphibs parked at the State Building downtown by the present Pioneer Theater.

Sinking ever deeper, we find a citation in the *Reno Evening Gazette* of the complete draining of the lake in October of 1954, some 16 years after it filled, to get rid of an accumulation of junk and sick fish. The Cochran ditch supplying it was shut off for the season, the outlet penstock was opened and the lake did indeed fully drain. My family lived a block west on Watt Street, and each day brought new treasures to light after school. The *piece-de-resistance* was a small pre-war coupe, not near the shore but well out into the lake – records of the car's blue license plate indicated it had been reported stolen some years earlier. The unimaginative were perplexed – how'd it get there? – but the fun crowd speculated that someone was out cutting doughnuts on the frozen lake one wintry night and, well, you know the rest. I'd have reported it stolen too that night were it my family's car – "Yeah, dad, they bagged the Buick right out of the Christian Science Church's lot while I was inside reading Mary Baker Eddy." And yes, newcomers, our valley used to get that cold in the winter.

From junk fish to bad birds – not in the Historical Society's records but in my own noggin, was in the year following the drain and refill that Washoe County Fish and Game had had enough of the cormorants devouring the newly-planted trout in the now-clean lake. They put a bounty on them, a buck-a-beak for a double-crested cormorant's sleek black head. The first light of many days echoed like the OK Corral around our house, as the mighty hunters bagged 'em in style with shotguns. No one was happier about that program than longtime Reno attorney Miles Pike and RHS basketball coach Lloyd Trout, rest their soles.

If you're still with me after that line, I'll note that sailing was briefly permitted on the lake, thanks to late attorney Tom Cooke's 1962 efforts, and a water ski festival was held there in that same year.

Here, I'll make the admission: I'm no closer now than I was ten, or twenty, years ago to the federal ownership angle of the island, either at the time of the lake's creation or the present. Maybe I'm mistaken. I'll gladly take help, if a reader can point me to the right agency. *[None did]* Someone has to take responsibility for the island's ownership and fix this high-profile civic blight…

And later I wrote

OK, OK, how could we mention Virginia Lake memories last week without including the 1972 fountain? Ranking high in the great pantheon of civic cultural brilliance alongside the National Bowling Alley, cobblestone sidewalks and the ever-uglier renditions of the Arch, was the pump shooting streams of water backlit by multi-colored spotlights despoiling an otherwise pleasant summer sunset over the lake. The ducks, as if to say "get this abomination off our pond," ate the Styrofoam the contraption floated on, twice, and it sank, twice, and it's now, last I looked, behind the City maintenance building in Idlewild Park, a good place for it. Reno City Public Works threatened the wildlife leadership for monetary damages, but one duck told them "to put it on his bill."

Two popular Reno residents create a landmark...

The blooming of Arlington Nursery

Last Saturday's *Homes* section carried an excellent account written by Holly O'Driscoll about the former Benson home south of the present Arlington Gardens on West Plumb Lane. It triggered some pleasant memories for me – apparently for several Homefinders also, as I got a couple of e-mails calling it to my attention. (I do read this *Homes* section occasionally.)

The late John and Dorothy Phillips Benson were a popular Reno couple – a little cowboy, a little Bohemian, formidable bridge players, and Nevadans to the core. At the onset of World War II John shipped out, leaving his bride Dorothy minding the Phillips family ranch on the southwest corner of West Plumb Lane at its dead-end into Arlington Lane. (In actuality, her father was a dentist.) Dorothy passed the war years by gardening, making it her business to aggregate one of every plant known to man (well, almost). A tribute to her success is the remarkable number of species (over 60) enumerated on the listing agent's brochure for the property, part of which is now for sale.

Gardening led to cultivating plants in greater numbers than she could find room for, and soon Reno residents were invited by to take a few home. Which led to ordering from the few wartime suppliers 'way more than she could use, for friends popping by the "Arlington nursery" to pick up a few ornamentals or trees and shrubs. Protective sheds were built to house the more fragile stock, and eventually row after row of tubs of trees and flats of flowers, and a few birdbaths and other garden statuary occupied the corner.

The war was over, and John returned and saw the family acreage. "Holy Cow," he exclaimed, or something to that effect. The nursery on Arlington became the Arlington Nursery – blooming from an avocation into a business. I'll stick my neck out here and say it was only one of two nurseries in Reno and Sparks in the years following the war – the second being the Fujii family's Nevada Nursery on East 2nd Street. *[That brought no e-mails of protest, so it must be true.]* With the war effort returning to a peacetime economy, more nursery stock and garden merchandise became available, the valley was mushrooming with the new homes of relocating folks trying to replicate the lush landscaping they were used to in California (with some climatic frustration), and Arlington Nursery was well underway.

The Bensons enjoyed foreign travel, and so they did frequently, not to the once-touristy European capitals that were rebuilding from the war, but to the mystic unknown of the Far East. They had a taste for the unique, akin to gift shops like Gump's, or locally Better Browsing and Norfolk in years to follow. They shipped their treasures home. Adding to the ambiance of their growing shop were two exotic young ladies straight from the album jacket of Broadway's *The King and I* – Balinese or Siamese as I recall – who glided around the little cottages for many years, helping the customers. Those cottages now form the core of the Arlington Gardens. (Dorothy later donated that part of the property to the Junior League of Reno.)

[A reader contribution to my friend Guy Clifton's second volume of You may be a Nevadan if…, *reminded me of one of the Siamese ladies' hobbies: A Koi pond, well stocked and slowly diminishing in Koi population. No one knew why until the Great Blue Heron landed, swooped up a fish like a herring and flopped her big wings off into the sunset. And that signaled the end of the Arlington Koi pond…]*

Dorothy's first love, even more than her plants, was for animals. Few customers didn't know of Mr. Rabbit, the oversize cottontail who grazed on the inventory whenever he could escape his cage. Dorothy and Mr. Rabbit still grace the Gardens in a hare-raising portrait she had done of the two of them. On one occasion, the Bensons were staying at a Palm Springs motel where a big 'ol hound dog had been abandoned by his owners. They adopted him and he too roamed the place for years. Many of their old customers remember him, named simply Hyatt, for that's where they had first met him. (And it's a good thing they stayed where they did; "Motel 6" would be a strange name for a pooch.)

Their community benevolence was legendary; the most notable one remains as the "Benson Gardens" adjacent to the doomed Fleischmann Planetarium at the University, hands-on, physically planted by John and Dorothy themselves, who then endowed its maintenance, and named for them, some say, against their wishes. One would hope that somebody on the Hill short-sighted enough to demolish the Planetarium has the good sense to perpetuate the Benson Gardens alongside the relocated Planetarium.

• • •

The second recollection – somewhat fowl – was a bright morning in maybe 1960, when I had deposited a school bus load of little tykes at the almost-new Jessie Beck School on West Plumb Lane and was proceeding to my studies on the Hill. (Bear in mind that West Plumb was then two-lane, sort-of-paved, lacking curbs and gutters but with a shallow ditch on either side of the street.) A peacock, one of several harbored by John and Dorothy at the Arlington Nursery, scooted in front of my bus. In a split-second I weighed either facing my dispatcher Al (Charley) McVey, or John Benson, a hulk of a guy who had played interior line for the Wolf Pack in its glory years and who bounced me on his knee as toddler, for doing in his peacock. I elected to veer into the ditch and let the glorified turkey live (had my kids still been on board it would have become roadkill.) This at the expense of gaining the dubious distinction of being the only school bus driver in the district that ever beached a bus to save a peacock. I called McVey for a tow truck (he and wife Dollie still read this column) and some of my young bus passengers that morning might be also be reading this, then sending it on to *their* children. Final thought: I lived not far from the nursery, and can report that a nocturnal squalling peacock sounds more like a crying human baby than does a crying human baby. But louder...

• • •

[University of Nevada alums unite: May the Benson Gardens and the Fleischmann Planetarium still be standing as this book hits the shelves...]

He's done so much for our town, he gets his own segment...

The Real Neal

"Those of us who gather to reminisce and enhance the lore and history of our valley all take our places somewhere on a wagon wheel like this," I spoke, clutching at my wagon wheel bolo tie for emphasis. The audience fell agape.

Turned out I wasn't wearing my wagon wheel bolo, or any other bolo that night, and the crowd of a hundred or so at the January Westerners' Corral meeting questioned why I was fumbling with my unadorned throat. But I pressed on at my task of introducing that night's featured speaker – a lifelong friend of mine.

"Around the rim of our wagon wheel are those in clubs like the Westerners, the Good Old Days, the Newcomers, the service clubs, Eldercollege, the City's Historical Resources Commission, school classrooms, the Historic Reno Preservation Society – (HRPS) – and a myriad of other groups." I should have mentioned *Homefinder* readers...

"Like any good wagon wheel, our wheel has spokes – in this case, the wonderful contributors to our landscape of knowledge: Richard Moreno on Nevada's trails, David Toll, Stanley Paher. Phillip Earl; they don't get any better than Phil. The railroad guys: Richard C. Datin and Dale Darney. Dwayne Kling, archiving the history of our once-major industry – the real gamblers in early postwar Reno. The University's Oral History Program.

"Frank X. Mullen, who's series in the Gazoo made the Donner Party come alive again for us for weeks on end while turning Tamsen Donner into a 19th century hottie. A magnificent effort." (Hell, Roseanne would have been a hottie after 40 snowbound days with the grub long gone, but I didn't mention that...) "Two of my old RHS classmates: Pat Ferraro Klos, the driving diva of HRPS, and Leanne Stone, keeping the heritage of the University of Nevada straight. And a third classmate: Skip Hansen, for his tireless work on local Chautauquas."

What I didn't know that night, but do now, is that HRPS has partnered with RSCVA in a project to make their popular Reno walking tours available at times favoring slack-times of conventions in Reno and Sparks for conventioneers and their spouses – what a great venture that will be for tourism!

I droned on: "And we've a lot more spokes: the videographers, Jack Sutton and John Tyson, taking us on fascinating graphic tours of our state. And the still photographers on our wheel, Don Dondero, with a basement full of six decades of photos of stars and less so, frolicking in our town. Neal

Cobb, who I'll introduce in a moment, with a monstrous trove of photos of old buildings from his parents' Modern Photo shop in old downtown Reno. A third photographer whose news work will define our history in time to come – Marilyn Newton, the best at news work. How 'bout Linda Duferrena's work? Breathtaking photographic artwork of the unique beauty of our state. And music? Well, we can't forget Citizen Sam Dehne, off the wall a bit, but his tunes at public meetings still a part of our lore.

"We've got two Guys, neither from Italy that I know of: Guy Clifton, y'all, with his comprehensive tome of our long rodeo heritage, and State Archivist Guy Louis Rocha, holding me on the straight and narrow trail when I incessantly try to insinuate that Butch and Sundance robbed the First National Bank in Winnemucca." (They didn't, but Julia Bulette was in truth the first CPA in the Comstock.) And sadly, another Guy added to the spokes only an hour before the meeting started: "Guy Richardson, the longtime RGJ reporter who complemented with text the life, love and lust captured in Dondero's graphics. What a pair of dandies – we'll miss them both.

"I missed a few spokes, too many, and I'm sorry, but we could be here all night. What I'd like to do now is introduce the hub of our wagon wheel, the glue that holds us all together, a man who has the respect and admiration of all the names I've just mentioned. I drive him crazy by using *about*, as in Mary S. Doten School was built 'about 1911' in a column. 'About' is not in his vocabulary. And notwithstanding the fact that he's lived in our Basque country for 63 years and still can't pronounce 'Arrizabalaga' the same way twice, he's a stickler for detail." (There's a couple more artistic spokes for us, Ramon and Joan Arrizabalaga.) "If a *Homefinder* reader sends me a picture, Neal will copy it, making one for himself, one for me, the original back to the reader, and finally one for the Nevada Historical Society – he's added a tremendous number of recently-discovered photos to the Society that way. And if the Sparks Lions Club or Jessie Beck School wants a lecturer about our history, he'll twist some spoke's tail and get them a speaker. I've got a few knots in mine to prove it.

"Thirty years from now, the Westerners will meet and speak of a powerhouse of a guy who was the quarterback during the decades preceding and following the turn of the 21st century, of all things historic and fun about our towns since the first train rolled through." (I couldn't resist speculating that they would meet then at the Liberty Belle, still in its 2003 location; the RSCVA would still be rattling its condemnation sword and Marshall Fey would still be dishin' up prime ribs and chocolate sundaes. The Westerners cheered – these folks were Belle diners, all.)

"I'd like to bring to the podium now, my friend from our childhood days, growing up on the fringe of the University of Nevada campus together, a guy I regard as the driving force in Reno's history today, the one who holds the spokes together. Please welcome Neal Cobb."

And did they ever…

No, he's no relation to Ty of *Cobbwebs* fame, and yes, agape spell-checked so I left it alone

The next week I wrote:

OK – enough of that – we promised last week a tale of 1950s juvenile justice, Nevada-style, inspired by our walk downtown. Word comes that a man known well by many of us in this town (and it's not yrs. truly – our Whitaker Park neighborhood's a coincidence), happened into the Payless drugstore in the early 1950s on our lunch hour from Mary S. Doten School (at West Fifth and Washington Streets), where a Master padlock, the long-shank bicycle kind, just happened to fall into his pocket as he walked out the door onto West Second Street.

He was busted by the druggist, who took him to an upstairs office. Our friend feared impending arrest for shoplifting, but the druggist thought different. "I know who you are, and where you go to school. I know your dad, and where he works; I know you live up by Whitaker Park and I know just where to find you. Turn around."

The druggist opened the padlock, looped the shackle through our friend's back Levi belt loop, and closed the shackle. "I'm going to be watching you for a week, and you better have this padlock on your britches for the whole week, or first I'll call your dad and then you're going straight to jail for shoplifting. Be back here in one week."

Our friend hid those Levis outside his bedroom window, and wore another pair of jeans around his house to avert questions from his parents, leaving each morning, sneaking around to his bedroom window and pulling on the 501s with the long-shackle padlock. Then he'd head for school. He recalls that several times he saw the druggist, lurking on a corner, checking him out. The shackle banged into the wooden desk backs at school, and his buddies yanked on it and asked him questions about it.

He grew to hate that padlock…

In a week, he reported back to the Payless drugstore. He went upstairs with the druggist. "Have you learned anything?" the druggist asked. "Yessir, and I'll never steal again." "Then turn around." Our friend did so, and the druggist unlocked the shackle. He then handed the lock, with the keys, to the young miscreant. "You earned it. It's yours. Now beat it." And so our friend did.

He told me this story recently, reminded by the Payless reference in a column. As I listened to him I tried to recall whether I too saw him roaming around the schoolyard with a Master bike padlock banging him on his butt five decades ago."That tale's a keeper," I said. "And I bet you still have the padlock?"

"Hell no, I threw that thing into the Orr Ditch five minutes after he unlocked it!"

Master padlock, $1.49. Hole worn in Levis, $2.50 for a new pair at Parker's. Cost to taxpayers, zero. Neal Cobb's lesson in life, priceless.

• • •

["501s," mentioned above, were the button-fly shrink-to-fit Levis we all wore, three bucks at Parker's downtown, four-bits off if you brought in the red tag from your last pair.]

I wrote this for another publication in early April of 2003 and sent it to the RGJ almost as an aside. I was shocked at the response, from readers who knew as little as I did about this center of world attention.

Baghdad-by-the-Bay

The Arabian Nights – a 12th century fable and a 19th century state of mind. Veiled maidens with rubies in their belly buttons darting furtively through arched portals, camels kushed outside darkened houses heavy with the odor of strong tobacco burning in a hookah and cuisine based on God-knows-what cooking in an earthen kettle; threatening-looking men with bold moustaches, loose garments and heavy scimitars at their sides, and nary a sound to be heard other than music with some unsettling tone and meter in the background. A crescent moon – always a crescent, never full nor new – always overhead. A disdain for westerners. Safe haven for miscreants from all over the earth, akin to Butch and Sundance's Hole in the Wall a thousand years later. A foreboding night in a foreboding town.

Baghdad. Or, seen in many early western publications as Bagdad.

It caught the world's eye in the 1920s when it became capital of Iraq. Boundaries of faraway nations meant little to us – it was all the land of Arabia to the music lyricists, fashion designers and Hollywood writers, all capitalizing on its mystique. Few seasoned moviegoers can forget the sepia-toned scene, in Cinerama yet, when a tiny speck on the barren windswept desert appeared through a distant mirage, then inexorably, slowly, grew larger and closer to the viewer until the skirted horse and a turbaned Omar Sharif, his tattered burnoose streaming in the wind, dismounted to deliver news to (Capt. T. E.) Lawrence of Arabia. Many regard it as director David Lean's most memorable scene, ever.

But why did *San Francisco Chronicle* and *Examiner* columnist Herb Caen nickname San Francisco, and later subtitle his column, *Baghdad-by-the-Bay*? Baghdad and San Francisco are little alike; San Francisco built on seven hills, only forty square miles with water on three sides, but Baghdad basically level and spread out 20 times larger, its only waterfront the Tigris River; San Francisco, in a word, of breathtaking beauty while Baghdad, well, by Caen's assessment, less so – the sparkling white minarets exist mostly in travel brochures. Not an unattractive city, but no San Francisco. Why was it called *Baghdad-by-the-Bay* by a scribe who set Bay Area trends for seven decades, until his death in February of 1997?

Right about now, in case you're wondering what inspired this column: A reader asked me why, given my frequent references to Herb Caen, haven't I jumped on Caen's 50-year old reference to Baghdad. And I point out that I welcome many former Bay Area residents to this column, who loved or hated Caen but definitely read him daily. My simple excuse is that I figured that some other writer had already drawn attention to it, given the events of the world. But learning of none, I'll wrap up the explanation:

Caen drew his analogy based upon lifestyle, not the cities' appearances or geography. Caen's San Francisco was a wild, wide-open city in 1951, a town with colonies of a dozen ethnic regions that lived by their own cultures unabated, a dozen tongues spoken each morning on the 38-Geary bus line on the way downtown to work, not unlike a commute in Baghdad. Fugitives from other climes who lived less than savory lives were left alone, so long as they didn't cause any problems to either city's other residents.A large Bohemian presence thrived in both cities. And both cities had an unsung tolerance, ranging to admiration, for their diversity and colorful characters, the colorful rising to high places in Baghdad, and respected, if not exalted, in San Francisco. Remember, Caen coined the nickname in the 1950s; San Francisco perpetuated its no-holds-barred Barbary Coast district for a century after sailing ships gave up the ghost, and Count Marco endured as a local character well into the '70s. (And note the fabled "Barbary Coast" itself is of Arabian flavor…)

I hope I didn't break any reader's heart with this yarn – I was raised on Herb Caen's stuff, and frankly do borrow, usually with attribution, some of his gimmicks like "*Pocketful of notes*," "*These things I like*," and *"And then I wrote,"* and until unraveling his rationale, thought Baghdad was a gleaming sister city to San Francisco, appearance-wise. Guess not. But we still wish the Baghdaddies and Baghmommies all well, and if you read this last sentence Saturday morning, it'll surprise me to no end. *[I was surprised – it ran!]*

The big brick building across from the Sparks Nugget helped keep easterners in veggies...

The PFE Icehouse

A haunting reminder of the heyday of Bill Harrah's reign on the local scene remains visible – albeit fading, like its memory – high on the wall of a fairly substantial brick building south of the train yard in Sparks. *Harrah's Automobile Collection* the fading white block letters read. Many of us remember fondly the acres of painstakingly-restored cars in that building and the warehouses adjoining it, the Ford Tri-motor airliner stored there, the most comprehensive automotive library in the land, vintage wooden speedboats, and the streetcars that Harrah acquired to eventually rim the collection. (When the collection was first moved there from its original location on Lake Street in 1961, the admission was a buck and a business card.) Sadly, in the *[27]* years since he passed away *[1978]* the heart of the collection has been decimated, and the building's one-time incredible lore is lost on many Homefinders and tourists as they view it from John Ascuaga's Nugget. I'll save recollections of the HAC for another day, and I have many. This morning the test following the column will be about the building itself.

To weave this tale about the building, necessity requires reciting several givens: California, the late 19th century, was the produce supplier to the nation. The predominant rail carriers were the Union Pacific and Central, later Southern Pacific Railroads. And produce, to be taken anywhere once it's plucked, must be refrigerated. But this column is not about railroads or veggies.

Produce grows in the summer, while ice, much to the consternation of the Pacific Fruit Express, a conglomerate owned by the two railroads, forms in the winter. Others have explored the great heritage of our neighboring town of Truckee, and its confluence of ungodly freezing temperatures, its proximity to the Truckee River, and to sawmills, which produced sawdust as a byproduct, which is dandy for storing ice in once it's been harvested from lakes like Boca Reservoir. Properly stored, ice survived frozen well into the summer months. But this column is not about Truckee's rich heritage either.

The growing volume of produce being moved by the PFE and the lengthening of the growing season due to improving irrigation management began to deplete the harvested ice 'way too early in the season to allow safe shipment. Ice production became a mandate. The PFE elected to build thick-walled buildings to manufacture and store ice in along the waypoints of their rail route. The granddaddy of PFE icehouses was in Roseville, California on the west threshold of the Sierra, and a smaller facility was planned adjoining the SP's railyard in Sparks. And here I better mention, just to keep Curt Risley happy, that the PFE, which operated autonomously apart from the Southern Pacific, bought ranch land from Curt's grandfather, along Glendale Road at Stanford Way (named for railroad magnate Leland Stanford, natch.)

The main building was erected by PFE in 1920; additions to the compressor and tank rooms were made in 1924, along with a bunkhouse, blacksmith shop, cookhouse, dining room and a well house. The plant could manufacture 330 tons of ice daily in the sub-freezing building (I recall reading once that when the facility was operating full-bore it was Sierra Pacific Power's largest electric customer.) Peak storage was 19,500 tons of ice, but the typical daily storage was 150 tons, with another 150 tons stored at the dock.

Old-timers can remember a roofed white wooden platform extending 1,800 feet in both directions from the icehouse, which could accommodate 86 produce cars on either side – 172 cars could be iced at once. The ice was delivered to the long icing platform by conveyor and then along its length by a conveyor chain. The conveyor delivered 37 300-pound blocks a minute (an ice-forming mold is on display in the Sparks Heritage Museum.)

When the trains were spotted, the men – all PFE employees – would slide the blocks off the delivery conveyor onto a hinged section of planking that could be dropped onto the edge of the hatch on the boxcar being iced. (The cars had bunkers in both ends.) The icing crew was usually 20 men, two men working on each car.

In the early 1950s small-scale diesel engines and refrigeration equipment had reached a point of cost and reliability that made it realistic to equip produce cars with individual refrigeration units, and boxcar icing began to go by the boards. By 1958 the yellow PFE rolling stock had been converted to mechanized refrigeration, the Sparks PFE icehouse was closed, and the long icing platforms were dismantled.

And in downtown Reno, Bill Harrah, whose auto collection was growing by Maxwells and Reos, struck a deal with the Southern Pacific/PFE and created the best all-afternoon two-dollar show in town for families and auto collectors alike, a civic treasure that would endure for two decades.

Many thanks to Reno railroad historian Dale Darney, for his help and research on this yarn…

John Ascuaga and Dick Graves – what a break for Sparks that they met...!

Leave Nothing to Chance

A recent recollection of Happy Bill Howard, the Nugget's flagpole sitter, brought a flood of calls and pleasant reflections about the Sparks Nugget from the Homefinders. This prompted me to recognize that we should probably spend a couple of weeks soon, poking around the little Nugget café in downtown Reno where the first Awful-Awful sandwich was built. That 1950s culinary technology was transported to the downtown Reno Nugget, from Boise, Idaho by John Ascauga, then Dick Grave's food manager, and finally east to the Rail City – the town, not the casino – where the Sparks Nugget started in a little coffee shop on the north side of B Street/Victorian Lane. It soon expanded next door into Baker's Grocery and later into Ed McDonald's adjacent furniture store that Dick Graves rented to house Trader Dick's Polynesian restaurant – a name some say he lifted from Trader Vic's (Bergeron) in San Francisco. The rest is history.

But, I'm getting ahead of myself. The stuff above is my own recollection but quite a bit of research beckons before that column comes out of the barn. I was reminded this week that the original Trader Dick's had several caged monkeys at the entrance to add to the South Sea flavor, that were eventually dispensed with because the little beasts kept escaping into the restaurant. No word as to where they went next, but some readers remember that there were some particularly good real estate columns written during that late-1950s period of time. *[No newspaper readers knew what I meant by that when the column ran; the inference was to the old theory "give enough monkeys enough laptops and enough time, and you'd wind up with a passable real estate column." I think it was biblical.]*

Another e-mail was of the legend, purportedly a Basque saying, that rimmed the four walls of the old (and present) coffee shop: "Heresto Pands Pen Dasoci Alhour Rinhar M Les Smirt Hand Funl Etfri Ends Hipre Ign Bejus Tand Kindan Devils Peaks of No Ne." Work on that for a week – many of you will readily remember it – and next week I'll offer a translation into English.*

One last Nugget item for this morning came from Les Conklin the Younger, who reminds us that when the City of Reno adopted parking meters in the mid-1950s, the Nugget's then-owner Dick Graves lost no time in acquiring a parking meter from somewhere, planting it in front of the Sparks Nugget, which was then still on the north side of B Street. He put a chain-link fence around it with a big scary sign *Do Not Feed This Animal!*

as a little in-your-face gesture of friendship to Reno. I labeled Graves as a marketing genius in last week's piece and this stunt drives that point home. (Several readers wrote that Graves' slow, almost stodgy temperament belied the wheels that were constantly racing inside his head.)

• • •

**["Here stop and spend a restful hour, in harmless mirth and fun. Let friendship reign, be just and kind, and evil speak of none."*

Dick Grave's daughter called later, to remind me that Graves, aside from being a marketing genius, was also a fine pilot, shuttling his own Ryan Navion between Sparks and Boise.]

In our lifetime, a neighborhood changes, flourishes, then wanes and rises again…

Walkin' Wells Avenue, ca. 1970

South Wells Avenue was once a happenin' little shopping area. New, modern buildings were being built to accommodate merchants seeking a compromise between downtown and the Park Lane/Shoppers' Square malls – then the only two malls in Reno. South Wells Avenue is 22 blocks long, too far to walk, so for this morning and probably a follow-up next week we'll hopscotch around instead of going block-by-block. The inspiration for all this? Twofold: The Reno City Fathers – and Mothers – are toying with a major redesign of Wells Avenue, with new landscaping, street lighting, and single lanes leading into traffic go-arounds at several locations. *[And we now know how the go-arounds went over…*] Secondly, a restaurant that opened during the heyday of the street, closed a week or so ago – a landmark that started and ended an era.

We'd like to recall what the street once meant to our town's economy and lifestyle.

• • •

Cruising through newspaper ads, old Yellow Pages, City Directories, county records and other clutter pointed us toward the mid-1970s as the glory years of Wells Avenue. It's seems eerie that McDonald's, which opened in June of 1975 on the corner of Colorado River Boulevard, recently closed. (Few businesses in the last century had better demographic foresight than McDonald's, and their closure is indicative of the ebb and flow of a neighborhood's viability.) The Wells Avenue McDonald's was the third in Reno, following closely behind the original store on Keystone and the second on Oddie Boulevard (both those structures replaced in recent years.) Across Wells Avenue was Wayne's Drive-In, soon to become a casualty of Mickey D's proximity. The Deluxe Laundry north of McDonald's was one of McKenzie Construction Company's first buildings in Reno, ca. 1952, and is still active in business and under the same ownership. *[At production time, it's for sale, business and building.]*

Restaurants – good ones – abounded on Wells Avenue. A favorite watering hole for business people was Posey Butterfield's, later the Rapscallion, on the corner of Vesta Street. A Mandarin Café was across from McDonald's, great Chinese, no relation to the classic Mandarin downtown. We once wrote of old service stations becoming the best restaurants in Reno, and the Gulf Oil station that became Froggy's Lunchbox, just north of McDonald's is one of them. (You may know it better as P.J. and Company.) A base chapel was hauled down from Reno Air Base to the corner of Vassar and Wells, bricked over and made into Little Flower Church, somewhere between 1949 to 1951, depending on your resource. Now a bank, it was banker Sid and Vera Stern's macaroni joint in Wells Avenue's heyday, proving that all good Wells Avenue buildings, including Catholic churches, start or end as restaurants. *[Sid and Vera Stern were Nevada First Thrift's philanthropic founders, putting a thrift branch in the old church soon after Little Flower opened on Kietzke and East Plumb. Wonderful friends both, Sid has left us; Vera's still a community asset and a fun one.]* Then we have the restaurant that became an office building, the Dairy Queen just north of Vassar; if you look real hard you can see the old building where we ordered Peanut Buster Parfaits. And we can't forget Juicy's on Ryland, for a great burger in the lube bay.

South of Posey's was Humphrey's Furniture, a fairly large store. Another major furniture store in Reno was Baker's Furniture south of Arroyo Street, which had its origin as an Eagle Thrifty drug store, with a pharmaceutical warehouse in the south end. It then became Baker's, then Good Morning Furniture, then closed. Eagle Thrifty moved across the street into a new building, with the greatest shopping variety in Reno, a true super-drug store. Name it, they'd have it in that great basement of theirs. That store, as did all Eagle Thrifty's, became Raley's, and that Wells Avenue Store is now an IGA outlet. *[And nearing press-time, an independent Mexican mercado.]* Many small retail buildings were built in the 1960s, some pretty clever and well-designed. Check out the building on the southwest corner of Wells and Roberts Street: architect Web Brown incorporated five distinct architectural styles into one retail building for the Eccles family. Landlords had little trouble finding quality, long-term tenants, in all categories of merchandise – Brundidge's Art Supply, Don Hackstaff at your service; GoodTimes Clothes with Pete and Linda Sanetra; Lear-Higdon Opticians, Roy Lear and Frank Higdon transplanted from Hamilton Opticians downtown. Frank fitted me with the first contact lenses in Reno, in 1956. Tapis Tree Needlework. Crown Electronics, Wok-on-the-Wild Side kitchen stuff, Whippy's Golf Shop, Reno Ski Shop. Pants Etc., Earl's Western Wear, Sierra Custom Sound, Greco's Music Store, Murdock's, Sierra Cyclery. Aids Ambulance operated out of a building at Stewart Street, their name proving to have an unfortunate connotation in years to follow.

And services: a half-dozen pet stores, another half-dozen cleaners, beauty shops and barber shops galore, Corrigan's and Ryan's saloons and the Wonder Bar, dentists and optometrists, Art Remple Television, a Valley Bank and a major post office (at Ryland, now a hock shop; it still has the brass federal postal eagle insignia in the southwest corner.) Many government offices – State and federal – in the small buildings around Posey's. A block-square vacant lot to play ball in north of Wonder Street, owned by LaVere Redfield, the water table about four inches below the ground hampering its use as a building site until relatively recently. Cornwall Insurance Adjustors, and two rhyming diners, Eato's Burritos and Pat-Your-Belly-Deli, and that's where I draw the line.

South Wells Avenue was a great street, and could be again. In the years following World War II 37.2 per cent of the schoolkids in Reno lived within two blocks of either side of the street and continue to harbor a fierce loyalty to the neighborhood even today. The Wells Avenue Gang – a group formally organized about a decade ago by the late Clark Santini – meets regularly and will probably read this and regale me, I of the Whitaker Park bunch, with tales of their youth.

But this is not a column validating their aberrant behavior, rather a plea for all to remember fondly the many businesses and merchants who populated South Wells Avenue, and hope that in time to come the municipal plans to revive it will meet with great success.

The Wells Avenue Trench

In the brouhaha over the downtown railroad trench, another forgotten local engineering masterpiece –that we also didn't get to vote on – would go ignored, were it not for the efforts of Don Richter, who contacted Carmine Ghia of our research department with facts about the Wells Avenue Trench. Actually, a tunnel, but I'm trying to salvage this lead.

Richter, we all remember, soared to renewed popularity last summer when we revealed him to be the parking valet at Eugene's in the early 1960s, who would always have the sedan awaiting precisely as a party of diners walked out of the restaurant. A Sigma Nu, he graduated from the University of Nevada and took a pay cut to leave Eugene's and sell insurance, as he still sells even today.

Last week we walked South Wells Avenue and I predicted a spate of lame Wells Avenue Gang recollections and promised to avoid writing about them at all costs, but Don's recollection is just too good to ignore. Every facet of it has been independently verified.

• • •

On a bright afternoon soon after World War II, two playmates whose names are Eddie Pine and Jim Miller left the brand-new Veterans Memorial School on Vassar and Locust to walk to their homes, across South Wells Avenue from each other on the corner of Claremont Street. Crossing Wells was difficult, even then, because the new underpass connecting Wells to Highway 40 – East Fourth Street – made it easy for a lot of cars to use the street to get to southern Reno. It would be easier for Eddie and Jim, and the hordes of other kids that lived on the east and west side of South Wells, to get together if they had a tunnel between their houses.

So Jim and Eddie began to dig, in Jim's front yard. They spent an afternoon digging, moving not a great deal of earth with only the one shovel that they had, taking turns. But they made a small dent in the task. The tunnel was underway.

Jim's dad, Walter, came home from his job managing the downtown Sprouse-Reitz department store, and assessed the new hole in his front yard. The boys explained their endeavor and then dove for cover, expecting the worst.

"You boys need another shovel? Maybe a pickaxe?" Walter offered. The boys concurred that more equipment would be good. While they were digging the following afternoon, Walter came home and brought them another couple of shovels and picks.

The dig continued; a few more of the Wells Avenue Gang – now comfortable that they weren't going to wind up in the soup for digging up the Millers' yard – joined in. Walter brought a few more shovels.

The hole grew – two, then three feet deep, from the size of a card table to a four-by-eight blanket. A rope ladder was fashioned to get down into the pit. Still more kids showed up each day to help, bringing their own shovels.

As the hole reached five feet in depth, a bucket-brigade type of excavation system was devised. Walter brought some buckets. Kids were making a pilgrimage from Veterans School to Wells Avenue. Grownups were starting to stop by and watch. Even the girls in the student body were chipping in; digging, hoisting the buckets, barrowing the dirt to the growing tailing pile alongside the Millers' home. The hole was approaching eight feet deep, now getting a little soggy during the day, easing the afternoon's dig.

Walter came home one day and noted that the hole was close to the requisite depth, and soon the direction of the excavation would turn toward the sidewalk, then under the street to Eddie's yard. The neighborhood excitement was almost overwhelming, and the whole education structure at Veterans Memorial was going to pot while this project moved ahead.

But, Walter said, could you guys just level the floor of the hole a little bit in *this* direction for a few feet before starting toward the street and the Pines' house? And so they did.

The time was approaching to start the stope under the street. They perfected the floor of their cavern, by now over eight feet deep, the work product of scores of their classmates. And all the while, the neighbors to the site and the teachers at Veterans Memorial, acutely aware of the excavation, scratched their heads in wonderment about what was going on on the corner of South Wells Avenue and Claremont Street, and why wasn't Walter Miller coming unglued?

Eddie and Jim decided that the hole was deep enough. The tunnel would begin.

• • •

Virtually the entire student body of Veterans Memorial School marched from the school on the afternoon that the hole would start becoming a tunnel, picks and shovels over their shoulders, boys, girls – researcher Ghia was unable to confirm that they were whistling "Hi ho, Hi ho…" but it could have happened that way – this yarn is basically founded on fact.

They approached Jim's house, ready to go to work and turn the bore toward Eddie's yard. Then they looked down into their excavation.

Resting on the floor of the pit was a tank – a brand-new, black furnace oil tank, about four feet around, and five feet long.It's probably still there.

• • •

The kids got a good laugh out of it, for they all knew deep down that a tunnel was out of the question, but didn't know how to call off the project. And we're told that Walter made it right for the whole neighborhood. He's since passed away, but is remembered as a pretty good guy by the Wells Avenue Gang…

God bless those who dug, Walter, and America.

Some folks, the University Mace, a mother's shamrocks from the Emerald Isle, theaters and darn good trivia...

FLICKS AND QUICKIES

[Often while cutting-and-pasting the old columns, I found leftover squibs too short for chapter treatment but too good to throw away. Here's some examples:]

How in the world would I know that Walter Baring worked at McMahan's Furniture as a salesman in the very early 1950s if one of someone didn't call me? *[This following a "why did you leave Walter Baring's name out?" of McMahan's on Commercial Row during a downtown text "walk."]* Baring was a dandy, went to Washington in 1956 as our Representative in Congress, our only one in those days as Nevada had only one seat. "No one likes Baring except for the voters," was the accepted mantra in Nevada politics – he served us in a long series of two-year Congressional terms until 1972, when he had a cardiac problem only days before the primary election. And true to form, Baring didn't hush it up. He got beat by a relative nobody in the primary by playing off his formidable incumbent's health problem; the nobody in turn got beat by another nobody in the general election. Baring could have covered it up, won both elections and remained Representative until today, (notwithstanding the fact that he died in 1976, but as we see in the CNN sound bytes of several dinosaurs every evening – presence of pulse, respiration and temperature are not necessarily requisites of congressional delegates.) The one-time furniture salesman got a major street named after him in Sparks, and in retrospect, he was a hell of a Nevadan.

• • •

A reader a recent column about downtown Reno took umbrage that I didn't mention Fenwick's (art supplies) on Sierra Street just south of the tracks – I pointed that store out in a column last summer but I don't mind saying it again: Fenwick's was a wonderful store, and Jerry Fenwick remains today a northern Nevada history buff and the keeper of an extensive bygone day-photograph collection, and who, like historian Neal Cobb, is happy to let the community enjoy the old photos and has arrived in the 21st Century ahead of most of us – computer-wise – and is hard at work digitizing old local photos.

• • •

Or, you might like this one – this firsthand from Clayton during our many "Tuesdays with Clayton" before he passed away: Two popular Reno couples, Virginia and Clayton Phillips, and Nevada and Sessions (Buck) Wheeler, were sitting around a campfire in northern Washoe County many years ago – four late Nevadans who knew our state like the backs of their weathered hands, and loved every acre of it. They dreamed up an icon that night: a baton, embodying all the elements of our state. Over time, they found a suitable piece of native mountain mahogany. Onto it they bonded some Carson City-minted cartwheels, some gold, silver, copper and other ores that Nevada produces; they affixed sprigs of sage and pine and fauna indigenous to our state and a host of other souvenirs embodying Nevada, like chips from some old casinos.

They presented the mace to the University of Nevada, where annually University Provost Alessandro Dandini, a legend in his own mind, raised it with great aplomb just as Professor Post cued the orchestra to begin Pomp and Circumstance. Count Dandini then carried the mace on high as he led the graduating classes onto the Quad for Commencement, as did Rollie Melton in the years to follow. At Clayton's memorial service a few years ago, where the featured music was *Home Means Nevada*, natch, the question was asked several times: *Where is the mace now…?*

• • •

Next time you're stop-and-going along Kietzke or Longley Lane, remember that either the guy behind you or the one in front of you, or both, aren't trying to go north nor south, but in reality to the east or west, but have to get around that great big long airport runway that a young Realtor named Karl Breckenridge (the Elder) wanted to tunnel under when the costs were still minimal. Ol' Dad about got a net thrown over him for irresponsible babble like that – how ridiculous! A tunnel or trench?

And the moral is that some ideas are wonderful, but become less so as the infrastructure grows and costs skyrocket. End of trench commentary, no position taken. *[For now]*

• • •

On the Saturday nearest St. Paddy's Day each year we usually run the story of a shamrock – this year we'll abridge it a bit to give it a rest. The shamrock in question arrived yearly from Ireland just before March 17th, to be placed on the grave of a young Irish U.S. Air Mail pilot who crashed in 1924, while trying to drop a wreath at an Air Mail mechanic's funeral service in the cemetery behind the present ATO fraternity house. The leaf was mailed until the war years from the Emerald Isle by the pilot's mother. After a number of years the shamrock quit arriving, but the tradition was resurrected a score of years ago by northwest Reno resident Barbara Rabenstine, who will journey tomorrow *[written March 16, 2002]* to Mountain View Cemetery to place a shamrock on the grave of William Blanchfield. Barbara, a friend and fine lady, has the dubious distinction of being a resident – three years old at the time – in the home that Blanchfield's DeHavilland mail plane crashed into. By the luck of the Irish, Barbara, her sister Betty and her family were away from the home at the moment of the crash on that hot August afternoon.

Next time you're riding about up by Whitaker Park, check out that home at 901 Ralston Street, the only residence in America built by the U.S. Government, appropriated following a debate that took place on the floor of Congress. The solons concluded that since a federal airplane wrecked the home, the feds should rebuild it, and so they did. If you're in that neighborhood, we'll point out another home with a story, at 752 West Street, a home designed by Death Valley Scotty's architect and later the residence of a University of Nevada president.

[Yes, the U.S. Air Mail airport by the present Washoe Golf Course was named Blanchfield Field in his honor, to be officially shortened in years to follow to the more obvious Blanch Field.]

• • •

A recent column "killed" the YMCA too early, in the words of Neill (two-ells) West. The boiler blew and the 1911 Delongchamps building was razed by the ensuing fire three years *after* our 1950 walk, which I meant but wasn't what the text conveyed. Neill was an Alpha Tau Omega fraternity pledge in 1952 and was working in the building, where he probably met Les Conklin the Younger, while Les was lifting weights when the building exploded. (No doubt buffing up for a career selling heavy fur coats a block to the west for 40 years.) Les questioned the date too, and I thank them both. (Too many notes – I was researching our walk downtown and the fatal Greyhound building fire at the same time, a fire that did in fact predate 1950 by two years. And I'm too old for multitasking.)

• • •

We'll throw this out to get the pot boiling a little: Realtor Paul Crooks supplied a 1958 photo of Crooks Bros. Tractor Co. on two-lane Glendale Road, which he reported to be the first building ever built by real estate magnate John Dermody (and I suspect was actually constructed by

McKenzie Construction.) It's still visible as the core building of mighty Cashman Equipment, your local Cat dealer.

• • •

And, to the flicks:

To hear from three favorite correspondents in one week is a thrill, and this week Pauline Carpenter, Neill West *[text preceding]* and Nevada history heavy-hitter Richard C. Datin all checked in.

Richard is a gentleman. A historian and prolific writer, and a nationally regarded authority on Nevada's railroads, he's more entitled than most to derail me for an error, but only pleasantly nudges me that "…the Reno Theater you mentioned last week as being next to the Wigwam cafe, was actually just south of the Overland Hotel on the east side of Center Street." He's right, of course; an old photo at the Nevada Historical Society shows the "Nevada" theater, not the "Reno," next to the Wigwam Café, from 1942 to 1948, when it became the "Crest." Mea culpa.

About 22 of you all claimed to have the neat clock, the one that we all remember over the fire exit of the Crest with the white hands and blue-neon rim, hanging in your dens. Several people recalled never, ever sitting under the massive chandelier in the Majestic Theater. (That chandelier's featured in 1920s brochure about the Delongchamp's rejuvenation of the Majestic.) Several readers mentioned the wide seats – about a seat-and-a-half/three buns) – on the ends of alternating rows in the Tower theater, so that no seat was directly behind another. Those who would neck in public places, the Pagans, generally grabbed those wide seats first.

I mentioned that the Granada had no loges in 1950, prompting Pauline Carpenter to scold me for forgetting that the Granada had loges and balcony seating until a 1953 fire trashed the inside of the theater, when it was refurbished with no upper deck. And I never argue with any lady who was a head Granada usherette during her senior year at Sparks High School (maiden name Pauline Keema). Nothing escapes you readers…

• • •

And then I wrote: Sarah Bernhardt would be hopping mad: The tiny 3,800 square-foot office building in Sparks that Joe Mayer and I eke a living out of has four handicapped parking spaces, with two or three usually in use. The new art museum on Liberty at Hill Street? Four handicapped parking spaces. Go figure…

This was a sleepy week with just too much time on my hands...

School names

Our *[late, July of 2003]* classmate Tom Jensen (RHS '59) won the Silver Pen award a while back for his letter to the editor of the Gazoo, regarding the naming of two new Washoe County schools. I've opined in columns past that that honor should be limited to a person who received at least one paycheck from the Reno, Sparks, Galena, Glendale, Nachez, Gerlach, Steamboat, or later the Washoe County District. After talking to Tom, I have changed my position. I realize now that some weight should be given to a foreseeable nickname of any named school's team mascot, worst-case example: the Echo Loder Odor-Eaters.

We could easily have been stuck with the Wooster Roosters, the Greenbrae Packers, or the Glenn Hare Cottontails. The Gerlach Holmes are elementary, Watson, as are the E. Otis (Vaughn) Elevators, the Donner (Springs) Partiers, or the Roy Gomm Bommbers, (opposed by Gomm's Moms' Club.) Or the Lemmon (Valley) Drops, the Lincoln (Park) Logs, the little Brown Jugs and the Lois Allen Wrenches.

We could have encountered the Alice Maxwell Smarts playing the Darrell C. Swope Dopes until they were all (Katherine) Dunn in; fortunately Swope inherited its "Panther" mascot from old Central Jr. High first. I was in the first Central student body, the one that chose that mascot. Our late classmate Margaret Eddleman (RHS '56) designed the Panther-head logo that's still in use at Swope even today. Then there's our coach Bud Beasley; surely the students at the elementary school honoring him might have been called the Beasley Batsmen, for Bud at 92 years young still booms out *Casey at the Bat* the way sportswriter E. L. Thayer meant it to be delivered: *Strrrriiiike Twoooo!!*

Pity that some of our favorite teachers and principals don't have a school named after them (yet!). David Finch's inevitable school's feathered mascot is obvious, (at least to everybody but the late Finch, a legend albeit a man not long on humor. Read the chapter.) But how 'bout the (Betty) Morris Chairs, a team to play against the Libby Booths? Betty was the dynamic kindergarten teacher for a score of years at Jessie Beck Elementary School, whose first principal was Jim Puryear, who was my nomination for a new school name in the last naming go-around. Central's vice-principal Chester Green deserves a school, surely to be the Green Hornets, as does Central's first principal – doesn't this school board realize that we could have a playoff between the Chauncy (Burger) Kings and Robert (Dairy)

McQueens? Seriously, Morris, Finch, King and Green deserve their own schools. And Puryear. And Gonda and Benson and Muth. And more.

But returning to the business at hand, if you don't like those fast foods above, how about a (Ted) Hunsburger (Elementary) with fries but not French, or a Big (Effie Mona) Mack? Or the great elementary school team, the Anderson Split Peas? From southeast Reno, the (Edward L.) Pine Nuts, Potatoes (Robert) O'Brien from Stead or a slam-dunk nomination, the (Glenn) Duncan Donuts. The late Nevada historian/author/RHS teacher Effie Mona Mack never got a school name, by the way. Should have… Pet peeve of Reno High alums: It's Huskie, not Husky; sportswriters and spellcheckers take note.

Galena High beat out Agnes Risley Elementary for the Risley Grizzlies. But Galena is a school that could easily merge with another school, as could Mount Rose Bullis Elementary, Florence Hunter Drake Lake, and Ga-Lena Juniper, whose mascot could be the Juniper Berries if the late Peavine elementary schoolmarm Bernice Berry doesn't get her own school named after her. Bea was a dear lady, a family friend for 50 years, who passed away just months after her 100th birthday last September. Rose Bullis is the reliable archivist for the school district – if Rose doesn't know about it, it hasn't happened yet. And Rosie don' know 'bout this column…

A few notes are left over, of our late favorites Marvin Picollo, P.E. teacher Ed Van Gorder, and Nancy Gomes. They got their names on schools – Van Gorder Elementary's mascots should probably be the SweatSox.Everyone remembers Marv Picollo as a fine administrator, and those of us who had him as an RHS English teacher recall that he could also ski our butts off come the weekend. This column started in fun but I now realize that there are scores of dedicated educators – many who don't have schools named after them – who deserve some RHS alumni attention, like our late contemporaries Neil Fockler, Becky Rose and Kenny Vaughn, who left us, too young.

I was going to wrap this up by throwing in the (Mamie) Towles – a boxing expression, and pointing out that it's a (Rita) Cannan – a premium brand of towel – but I won't ensnare these two fine old principals who both had elementary schools named after them with that sort of hi-jinx. (Miss Cannan was normally a warm lady – a Mrs. See's Candy-box look-alike – but I can still feel her icy stare when she cracked the whip at Mary S. Doten in 1948.) This ain't over yet – stay tuned.

Careful, there's a test at the end...

The big black Beetle on the fire station

While strolling East Fourth Street in a column a few weeks ago, I promised a story about the great big black widow spider atop the old Morrill Avenue fire station.

Well, for openers, it's not a black widow or a beetle, but a scarab – we should have known, since it's made from an old VW, and it only has six legs (a spider has three more.) How did it get there? Away we go, all together on a Saturday morning.

In 1977, an artist named David Fambrough operated a business with his family – his mother is Jill Fambrough, who like many others was a stripper before she was a Realtor (with Prudential Nevada) – but not what you're thinking. The Fambrough business was The Stripper; it stripped furniture for refinishing and was located in a Quonset hut 'way out on South Virginia Street (it's still there), where if it blew high as a kite, as furniture stripping businesses all do, it wouldn't vaporize anyone but the Fambrough family.

David, an accomplished artist in bronze, marble and steel as well as restoration and maintenance of fine art (he was curator of the extensive Wilbur May collection and has cared for Picassos and Modiglianis), was also somewhat of an Egyptologist. One day while sketching a scarab, the national bug of Egypt, he noticed it's similarity of silhouette to a VW Beetle. He looked out of his window at the carcass of a Veedub sitting alongside a pile of irrigation pipe in a field on the Double Diamond ranch where his business was located. He looked at his drawing, and back at the VW. *Voila!* The cowboys at the ranch told Dave he'd be doing them a favor to get rid of the stuff, so the scarab was born and built, to sit alongside the Quonset barn for several years. (He later made several others, a duplicate of our Reno scarab that was placed in Mound House east of Carson City, and third we'll learn of in a moment.)

Enter now George Benny, who gained color of title to the Double Diamond Ranch and the River Inn on the old Lawton's site west of Reno. Before earning himself a stay in a federal gated community for several real estate transgressions gone wrong, George kicked The Stripper, David Fambrough, and all his bugs off the Double Diamond spread. The third beetle was loaded in a trailer when some miscreant stole the dismantled beetle, trailer and all. So – should you see a black '28 Dodge coupe atop six irrigation-pipe legs somewhere in *Homefinder* country, David would like it back. Or at the very least, his trailer.

The beetle received national attention, as the focus of innumerable magazine and API wire service stories, even a mighty National Geographic network inclusion in "The Volkswagen as Art." Bill Harrah, in what must have been the last few months of his life, was negotiating to acquire the scarab. David eventually gave the City of Reno the original bug, now resting on the fire station. For the edification of the goat-ropers out in the middle of the state who seem to enjoy this column, I'll try to put an image of it up on my website.

Is David done building scarabs? Not on your life – he'd love to increase the collection. Leave us not forget that a certain percentage of the cost of a public building must now be spent on durable art – David would like to try a Fiat "Spyder" and a Hudson "Hornet" with a giant pin through their backs like a true insect collection. Maybe a DeHavilland "Gypsy Moth" airplane.

A word to the wise to David: a Caterpillar would also enhance the collection, but that big ol' yellow D8 bulldozer may need more than irrigation pipe for legs.

And readers: A spider has eight legs – just testing you…

• • •

Subsequent e-mail from David Fambrough: Thanks for the great write-up, enjoyed it much! especially how mom [Jill] like many others, was a stripper before becoming a Realtor. P.S. almost forgot, Jill is talking to her legal staff, for defamation of character!

[More of David's work can seen on the southeast corner of Moana and Baker Lane – the iron dragonflies. Jill's kidding. I think.]

A Saturday of readers' questions, and text leftover from a few downtown walks...

Walkin' downtown

In an unguarded moment a few months ago I mentioned that if I ever bound these thoughts into a book I'd probably title it *You're going to do* WHAT *to the Mapes?* A better title might be something as boring as *Strolling Downtown Reno*, for it is those strolling columns that seem to draw the most reader response. *[And that I love to write.]* Following a few downtown strolls some notes, questions, and recollections piled up so off we go, the Saturday morning movie at the Tower Theater is just letting out; John Wayne and Richard Widmark beat the bad guys again and The Thing didn't catch us so we'll walk around downtown some more.

Most of the questions that arose were of the "where was the…?" category and while neither I nor my research assistant Carmine Ghia laid awake any nights over them, we can respond to a few: The Club Frisco – don't call it that around Herb Caen – was in the Harrah block of North Virginia Street. Walton's Town & Country Décor was on North Sierra, no known connection to the funeral home of the same name. That brings to mind the new office complex being built south of Del Monte Lane called Mountain View, a name that some out-of-town developer may come to regret. I for one already have too many friends residing in Mountain View, and they don't keep office hours. Someone asked about the Red River Lumber Company; look out East Fourth Street in the 300 block, but call ahead to be safe that it's open. Martin's Cash Grocery was at East Fourth and Evans, and yeah, yeah, yeah, a good column might be of old mom-and-pop grocery stores – I hear that all the time and you're right. Before families had 23 cubic foot refrigerators a trip to a corner grocery – not a supermarket – was *de rigueur* once every couple of days, and I'm cataloguing nearly 60 corner grocery stores in 1950s Reno and Sparks.

The Elk Hotel? On Commercial Row by the Arch Drug, and it had nothing to do with the Elks' Home by the river. (Across Virginia Street was the Stag Inn, a good corner for the antlered.) "What was the Huskie Haven you mentioned in a Center Street walk column?" 'Twas a social, after-school club for Reno's only (public) high school (can you tell that I tangled with Manogue's alumni over a "Reno's only high school" reference a few months back?) Huskie Haven was former fire station on the corner of Center and Ryland, great pool tables, darts, study areas – a good place to hang out.

It closed as a school district-sanctioned facility during the mid-1950s when the Reno School District became the Washoe County School District, but continued on an unofficial basis, hosting dances most Friday nights at the California Building or State Building, and ice skating at Idlewild's ponds during weeknights in conjunction with Parks & Rec. Life was good. And the Huskies welcomed the Sparks and Manogue kids. Primarily their women.

The Western Milk Depot, you asked? East Fourth near Evans, getting the milk cans off the Western Pacific Railroad cars arriving from Sierra Valley every day. When the excellent Washoe (Period) restaurant opened in the old Glory Hole recently, a reader wrote, "wasn't there a Washoe Restaurant in Reno years ago?" Sure was – on Commercial Row. A radio station on Stevenson Street? KOH, on the west side of the street, torn down when the topic of another reader question, the Greyhound bus depot was built. Harrah's wanted the downtown bus station site next to the Santa Fe hotel, primarily so the intervening alley could be abandoned and their properties joined. They acquired the half-block between West First, Second, Stevenson and the alley, then designed and built a bus station then exchanged it for Western Greyhound Lines' terminal on Lake Street, (which curiously was never razed). That transaction was not without public rancor, for a few narrow-minded souls didn't really want a bus station by a beautiful park and the river, knowing as they did that some discerning bus riders feel that there's nothing more satisfying than fine wine and a snooze in a park after a long bus ride. Harrah's prevailed. Imagine that. And closing out Stevenson Street, the early YWCA was on the northeast corner of Stevenson and West First.

The original name of early Reno's premier law firm? Try Hoyt, Norcross, Thatcher, Woodburn & Henley, and why do you ask me questions like that? I'm a street guy, not a name guy. Researching this, Carmine also found an ancient reference to the firm of McCarren & Wedge, proving that we've been misspelling Senator Pat McCarran's name for over half a century now. McMahan's Furniture was downtown, as a reader recalled, on Commercial Row well into the 1960s. *[Somewhere in this book we learn that later-congressman Walter Baring sold finer parlor furniture there.]* No one asked, but Whitehouse Clothiers, Jacobs (clothes) and yikes! – a hock shop were also on early Commercial Row. Soon we'll gather at the all-new Shoofly Saloon near the location of the old Nevada Turf Club.

Harry's Business Machines – a sure Great *Homefinder* Longest-Running Business candidate if I ever get back on that kick – was and is on West Street, just north of the tracks. (Following a couple of GHLRB columns, I was accused of selling out accolades for goods and services, like

I need fuel oil from Washoe Keystone for my gas furnace or Peerless Cleaners to press either of my Oxford shirts.) Harry's owner Gordon Foote is a friend and a frequent contributor. *[GHLRB = Great Homefinder Longest-Running Businesses. Not one of my brighter ideas, in retrospect.]*

Closing notes: The old Temple Emmanuel? I'll mention it again: on the east side of West Street across from old Reno High/later Central Jr. High School. I can't resist including that Kay Fujii's Nevada Nursery was on the south side of North Street, and the Western Pacific tracks ran along the west side of East Street. (East Street, never a dedicated street, actually the NCO/Western Pacific railroad right-of-way, mysteriously became known as *Record* Street relatively recently.)

Keep the questions coming – they're my job security. The Accident-Free Day count at Ralston Foods on East Greg Street, which we're still planning on touring soon, is up to 673 days. You read this first in the *Homefinder*: Greg Street was named for Greg McKenzie (true) and Picabo Street (possibly). Have a good week; go buy a house, and God bless America.

It hasta be pasta

I was reminded by none other than Buddy Sorensen at a recent convening of the Seven-Ayem Senior Moment Krispy Kreme BS and Coffee Klatsch that if I'm going to go carousing around town on Saturday mornings talking about old markets as we have been on-and-off for the past few months, that I'd darn well better pay some mind to the Ferrari family's Food Store, and particularly to include the nickname of a popular member of the family.

That family member's name is Bob Ferrari, who graduated from the original Manogue High School by East McCarran Boulevard at its Truckee River crossing, and went on to letter for four years in both baseball and basketball at the University of Nevada. He enlisted in, and later retired from the U. S. Army, then returned to teach at Sparks Middle School and eventually retired also from the school district. He's now anything but retired in land development – his family recently donated a significant parcel to the Food Bank of Northern Nevada.

But all that pales in comparison to his duties in the 1950s as a grocery delivery driver, taking vittles from hither and yon to the Food Store's customers. On the tailgate of their 1946 Chevy truck was lettered, *Noodles – free delivery*. Thus our friend and Sigma Nu fraternity brother, following a career facing military combat and later the trenches of a middle school – which together should merit sainthood for anyone – came to be known by his friends as "Noodle."

I asked him whether any middle school students called him that or "Mr. Ferrari," and he indicated "Mr. Ferrari, heavy on the 'Mister.'"

• • •

OK – it's fine to have a little fun at Bob's expense and anticipate him walking in to the Coney Island next Monday to a chorus of "Hey, Noodle!" but I owe the family more – the market was one of the stalwarts of our town. It was located in the venerable brick building on the southeast corner of West Second and West Streets, that building itself the subject of a Roy Powers painting in years past. I suspected that the Ferrari family brought their pasta skills from the old country, but learned that no, the family men were railroaders, coming to Reno from Palisade in eastern Nevada. The market was operated by several of Bob's aunts and uncles and finally taken over by his parents, Ben and Nora. The family all pitched in, Bob and his sister Marilyn, who now operates the family's motel in Kings Beach, and their younger brother, the late Ben Jr. – all taking their places in the store's operation while going to school and college.

Bob remembers a great trade within the fashionable Colonial Apartments around the corner, delivering there frequently to some shut-in residents. He recalls a small strongbox in the market that had been ignored for many years being opened one last time when the store closed in 1958. In the box were I.O.U.s from many local residents who had fallen victim to the Great Depression, families that the Ferrari family stood behind in a time of need.

The Food Store was an integral part of early Reno, and I'm glad we finally worked it into a column. Several e-mails asked why I hadn't included it; the simple reason is that we hadn't arrived at any downtown mom-and-pop markets yet. I'm glad Buddy got me moving on it, particularly with the nickname angle. But if you encounter Bob and call him "Noodle," don't tell him you read it here – I think he might have boxed a couple of rounds for Coach Jimmy Olivas while at the University, and I have a glass jaw.

Order in the Courtroom

The columnist's milieu obliges an economy of words; the most critical is during the strolling tours we take about our valley. Occasionally that economy runs completely amok, most recently in a California Avenue walk wherein we learned approaching Creek Place that "...Ellen Creek would later wed the late federal judge Bruce Thompson." Several of you contacted me, but your thoughts, always appreciated, were unusable in this Saturday family outing.

Ellen Creek in fact married Bruce Thompson the very much-alive and vibrant weekend horseman and weekday law partner of Springmeyer & Thompson, who would later be appointed a federal judge. Better?

Now, having the Thompson file open, a few anecdotes about the storied jurist that demand chronicling in these proceedings. The first is of the out-of-town attorney, in Reno to try a case in Judge Thompson's court. The judge's eyes, as was his wont, remained closed for an extended period of time. The visiting attorney, unfamiliar with the judge's proclivity to close his eyes, the better to digest the testimony, stopped and objected vehemently that the presiding judge was sleeping through the trial.

Judge Thompson opened his eyes, looked in the direction of the court reporter, told her to peel back a couple of pages from her Stenotype machine and track him. He then recited, *verbatim*, the last two or three questions posed by the objecting attorney, with the witness' responses, also *verbatim*. He looked at the reporter. "Close?" he asked. "Dead on, Your Honor," she replied. The judge then swept his hand in the direction of the chagrined attorney and, returning his eyelids to their restive state, bade him to please continue. I can't speak as to who prevailed in the eventual outcome of the case, but would surmise that that attorney was on his toes for the balance of the trial.

A second story deals with a trial in Judge Thompson's court involving a heady regional issue and attended by a relatively large number of out-of-town heavyweight attorneys, several accounts at nine, others closer to a dozen – all teeming around the parties' tables in the courtroom.

Things were not going well in the opening hours of the procedure – neither the judge nor the court reporter could sort out the names of this assembled mélange to give instructions or attribution to. The judge declared a recess, and set his clerk to a task.

When court reconvened, the gaggle of counsel reentered the courtroom, each wearing a postcard-sized tag, suspended from his or her neck by a rudimentary piece of twine. On each tag was a number, of a size sufficient to be seen by the judge and the reporter. They wore them for the rest of the lengthy trial. Court watchers are in agreement that it was humbling experience for some, to arrive in our town as legends in their own mind, their names household words in their home venues, to become known as *Attorney No. 11* or simply *7,* if they arrived at a first-name basis.

Such was Judge Thompson in his court. Yakking up this yarn with an elderly Reno woman (oh, OK, my mother), who played bridge almost weekly with the Thompsons in the 1960s and '70s, she appraised the judge as one of the two best bridge players she had ever known, and she's known a few – an invaluable partner but deadly opponent – and ranked Ellen right up there near him. She too recalled his eyes-closed-to-concentrate trait during the opening bidding, and when a slight smile creased his lip, all at the table knew that he was going for a small or a large slam, maybe even a rare grand slam. And he'd make em'.

Many of my contemporaries grew close to the Thompson family through their children, who were our classmates, Dr. Jeff, Judy, and Harold, a prominent Reno attorney. They always welcomed us to their mini-ranch on remote West Plumb Lane, and Bruce and Ellen remained treasured friends as we entered adulthood.

And *that*, Homefinders, was the verbiage that didn't fit into the California Avenue walk column.

•••

In the recent Tombola Day piece, I wrote "…community ladies and doctors' wives." The two are not mutually exclusive; a lady could be both. And I'm not lacking political correctness, heaven forbid, as was suggested by two readers; Doctors' Wives was the name of the hospital auxiliary. And John Iratcabal barbecued lambs for 19 years, not pigs, as you read here. Why would a Basque barbecue a *pig*…?

Big weekend coming up, Homefinders; make it a firecracker, and a safe one. Ride life's bronco to the eight-count bell, and God bless America.

A Grand day at Ralston Foods

Inside what might be the only building in town where an employee could drown in a 200-gallon drum of clover honey, 150 souls have worked together for 1,000 straight days as of last Wednesday, often 24 hours each day, without incurring an injury grievous enough to necessitate any lost time, let alone killing one another. *[We'll update that to a final number closer to presstime*

It was 1,540 days in early May 2005.]

About 1,030 days ago I started watching the "Accident-Free Day" readerboard on Ralston Foods on East Greg Street grow, day-by-day, to about 270 days. Then one January morn early in 2001 it fell to "001." Rats – someone got hurt and the tally had started over. That September I called attention to their 260-plus days of safety in this column, fearful that it might carry the "Cover-of-*Sports Illustrated*" syndrome and trigger an accident. Since then I've frequently noted their progress at the close of the column, often getting an occasional reader call checking on them when I went too long between updates. Somewhere on a computer disc is the text from a column I can't find, wherein I speculated that to keep the "Accident-free" count climbing, an employee's carcass was converted into bran flakes and the evidence resides in 37 supermarkets all over the nation. "Not so," responded George Smith, Ralston's Guru-of-Grain. "That person was from the HR department, and was loaded on Dave Stix' trailer, spread out in the pig pen at the Damonte ranch, but the pigs caught on and grazed all the way around him." Dave Stix is the south Reno rancher who buys unusable or spilled cereal for his feed lot. And this tale, is obviously false. I hope.

How 150 people could escape injury in any facility, let alone in Ralston Foods for 1,000 days boggles the mind – I know of a 30-person office where the acrylic lens of a light fixture fell and put an employee into the hospital overnight. When you visit the plant and watch a railcar load of oats get converted into stacked boxes of little doughnuts that look a lot like cheerios, the 1,000 days of safety take on real significance. Note that I use no capitalized brand names in this column, as Ralston makes cereal for all the grocers, the mighty and small alike.

A bulk-commodity railcar is rolled into the building – railcars roll silently and your visit could terminate right there as it goes over the top of you. A stainless steel, food-grade hopper is slid under the car's outlets – the product is in a sterilized environment from the time it leaves the railcar (and presumably when it was loaded into it.) The car's chutes open and compressed air takes it from the hopper to one of the score of silos in the tower on the east end of the building (the tower with the checkerboard until Ralston Purina – pet food – was sold to Ralston Foods in April of 1994 and the building completely revamped in a mega-million overhaul.) Since the plant's set up right now for a run of rice crispies or corn pops that might take several days, the oats will remain in the silo, then for a day longer while the plant is cleaned and reset to make cheerio-like cereal. An independent nationwide inspection contractor familiar with industrial food plants regularly monitors sanitation. I still have the bump-cap, safety glasses, elastic booties, hair net and earplugs that I wore during my visit, both for my own protection and the preservation of plant cleanliness Struck quite a figure in my booties and hairnet, if I do say so myself. Wish now that I'd remembered to take the hairnet off before I went into Tom Young's Great Basin Brewery after the tour – I the only man there with a hairnet.)

The oat run may start at noon or some wee hour of the morning. The production line, spread over an acre and several levels of the plant, takes life as the silo is vibrated to start the oats flowing onto a belt. Computers guide the conveyor belts' speed, the steam heating the huge cooking vats' temperatures, and the little jets that extrude cooked oats in circles the size of cheerios onto a baking surface where they cook and harden and are then vibrated off into a conveyor – picture an endless stream of cheerios pouring onto the luggage carousel at the airport. That much cereal. If it's nut-'n-honey, lowercase, the computer may have released honey from one side and nuts from the other while a mechanical arm stirred it. There's been very little human intervention, save for keeping an eye on the many computer stations along the route. But those humans have been constantly exposed to steam, scalding hot water, huge stainless kettles far beyond red-hot to the touch, conveyor belts grabbing at loose clothing, compressed air escaping, and an occasionally serious racket at some stops along the oats' journey.

The sea of cheerios moves above us, now being separated into chutes of ever-decreasing size until their opening matches the size of a cereal box. Cardboard flats – supplied by the end-user grocers and preprinted somewhere beside this Sparks plant – are machine-folded into boxes. Rolled waxed paper is mechanically sized, folded and glued into a sack as the cheerios pour into it, and the whole thing falls into the box which is then glued shut. And this doesn't take forever – the boxes fairly fly off the line and are mechanically stacked on pallets, then taken to the west end of the building for shipping. A dry-bulk railcar of grain has been converted to a boxcar of cheerios, and the plant will retool for corn flakes. If you've escaped the rolling railcar, the mile of conveyor system, the steam kettles, the compressed air transfer system, remember a forklift still might get you right here so don't drop your guard quite yet.

Ralston Foods and its predecessor have been outstanding community neighbors and employers in our valley, and in the brevity of this column it's hard to overstate their diligence and commitment to industrial safety – or maybe writing that 1,000 safe days in a plant as complex and fraught with peril as any on the West Coast, says it all. I thank Dan Kibbe, the facility's manager, Steve Smith from Human Resources and the aforementioned George Smith, no relation, for their input and hospitality. They're shooting for two grand on the readerboard above the guard shack on East Greg Street, and we wish all 150 employees good luck.

Now – go eat your morning bowl of cheerios, lower case, with an expanded appreciation of the veritable art forms floating before you.

• • •

[It was the George, the guru-of-grain, that told me that the chicken crossed the road to see his brother Gregory peck.]

On the Loose With Realtor Suess

I once lamented in the column that the street name "Locke" (for long-time pharmacist Bill Locke) was ixnayed by the City of Reno in 1981 because it might sound like "Rock" to a speeding fire truck driver. If that's so, the capitalized street names that follow – all for real and all in Washoe County – should sent the local street-naming committees into overtime for the next few years:

We've a Quail and a Vale, a Dale and a Ruth; a Swaledale, a Gale, a Muth and a Booth;
Ralston and Purina, Sandra and an Arbor; a Marina and a Sandy and one called Harbor.
A Ron and a Dawn, a Von and a Velerie; a Fawn, a Jon, a Hahn and a Mallory;
Stine and Line, Rhein and Pine; Damon and Pythia, Forsythia and Vine.
Molly and Polly, Sally and Rilla, let's not forget Jolly, Valley and Villa.
Suzy Lake and Sphynx, Suzanne and Sue; a street named Lynx and one named Larue.
We know Mall and Fall and Ball, y'all; and Tholl and Wall and (close) dePaul;
(Who sang puff de dragon with dePeter and deMary).
And all of this starts to get scary, with Cherry and Lymbery, Geary and Gary.
We've a Haley and a Bailey, Robb and Clover;
To a fireman they might sound like Cobb or Plover.
Rye and Sky and Nye and Champion;
A Whistle and a Thistle, but what is a *Rampion?*
Bates and Gates, Kate, State and Leather; all seem to rhyme with Tate, Feather and Heather.
Dow Jones or Jones might mislead the man in the firetrucky,
But not half as much as Buck, Tuck or Lucky.
Caballo, Denio, Rio Tinto and Cello; Papoose and Caboose, Pinto and Mello.
Marne, Tarn and Barnes, Carlin and Hodge, they all sound a lot like Marvin and Lodge.
Prater and Slater, Pearl and Earl; Oh! How I wish we'd a street called Squirrel!
Brook Drive and Brooks Circle, and a third street called Brookie;
And if Brook rhymes with *Nanook*, then what rhymes with *Brookie*?

We have Lacy and Staci, Snow and Coe; Tracy and Casey, and old Latigo.
There's a Little Ford and Ford, and indeed, a Taurus;
But Prior and Dyer don't do that much for us.
A Duke and a Prince, a King and a Queen;
Daniel, Daniel Webster, plain old Webster and Lean.
Ben and Ben Franklin, Franklin and tough rhymin';
Bank, Robert Banks, Roberts and Lyman.
Sandra and Dee, Bobby and Darin – this is the place to throw in McCarran.
(Or the towel...?)

• • •

[No one caught me; I had to go to Carson City for "Nye."]

AROUND THE HORN

This morning to break up the boredom, we emulate CNN's Aaron Brown, my favorite newscaster (national, Tad, national), and go "Around the Horn," from the *Homefinder* bureau in Sacramento this week where I'm working, to our far-flung correspondents around the globe.

First, Dateline West Second and West Street, to Sandy Saviers Halley, in response to a recent column about KZTV, precursor of KOLO-TV. Sandy, a headline from you, please.

"I remember when we got our first TV in 1953 – it was a Capehart." A *Capehart*, I scoffed. "Saviers Electrical Products, synonymous with Westinghouse in Reno, and you watched a *Capehart*?"

Closer investigative work from Sandy indicated that Saviers also carried Capehart, and I found some old Saviers ads for not only Capehart, but Blaupunkt, Zenith and Fisher radios and TVs. We could do in-depth research with former Saviers employees Jackie Manoukian Powers, Gary and Janice Lubra, and Jack Hargrove. But our reporter Sandy is always on target.

Next, Dateline University of Nevada, to Reno railroad historian Dale Darney. Dale, your headline please:

"The original tram across Manzanita Lake was wooden – I have a six-foot section of it in our backyard. And my wife Lynn's father proposed to her mother on the tram."

Thanks, Dale. His report was filed after we wrote about the tram, a column that brought a few what's the *tram*? queries. The tram, before the University was developed near the turn of the century, was a timber viaduct carrying the Orr Ditch across a chasm near the south end of the (future) campus site. The chasm was bermed to create Manzanita Lake, with the tram allowing pedestrian passage along the ditch across the new lake. It's actually about 40 feet high above the floor of the lake. And Dale's report triggered an old recollection – the tram was a traditional place, far from the madding crowd, for a young swain to pledge his troth to a nervous coed – quite a few popped the question on the tram in the campus' early years. Later, it became simply "My place or yours…?" And someday we'll tour Dale's back yard; I have the feeling it's a doozy.

We go now to the north end of Valley Road, where *Homefinder* correspondent Misha Miller is standing by. Misha, a headline from you:

"Several weeks ago, when you did the story on Sterling Village, I wrote you about Howard Sanderson, and his barbershop up there. (He's since "relocated" to Vine and the tracks, across from Walton's....) You always knew when Howard (Sandy) was there, because his red Chevy (vintage 1950 or 1952) pickup would be parked in front... My daughter took the grandbaby to have his hair cut, and a sign in the window said he was "closed, but hoped to be back soon." There is now a For Sale sign in his window and a number to call….looks like another Reno treasure is about to "fade" away. Back to you, Karl"

Three generation of shorn locks by a tonsorial artist many locals remember fondly. Thanks, Misha.

Speaking of the surname Sanderson, Dateline Booth Street – a while back we pleaded with school superintendent Jim Hager to replace the "Reno" above the main entry of RHS, where only "High School" remained. Thanks to Dr. Jim, to Dale Sanderson, who, as the facilities manager for the school district is probably the biggest property manager in the county, and to the Buildings and Grounds guys, a shiny new "Reno" stands again over the entrance.

Next, Dateline East Fifth and Wells Avenue and to Don Stockwell, Don, a headline if you will:

"When KZTV first hit the air 50 years ago, one of their popular features was "Home State Sunday" – once a month the station would pick a state and invite former émigrés from that state to the studio on a Sunday afternoon, where the group was televised, a few spoke of some anecdotes and history of the state, and old neighbors were reunited and new friendships were made. It went on for several years after the station went on the air."

Many thanks, Don, good report – were they to rekindle the show today they'd probably have to move it to Mackay Stadium when the California residents convened on their Sunday.

Finally, Dateline Del Monte Lane, to old friend and correspondent Russ Schooley. Russ, your headline this morning:

"An El Reno apartment that I lived in on Del Monte Lane was removed in 1966. It went from Del Monte to Byars Construction's yard at the south end of 21st Street in Sparks, near the river." A check with Terry Markwell, an engineer in those early years with the late Marv Byars, and with Marv's widow Tosca, confirmed that there was indeed a little metal home there, used as a construction office. A visit to the yard, now the home of Lucky Concrete, reveals no building, but a concrete pad with pinnings spaced corresponding to an El Reno's foundation.

Readers have found all thirteen homes shown on the Sanborn map, which seldom misses – is it possible that El Reno developer Roland Giroux bought an extra unit and built this 14th one on his property on Del Monte Lane? The El Reno mystery lives on.

And with apologies to Aaron Brown, that's "thirty" for today, friends (an expression arising out of the old newspapermen's convention of typing *XXX* at the end of their copy, and, aw – who cares?) Have a good week and a thought for our friends in the path of Southern California's wildfires, remember with the Great American Smokeout coming up that 93 per cent of doctors who try Camels go back to their wives, and God bless America. *[And that line never saw print.]*

• • •

[Regarding Dale Darney's mention of the Orr Ditch Tram at the University of Nevada, here's a note that's defied inclusion in a column, but I want it to be in the book:

Readers have asked about the Orr Ditch's "inverted siphon" at the University. In 1959 the Regents approved a tunnel, if you will, from the south parking lot by the Fleischmann Home Ec building, under the Aggie building's parking lot and across Evans Avenue, and resurfacing east of Evans.

The Orr Ditch, which previously traveled 3,100 feet at grade through the campus, was routed into this tunnel, and the weight of the entering water pushed the water in the tunnel back to the surface across Evans Avenue to return to the existing – (100-year-old) – Orr Ditch channel.

This siphon freed up the abandoned channel through the campus, on a route vital to future campus construction. You can easily see both ends of the siphon (when the ditch is running full you can also hear the inlet end!

And, to really get down to the brass tacks of the Orr and siphons, there was at one time a siphon from the Orr on the north side of the railroad tracks, to the Chism ranch on the south side. Gonzo.]

Walkin' South Virginia Street, ca. 1955

So, it's a 1950s walk y'all want. The Homefinders haven't taken a Saturday morning walk for a while, and although there's frost on the pumpkin as I write, by the time you read this it could be a brilliant fall day. Or the dead of winter…no matter, we'll meet on the lawn at the Lake Mansion on California Avenue and South Virginia and trek south to Mt. Rose Street, and return next weekend. Remember the walk rules: Space doesn't permit including every man, woman, child or business along our path, nor a time span from the Civil War to today. We're in our usual 1955-1960 *Homefinder* time warp.

Onward we go across California Avenue with no stoplight, much to the consternation of the firemen in Station 3 across the street. We'll walk by Lyon's Signal service station on the corner (this is an era when almost every corner had one, if not more, service stations, heavy on the *service*.) Past there, Ham McCaughey's Reno Motors was selling Lincolns and Mercury's, in a showroom that would later serve as Codding & Wetzel's ski shop – Hal and Jerry, great guys – then later to become the casino area for the Ponderosa Hotel that would be built to the west of it.

We pass Reno Motors to Con Priess' Kit Carson Motel and its expanse of lawn second only to the University's Quad – many tiny rooms, stretching west all the way to Forest Street. It would later become the parking lot for the Ponderosa. Southward we pass Royal Tire, to have a few other names in years to follow, to the corner of St. Lawrence Street, and popular Glenn Turner Florist.

We'll look both ways and cross St. Lawrence to what my contemporaries knew best as the Del Mar Station, but on the morning of this walk it was Heric's Café, and would remain so for many years. *[We'll learn soon that it was also the Peppermint Lounge.]* The Mt. Rose Market, one I wrote about in columns past was in the south end of that same building; a neighborhood grocer, as most were in that period of time. South past another bar that's had a dozen names, to the Penguin Café, a favorite hangout until well into the 1980s, black-and-white checkerboard floor and all, their fare rivaled only by Ramos' Drug around the corner. Now it's Luciano's original location, still great food. Reno Pet Food was the baby of Don Combs, an incredibly funny guy whose widow Rachael still charms all that know her. Once upon a time a guy could work on his own car and might have gone to Ayres Auto Parts, south of the pet food store, for his plugs, points and condenser. (Do cars still have those gadgets??)

Across Taylor Street, a structure once the Dondero family home, later a laundromat, later still the American Red Cross, still later the KSRN-FM radio studios. South Virginia Street was used-car row in the post-war days, and we'll just stroll past a few car lots now until we get to the corner, once a Richfield service station, later Tom and Suzi Jensen's taco stand.

More car lots as we cross La Rue Street, translating from the French to Street-Street, the most notable lots were Hermann & Wilson's (Chryslers), and Pio's – Pio Mastroianni was an immensely popular Reno businessman whose surname I've never spelled right yet on the first try. At Martin Street, one of the earliest Eagle Thrifty Drugs then the Ox-Bow Motel, Harry's Coffee Shop (later the Olympic) and a Shell Station. (Note the proliferation of great little coffee shops before the fast foods took the viability out them.) Beyond Mary Street, the Pet Emporium where good ol' Tom Jamison now has his Pro-Serv printery and clock shop (clockery?), the Ho-Hum Motel, then Rauhut's Bakery's final location, now an open shell in the building. Two premium furniture stores: Freemont & Humphries, and Sellman & Gravelle Furniture and Décor a few doors to the south. Harry O'Brien, the Smilin' Irishman was in that block before moving out to Glendale Road, Ma Bell had a phone truck garage there for a time, Nevada Traction sold tractors in this block, and we had two bars, Klub 1091 under the Arthur Murray Dance Studio, and the 1099 Club on the corner, and you don't want to confuse one with the other if you're pub crawling. And, a Wash-a-Mat, when "Laundromat" was a copyrighted term. The 1000 block was a busy one.

South of Caliente, the South Virginia Deli and Liquors owned by the Games family, who would build the new Washoe Market on the other end of the block – (it's now an antique store). In midblock was Sprouse-Reitz, ditto antiques presently, and a little building that some say was bootlegged onto Sprouse-Reitz, years ago. In the time of our walk there was a long gap from Arroyo to Pueblo Streets – the El Reno Apartments that once occupied it had all been removed, and the block was vacant for a time before the Sewell family built Sewell's Market and joined the Bates family opening Nevada Bank of Commerce, both in the same building now occupied by Statewide Lighting and more antique dealers.

Another bank across Pueblo was an early First National Bank about which I touched off an e-mail riot sometime back, saying it had the first drive-in window in the state, while even admitting that Joe Sbragia's FNB on Pyramid and Greenbrae, or an FNB in Las Vegas might have preceded this one by a month or two. Touchy, touchy… Rauhut's Bakery occupied the southern part of that building, the best-smelling bank branch in Reno, later moving to their final location to the north, mentioned a paragraph or so above.

I think there was an occupant in what is now Miguel's restaurant prior to Miguel Ribero but can't pin that down. Miguel's became a Reno classic, moving to a building across from the Peppermill for a time in the early 1970s, retaining the older location as the "Cove." Before he passed away he beamed back to the old site; the food there better for extraterrestrials and mortals alike. A good hombre, Miguel was. We'll end this tour at the Office Bar, now Mr. O's, and cross Virginia Street next Saturday to Bill Stremmel's new Volkswagen dealership, then catch lunch at Landrum's – the Gazoo's buying.

Have a good week, take a Realtor to lunch and the family kayak down to the Truckee's banks and enjoy our new park; congrats to my buddy Skip Hansen, named a Life Member of the Reno/Sparks Board of Realtors, and God bless America.

Strolling the east side of South Virginia

When last we met, we huddled over the shuffleboard table at Paul O'Gorman's public house at South Virginia and Mt. Rose Streets, with a promise of walking north to our cars at California Avenue. I might have stopped too soon last weekend – several readers mentioned the early Safeway superstore in the "Val-U-Mart" Center across Mt. Rose Street, now an auto parts store, and the early Eagle Thrifty Market, later a Raley's, in the present Sports West gym; how could we forget the Cork Room and Spaughi's? and the golf driving range south of Walts Drive bordering the early Vario's, later Cicero's, now Bricks, no apostrophe. Bob Helms and his group attempted for a time to build a hotel-resort on that block-deep site.

Now we can cross South Virginia, near the New York Deli not far from the present IHOP, and Warren's Sav-Mor store, that would later move to Moana West. A slumpstone building next, housing a used-car lot, nearly across from the Continental Lodge, drab now but at one time invisible beneath a façade built around it to replicate a stagecoach, wheels, drover's seat, luggage rack and all – looked like it should hve been on the roof of the Liberty Belle. It was a Richard Graves creation, he the son of the Nugget's Dick Graves, opened as a restaurant with chuck wagon vittles, whatever they are. It did well for many a year. Bill Stremmel built his Volkswagen dealership, Bugging out of his original West Second and West Street showroom. Walking north across Pueblo Street, we find Applewhite Motors, notable only for their pre-FAirview (32) prefix phone number, 3-0000. We have to remember the late Ted Mattson's little office on our path, Ted a fine Realtor, as were Ted's office neighbors Gene LaTourette and the octogenarian Tom McKeown, now running a golf resort in Maui, the poor soul. The Lord smiles down on a few old Realtors. Walking north, Circus Potato Chip's factory, next to my classmate Roy Walker's Thriftee Seat Covers auto upholstery, and the venerable Landrum's – with only seven stools, we strolling Homefinders may have to eat our chili cheese omelettes in shifts.

Crossing Arroyo, well-nourished, we find what was once a White Spot grocery, replaced later by an early post-war retail building that housed a number of shops and restaurants – Martin Furs, Ma Rue Beauty Shop, Brookie's Grill, and every guy in Reno's favorite, Builders and Farmers Hardware. Upstairs was the greatest hardware store known to man, downstairs the most intricate model railroad ever built in Reno – few will ever forget the smell of artificial smoke puffing from the O-guage locos' stacks, mixed with ozone from the big Lionel engines' single-pole motors, plodding their cargo around a couple of hundred feet of track. What a store…

We'll walk past Reno Frozen Foods north of the retail shops, later occupied by Flowers Distributing, which distributed not flowers but OJ and other cold stuff to grocers (kind of like Eagle Service a few blocks to the north during this time period, a mortgage broker, not a place to take your eagle every 5,000 miles for a tune-up.) On the corner, a Standard Station, and have I ever written that in our mid-century time period, a Standard Station was owned and operated by Standard Oil, and a Chevron Station a Standard Oil franchise? I didn't think so. Standard closed this station, and did the only logical thing to do: park reefer trailers all over their lot to be used by the meat-packer next door. In a moment of civic pride, they flashed the underpinnings of the trailers, an only-in-Reno neighborhood cleanup display of solidarity.

Crossing Vassar Street, another service station, this a Signal. Further down the block in a handsome two-story brick building with offices above, the Hansel & Gretel children's apparel shop, I'll write at some peril the largest then in Reno, and one destined to stay in business for many years hence (in Moana West). That South Virginia store became John and Janie Oliver's waterbed store in years to follow and is now an adult bookstore. To the north, a Richfield station through the block to Center Street, later a drive-in, then yet another service station on the corner at Center Street, with a dozen names and operators.

We cross Center Street with some caution, because on this morning of our walk it's still a two-way street with traffic entering from the north toward South Virginia. One of my favorite buildings in Reno was the classy brick Shoshone Coca-Cola bottling plant, the gleaming stainless steel bottling line visible in the huge south windows, a parade of pale green Coke bottles being squirted full and capped right before our eyes, boxed in wooden cases, and loaded onto the yellow, red and white delivery trucks in what's now Restaurant Equipment and Supply Company's parking lot. A modern industrial miracle when the Farr family, nice people, opened it right after the war. Down the street across from Martin Street was and is Pangborn (then Pangborn & Douglas) CPAs, now the lair of my buddies David Morgan, Harry Parsons and Roberta, the Grinsell Who Stole Christmas, and onward to the Arctic Circle Drive-in at the corner. Onward to the next corner to the Q-ne-Q Diner – a stainless steel structure right out of a James Dean Hot August Night poster, where I had dozens of those new "hamburger" things with my dad right after the WWII while he met his buddies for coffee on Saturday mornings.

We see, from the Arctic Circle across LaRue Street, the neon "Barnes Radio" sign that would look so good in my backyard; Jim Barnes a radio pioneer in Reno who at one time had blue license plate W1, and also owned Barnes Cash Grocery on West Fourth Street. During the days when few locals had radios, Jim hooked up his set to loudspeakers and broadcast news of the day and prizefights to a crowd that assembled in front of the store on the Lincoln Highway. At the Cheney Street corner, we opine that the Giller family might have named their defunct ambulance service on that corner anything but "Aids Ambulance," and a few steps to the north, the new Caravan Motel and its legendary cocktail lounge where if the walls could talk, I could write another book. And looking across the street, I'm reminded by my childhood friend Bob Busey that post-Heric's Coffee Shop and pre-Delmar Station, was the Peppermint Lounge, where presumably one so inclined could do the Peppermint Twist. (Other landmarks I forgot last week were the El Borracho watering hole and the adjacent El Dorado Motel. Check out the incredible rockwork on both of them. They were all in my notes – who knows why not the column?)

Approaching the end of the walk lays Savage & Son Plumbing, Nevada contractor's license #10, with its basement chock-full of oddball obsolete fittings and parts awaiting those goofy enough to want to buy and remodel old, picturesque homes with hundred-year old plumbing. *[Savage is still hard at it on Wrondel Way – no basement anymore but their terrific inventory lives on.]*Finally, Dick Dimond Dodge in the attractive, San Francisco-style brick building, later known briefly before its demise as Les Schwimley Motors. And lo, we cross South Virginia Street to the Lake Mansion, our tour completed.

Have a great week, a great Holiday season, and God bless America.

The Levy Mansion

A few weeks ago this column made an almost passing reference to the grand house at 121 California Avenue – the Levy Mansion – and whether the house had been turned on its foundation from Sierra Street, to face California Avenue. And in a second column: why, and when, and by whom. The story came out of the barn in a hurry and brought correspondence with reasons and recollections going six ways to sundown.

As I write this, I have used the famous Ctrl+A+Del keystroke twice, computer geek talk for tossing the whole enchilada and starting over, this third time for keeps as we try to add a little to the local heritage. We'll turn back the clock to the Comstock era of the 1800s:

William Levy emigrated from Germany and opened a dry goods store in Virginia City, later journeying to Reno in 1887 to open the Palace Dry Goods store at 211 North Virginia Street (later the site of the Palace Club.) He had a partner, Herman Morris.

Abraham Goldsmith and his wife had a daughter, Tillie, who would marry William Levy. The year of their wedding is unclear; her name was just-plain Tillie, not Matilda as I speculated, and our newlyweds built a fine house at 471 Granite Street (now known as Sierra Street.) It would cost $14,000 to build; the year of completion is listed variously as 1906 or 1907; I'll go with 1906, a year which enables me to drone on mercilessly about an earthquake taking place to the west in San Francisco, while the architect of the University of Nevada's Mackay School of Mines, Stanford White, was being murdered *in flagrante dilecto* on the roof of Madison Square Garden, which he also designed, only blocks from Tillie's birthplace in Brooklyn…

Contrast that to not a damn thing happening in 1907…

• • •

William Levy passed away in 1920. The Palace Dry Goods store would remain in business for 12 more years.

William and Tillie had two daughters, Mildred, and here it gets a little vague: I have found references to a Fritzi, the other daughter; annoyingly one source shows Fritzi as a nickname for Tillie. I'm staying with Fritzi as the second daughter as I believe the source of that information, accredited below, is superior. Fritzi married William Coblentz, a San Francisco attorney; Mildred never married.

Tillie died in 1938. The two daughters had disparate interests; Mildred chose to live in the family home on Granite Street, while Fritzi, a resident of San Francisco had no interest in the family home. They elected to sever the property into the east and west half of the lot, each daughter keeping one half. The grand home was moved from the easterly half of the lot, to the site of a once-expansive garden to the west. Most sources show this project being completed in 1940 – allowing for lags in telephone books, City Directories and Sanborn maps.

The home was not simply turned ninety degrees, according to Romolo Bevelaqua, who has moved half the houses in Reno for the last half century, is an invaluable source for me, and has forgotten more about Reno than I'll ever learn. *[Rom passed away a year after this column was written.]* A new poured concrete foundation was laid, and the house moved the short distance west onto that new foundation. Several exterior features of the home could not be replaced, accounting for a large set of French doors opening out onto a post-move, non-existent balcony when attorneys Ron Bath and Larry McNabney bought the mansion in 1976. One bathroom was never replaced, but the chain-pull tank high on the wall of the bathroom over a non-existent commode remains. The icebox, huge but not quite a walk-in, was loaded with ice from the exterior of the home in the early days and remained as a storage area after the move. Mildred Levy lived in the home until her death in 1976. The vacant lot created by the move to the east of the home's new location was leased to Lyons & Maffi as a Signal station in 1940, ending its career as a Chevron operated by Obie Dunn when the City of Reno widened and realigned Sierra Street to connect to Plumas south of California Avenue in the late 1970s. The small parking lot east of the building was left over from that realignment.

• • •

The postscript to all this is that research takes strange forms: Recall a recent column when conflicting research of the usual sources took me all over the map, I walked in the Levy mansion in desparation and simply looked around, hoping to jar my memory. Legal secretary Michelle Peinovich, who works in the mansion, was immensely helpful. Now it gets weird:

A Bay Area resident happened to be in Reno a few weeks ago, picked up the RGJ *Homefinder* and idly glanced through, looking at our relatively low home prices. The Levy piece caught his eye, and he took it back to Novato to a friend whom he thought might enjoy it.

His friend's name is Peter Oser. Peter is Tillie Levy's great grand-nephew, and had done his homework before he called me. We had a great talk and I'm deeply indebted to him, as he provided accurate information that might have been lost forever about this great old house and an historic Reno family!

And what luck, that Peter's friend visiting Reno didn't get hung up on the sports page or the Car Guys column, never to make it to the *Homefinder* and get the story back to Peter…

Back to Reno We Go

One of the bright spots in taking walks downtown is that you readers always prompt the next few columns that follow one, and this week we're finally getting to a stockpile of "you forgots" and "where weres?," thanks in advance to phone books, Sanborn maps, Polk City Directories and newspaper ads and a few friends.

You forgot Bello's Tamales, capitals optional because I don't think it never really had a name, just word-of-mouth advertising. The best tamales in town, out on West Second near Washington in an old brick house, corn growing in the back yard, chickens to the west, with a gleaming pressure cooker in the immaculate basement. Father would travel from Ralston Street and place an order in the morning, picking a plump Rhode Island Red sunning itself in the side yard, then return, probably have an Acme beer or two at Brickie's across the street, then take the tamales up the hill to home.

A tamale always tastes better when you look the major ingredient in the eye on the morning before you eat it. And the steel Acme beer can is worth more now in an antique shop that both the tamale and the beer were in 1950.

Where could you buy a Willys Jeep, now in civilian production following WWII? Why, at Steinheimer Bros. Studebaker at West Fourth and Sierra. And don't confuse that with Wiley Brothers Cars, on Plaza Street. Where was Dermody Appliance? On Arlington, then "Belmont," between West Second Street and the tracks. John A. Dermody went from Whirlpools to warehouses, and I'll stick my neck out by saying that Dermody Partners is now probably the biggest real estate taxpayer in Nevada. And he's still a great guy. You forgot Duffy's Tavern. Not really; we didn't walk Commercial Row, between Belmont and West Street, where William Bendix tended the bar. Not really. The main fire station was across West Street, on the northeast corner. Longtime Reno Fire Chief Harry Van Meter saved the bell when the belfry was removed, and it's now displayed on the corner by the new main station on East Second and Evans.

You forgot Chism's Ice Cream. I could never do that. Chism's was the dominant supplier of home and fountain ice cream, a popular, longtime Reno family's business on West Street, in truth existing as a dairy before the turn of the 20th century. Their 1950s patriarch John Chism was an effective Mayor of our town. John and his wife Miriam have passed away, and their daughter and sons' families remain active today in local art circles. Chism's was next to 7-Up Bottling, in their attractive modern glass-fronted building.

What does 7-Up stand for? I don't know, but I'm sure a reader will tell us. *[They didn't.]*

Faithful reader Kellene Gallagher asked once about the USO clubs; one venue they used was the Tropics on Center Street, which I think I tangled up in one column with the Palm Saloon on Lake Street (in Bill Fong's casino.)

You forgot Reno Mercantile, better know as Reno Merc. No, we wrote earlier that it was on the southeast corner of Sierra Street and Commercial Row, in the oldest commercial building in Reno. And I didn't even get challenged for that statement; the Masons built it in the 1870s. Landa Electric? On West Street south of the tracks – once upon a time if your clock or mixer would quit you'd take it to Landa Electric to be repaired. Once upon a time a clock or a mixer could be taken apart and fixed – now they're molded in one piece and we buy a new one. If it was a bigger electric motor, we'd take it to Brown-Milbery, then on Sierra, now on Gentry Way, (known then as Airport Road – couldn't resist throwing that *bon mot* in…)

The one person in town who remembers T.D. Tuthill Inc. asked me where it was. Never heard of it, but finally found it in mid-block on West Fourth Street next to Ruth Ryan's Dance Academy. A fine little lady, Ruth was, taught us all the waltz and fox-trot with the help of pianist Melba Manzo. Many remember her brother-in-law, Gordon Sampson, a much-decorated stuffy Canadian of great swagger who was the president of the Virginia & Truckee Railroad at the time it suspended operation, which was either an honor or a career-ender, depending on your point of view. He wrote his own flowery obit. His life would make a good column for my RGJ compadres who write about legends in their own minds. (That's why I'm a street writer – streets don't try to snow me.)

An argument, and glad it came up because others might have noted it so I can clarify it for the test at the end of the book: "The California Market was on California Avenue, not North Virginia Street as you wrote." You're right, sort of; there were two colloquial California Markets, one downtown, the other at California and Lander which was formally named, but seldom called, the California Avenue Market (another reader suggested it was the California Grocery, also its frequent colloquial name.) It's now My Favorite Muffin. My father worked at the market – rode a bike delivering groceries to the residents of that neighborhood. George Minor opened it, butchers Charlie Bradley and Fred Antoniazzi owned it later.

You forgot the Bundox. OK, OK – that great restaurant and bar, where not a few business deals were cut, was opened by the late attorney E. F. "Bud" Loomis and his wife Cebe, and stocked with Chinese artifacts that

Bud brought out of China when it was closed to Westerners before WWII (he had been overseas as an envoy to China.) He also owned the Oriental-influenced River House Motor Lodge. Another great story for a people-writer. *[Oh, to hell with it – I wrote my own column about the Bundox when they tore it down. Find it in this collection.]*

Roy Stagg's Roaring Camp? Across East First Street from the Bundox in the triangle of East First, East Second and Lake Streets, (and much earlier than the Bundox). That's where Stagg housed and displayed his antique gun collection, which he later sold to Harolds Club for display in the Silver Dollar Bar. The site was the Reno Bus Lines terminal and shop for most of my youth.

• • •

[And if someone tells you that East First Street was originally called Water Street, they're right.]

2 hot 2 rite

Late one evening early this week I take beach chair and aging laptop out under the stars, listen as an airliner in the distance strains against the heat-thinned air for the length of RNO's runway trying to slip the surly bonds of earth somewhere north of Meadowwood Mall, and when the shadow of the grasshopper falls across the trail of the field mouse on green and slimy grass as a red sun rises above the western horizon silhouetting a demure but tautly muscled Indian princess perched with bow and arrow cocked and aimed straight at you it's time for another Corona and man, it's hard to write real estate in the heat of the night and still keep a train of thought.

Veteran *Homefinder* readers know that when the mercury climbs to triple digits this column goes into triple dots – or, an ellipsis, an educated reader would call them – a device freeing the writer of adherence to any known language form, and where did we come up with *mercury* anyway? When's the last time you learned the temperature from *mercury?* I've an analog dial on my fence, a digital gauge in my pickup and lass on the weather channel all reading a hundred degrees...*mercury* indeed – that's kind of like a *dial* tone on your phone...when's the last time you dialed your phone on the little round thing on top with the fingerholes in it? Move over, Andy Rooney, this laptop's cookin'.

My archived e-mail often resembles correspondence from an outpatient clinic for the disturbed – do readers send questions like I get to The Two Guys From The Gazoo also, they being Guy Rocha and Guy Clifton, or save them just for me and my researcher Carmine Ghia?...the natural segue there is to the Two Guys From Italy, and carry the thought forward that at Two Guys' predecessor restaurant, the Big Hat on South Virginia at Moana, the big six-foot white Stetson hat atop the building was rotated by a radar antenna, taken from a naval ship in the infancy of radar after World War II...while on restaurants, where was the Circle RB?...we know it now as Micasa Too (read Two) on West Fourth at Stoker ...and was there a Micasa One?...sort of; it was simply Micasa, in the building on the southeast corner of Mill and Terminal, and if I'm not mistaken Greg Street, the extension of Terminal Way to the north, didn't exist during Micasa's early days...and Greg Street was named for our buddy Greg McKenzie...and the RB in Circle RB (which was a cattle brand) stood for Reno Browne, wife of bullwhip-cracking cowboy actor Lash Larue...isn't three-dot journalism fun? You've read half the column, haven't seen anything that hasn't been here before; the jetliner's about even with Gentry

Way now on its climb, sounds like the nose wheel's finally off the runway, and the Corona's empty.

It's a perspicacious night to bring up old Realtor John Sweatt who actually paid good money to put "Let Sweatt sweat for you" on the side of the old orange city buses; now there's a motto to worm its way into the psyche of homebuyers…ballerinas glow, ladies perspire, John Sweatts for you, what a guy…actually a great guy with a dumb motto…a reader, while I was writing about old businesses, asked why Savage & Son plumbers got rid of their cute little cannibal trademarks on their trucks…gosh, now why could that be?…was there a Cal-Vada *and* a Calavada Motors? another asked… yup, Cal-Vada Jeeps and Calavada Fords, decades earlier, later Richardson-Lovelock, then Bartlett, now Jones-West, no ties in ownership. Reader: I've heard the brick building on Kuenzli west of Wells Avenue housing Street Vibrations has never flooded, even in 1950 and 1955. True?...I'm told that's true; the Truckee channel is at its widest there so the water didn't rise to the building…which, while on the subject, was an old creamery, last used as such by Velvet Ice Cream and Mount Rose Dairy until the late 1950s…note for a future column, in cooler weather: there's a remarkable history of agricultural and livestock-related land usage in and around early northern Wells Avenue's history… *Jeopardy!*, hot night style: to the reader who wrote a couple of weeks ago, your answer is Windmill Dairy, I can't find your question but you'll know (probably prompted by Old Home Milk's inclusion in the Saturday morning movie piece)…

My column on the 1948 Lake Street fire mentioned a tannery, sparking a reader to question whether tanning parlors were really around fifty years ago or I was spoofing you. Think leather, dear, like saddles, no booths…I never spoof…the heat's making me grumpy so I have to ask rangy school superintendent Dr. Robert Hager, tied with petite County Manager Katy Singlaub as my favorite public official and labeled Yogi and BooBoo when they speak at luncheons together, why the stainless steel "Reno" preceding "High School" in my alma mater on Booth Street is missing above the main entry and has been for too long? *[The District fixed the* RE,*" which had apparently been stolen by a rival high school. Bob Hager's still tied as my favorite county official, with Katy.*

A reader chided me after this column ran for stealing a line – "…slipped the surly bonds of earth" – from Ronald Reagan, in his tribute to the shuttle Challenger's crew. Actually, Mr. Reagan and I both borrowed it from John Gillespie Mcgee Jr.'s epic poem High Flight, *known the world around as the Airman's Prayer (Sunward I've climbed…put out my hand and touched the face of God.) I simply have to start lifting my material from more obscure sources.*

And – no more than a week after adding the above footnote to this manuscript about the inclusion of High Flight *in the Challenger memorial, the poem was incorporated into Reagan's Simi Valley memorial service. McGee, a young RCAF pilot, died in 1941 before the poem was published – he'd be proud to be a part of the memorial to a president, over 60 years later.]*

Bud

The outlook wasn't brilliant for the Mudville Nine that day; The score stood 4-to-2 with but one inning more to play...

A cub sportswriter penned a ballad during his lunch hour one spring day, dropped it on his editor's desk – "Use it if you want it" – and forgot about it. Two weeks later, on June 3rd, 1888, the saga ran full-page in the San Francisco *Examiner* and twenty-four-year-old Ernest L. Thayer's *Casey at the Bat* entered the great pantheon of our national pastime, winning him an eventual berth in the Baseball Hall of Fame.

But it would be a half-century later that a true ballplayer would bring Thayer's work to life, from memory and at the drop of a hat, in ballparks, team buses, Little League award barbecues, school classrooms and wherever else the Boys of Summer gathered (that's not politically incorrect, but a collective for the girls and boys gathering for T-ball at Swope School through to Pac Bell Park because they love the game) – when Bud Beasley paused at Thayer's words, *But Casey still ignored it, and the umpire said:*, a delighted crowd of kids of all age and gender boomed out, *Strike two!,* for fifty years.

There was ease in Casey's manner as he stepped into his place; There was pride in Casey's bearing and a smile on Casey's face.

RGJ columnist Guy Clifton penned a superb bio of Bud last Tuesday and I won't even attempt to embellish it, but Bud was a *Homefinder* kind of guy – our teacher, mentor and coach for 38 years of us strong at Reno High School, and in later life deeply involved in many youth organizations, a stalwart of the RHS Alumni Association, a bastion of influence for the Good Old Days club, and a fireball to the very end.

We've got to include at least one Beas anecdote: On the ropes while pitching at Sacramento's Solons Park in a Pacific Coast League game in the 1930s, Bud returned a dinged-up ball to the catcher for another. He got it, but a couple batters later the new ball left the park on a pop foul. The catcher sent out the ball Bud had previously squawked about, so he returned it yet again to the catcher for a better one.

That ball eventually left the field of play, and the catcher threw out a replacement, guess what, the same bum ball Bud had refused twice before. Bud pointed to a fan high in the bleachers above first base and threw the offending ball to the lucky guy for a souvenir. The ump sternly summoned Bud to home plate to render an admonishment, and Bud recalled that he, the umpire, the catcher, and the batter all struggled to keep a straight face for the benefit of the crowd and the dignity of baseball. Such became our sport whenever he was in the vicinity.

Ten thousand eyes were on him as he rubbed his hands with dirt; Five thousand tongues applauded when he wiped them on his shirt.

On Bud's ninetieth birthday he visited Bud Beasley Elementary School – a gathering crammed with tykes agog over seeing the real Bud Beasley, right here in their multipurpose room. I think he spoke to every one of them individually. Inevitably a teacher toward the back said, "Mr. Beasley, how 'bout *Casey*?" and Bud, sensing that it was coming, as it had been in a thousand gatherings before, grinned and answered the call: *The outlook wasn't brilliant...*

If not ten thousand eyes, then at least four hundred, grew wide as the smallish man, already in his later innings, wove the tale of Casey in the animated, vibrant way that Thayer could have only dreamt that anyone would deliver it 112 years after he so casually wrote it. And I noted not just a few adult eyes growing a little misty and that wasn't from the chill December air.

And somewhere men are laughing, and somewhere children shout; But there is no joy in Mudville – Mighty Casey has struck out.

There should be great joy in all the Mudvilles of baseball this week, for we had the pleasure of Bud's knowledge, wisdom and humor, on and off the diamond, for 93 years. We all know that Mighty Casey fanned in the ninth stranding Flynn and Blake in 1888, but last Saturday morning Bud Beasley was ruled Safe, at Home.

Have a good week; tag up on the infield flies, the Homefinders' best wishes go out to Nellie Beasley, and God bless America.

[Bud died July 17th, 2004]

See you next time, Bill

Justice of the Peace Bill Beemer was – at the time of his passing a few years ago – one of the most knowledgeable authorities of the lore of our valley that ever passed through it, his wisdom usually conveyed in an atmosphere of side-splitting humor. The Judge used one long-standing remark to close the many memorial services he officiated. He would remind us that there is no expression of a lasting goodbye for death in the Paiute language; the closest expression that existed for that sentiment was "...see you next time," a pleasant euphemism for a farewell to a departed friend. He'd then recite the expression in the Paiute tongue. Those of us who had attended the many services that he officiated knew that the closing was part of the liturgy and we anticipated its arrival as the final compliment to a friend – the Judge bestowing that farewell upon them.

• • •

That's how it appeared in the column. Now, the rest of the story:

Having heard Beemer eulogize too many friends, always concluding with the Paiute farewell, I took the bull by the horns one night at a conservatively-libated Sigma Nu Christmas dinner. "I'd like to work your Paiute farewell into a column someday. Say it slowly in phonetic English so I can write it down." (The Paiute language has no printed form)

He paused. The assembled brotherhood awaited. I extracted a pen and found a napkin to record it for posterity.

Bill stared at the floor, then the ceiling. A hush fell. He spoke softly:

"I have no idea. I've never done it the same way twice."

Such was the humor of our friend, Judge Beemer. See you next time, Bill.

Remembering President Reagan

Our intended topic this week was Tom Swart and some of his railroad and Sparks yarns but the column got derailed with the events of the weekend. This column is not usually oriented toward personal recollections, [*President Reagan's memorial]* but this week I'm taking a little leeway, the Homefinders' forbearance appreciated.

We turn the clock back to 1982, in the early days of July. My wife and sons planned to travel to Palmdale, California. The high point of a normal Palmdale weekend would usually be the bookmobile arriving from Los Angeles, or tickets to the matinee performance at Western Auto, but on that weekend the space shuttle, the fourth mission STS-4, was arriving on Sunday, July 4th, astronauts Mattingly and Hartsfield at the conn.

That in mind, I went to Senator Howard Cannon's office on Booth Street and wrangled a VIP invitation to Edwards Air Force Base, where the shuttle was landing. No problem, I was a good Nevadan. We journeyed to Palmdale on July the second, and on the third, a Saturday, we went to the large NASA hospitality building in Lancaster – adjoining Palmdale as Sparks adjoins Reno. To give credit where due, the name "Cannon" rocked the staff, and the kids were treated like kings – tours of past Gemini capsules, "rides" on moon landers, and other courtesies – and we left with four human passes, one for my Suburban's windshield and some cool NASA baseball caps like the big guys wear. We were warned the landing had been delayed until 9:02 AM that Sunday (tomorrow) morning from 8:53 AM so we changed our plans accordingly.

The view of the Mojave Valley foothills that Saturday night was breathtaking – the firelight of Coleman lanterns and campfires ringing the valley – Caltrans estimated that a million people had come to the hills to watch what was planned to be the last west coast space shuttle landing, ever. At oh-dark thirty on Sunday the Fourth of July we left for Edwards AFB, and upon entering the base, the Suburban was checked from cellar to attic, and beneath with mirrors – for at 9 o'clock the night before it was announced that President Ronald Reagan was coming to witness the shuttle landing. We walked interminably across a parking lot, and I have a photo to this day of a large – make that huge – Rosey Grier look-alike Secret Service agent, who met all at the gate with "Take my picture!" then smiled a display of Ipana-ad white teeth – the purpose to make sure all cameras were indeed cameras and not guns or bombs or whatever. Nice guy.

At thirty minutes before 9 AM three tall young pilots, ramrod-stiff, flat-bellied in their powder blue NASA flight suits, arrived at their parked blue-and-white T-38 jet chase planes; the assembled ladies *en mass* all went ga-ga, the pilots kicked the tires and lit the fires, taxied out, rolled, and climbed out like a trio of homesick angels to points unknown. A moment later, the baseball-stadium-sized Diamondvision TV screens came to life, and the PA system carried the voice from NASA Houston, who was controlling the shuttle's landing. The shuttle was over the Santa Barbara Channel Islands, the chase planes transmitting images of it. "You are four miles downcourse, altitude one-oh-two thousand feet" – basically straight up from Edwards. "Valve off your hydrazine," and the shuttle complied with a vapor trail; the chase planes laid day smoke – all four aircraft now in full view from Southern California.

"We're coming down," announced Hartsfield, and did they ever – straight down, 40,000 people on the Edwards tarmac puckered, expecting the craft to bury itself in the desert. At the last moment, it leveled, the gear fell and the tail split into a brake, and the three T-38s strained to stay above it, using their dive boards, landing gear and full flaps. The shuttle stopped. 9:02 AM. How did they know that a whole day earlier?

Ronald Reagan, in the same western-cut informal duds he'd wear on his ranch on a Sunday morning, and his Nancy approached the podium and made a few remarks. He then cleared the NASA transporter for takeoff, a modified 747 with the shuttle Challenger recently completed at Palmdale's Plant 41 mounted atop it – both aircraft in a paint scheme similar to Air Force One's – to fly the new shuttle to Florida. The 747 rolled, and I watched it – it never climbed out – just flew across the desert. Interesting…

A few minutes later, joined by the crew of the Columbia that had just landed, Reagan made a few more remarks. Then, turning to the audience, he concluded his speech with that great Reagan smile and "Nancy and I want to thank you all for coming out in this hot sun, and we want you to go home now and have one Hell of a Fourth of Jul…."

The 40,000 people, and millions at home watching TV, never heard the "y" in "July," only the deafening whine of the transporter's four engines and the roar of the three T-38s, all four in a tight formation, coming up from behind the audience treetop high over 250 knots and pulling. They dropped their right wings in unison to the American flag behind the podium, just as the Marine band from NAS Miramar cued the *Stars and Stripes Forever* – John Phillip Sousa never heard it played any better. The planes leveled their wings then climbed rapidly over Reagan's shoulder as we viewed him, holding their formation in a left departure into the haze.

Our Fourth of July weekend had begun, the Challenger was away on its first trip to Cape Kennedy, and Ronald Reagan, in his western White House Levis and a goat-roper shirt on that hot Sunday morning, had shown us the nexus of presidency and showmanship in its highest form. Dry eyes among 40,000 people: zero. Photos of the flyover by the surprised crowd: zero. Offers to re-enlist into the services: 14,307. Pride in the US of A: Priceless.

• • •

Have a good week; thanks for that morning, Dutch, and God bless America.

Concordance

The cast of characters, from Ace Acres to the Zive brothers...